Demand Driven Strategic Planning

T0304241

Marketing is often seen as a facilitator for transactions that may occur between companies. Companies are more and more interdependent and related to each other, literally forming networks. Whenever a company is analyzed it needs to construct a network, to be used for research, or to work out the segmentation, differentiation, product, price, distribution channels or communication. And companies must understand this fact – that they operate in a complex network, interacting with suppliers, buyers, consumers, competitors, the government and other agents. This book explains why networks are crucial for strategic planning.

Marcos Fava Neves is Professor of Planning and Strategy at the School of Business (FEARP) at the University of São Paulo, Brazil and an international expert on global food and agribusiness issues. He graduated as an agronomic engineer from ESALQ/USP in 1991, with an MSc in 1995 and a PhD in management from the FEA/USP School of Economics and Business in 1999. He completed postgraduate studies in European agribusiness and marketing in France (1995), and marketing channels and networks in the Netherlands (1998/1999). He has given more than 400 presentations in Brazil and 150 in 15 other countries. His writing is focused on supplying methods for business, publishing 70 articles in international journals, and he is author and editor of 25 books from 10 different publishers in Brazil, Uruguay, Argentina, South Africa, the Netherlands, the United Kingdom and the USA. He is a regular contributor to *China Daily* and *Folha de São Paulo* in Brazil and has written two case studies for the Harvard Business School.

Demand Driven Strategic Planning

Marcos Fava Neves

Routledge
Taylor & Francis Group

NEW YORK AND LONDON

First published 2013
by Routledge
711 Third Avenue, New York, NY 10017

Simultaneously published in the UK
by Routledge
2 Park Square, Milton Park, Abingdon, Oxon OX14 4RN

Routledge is an imprint of the Taylor & Francis Group, an informa business

Library of Congress Cataloging in Publication Data
Neves, Marcos Fava.
  Demand driven strategic planning / Marcos Fava Neves.
      p. cm.
  Includes bibliographical references and index.
  1. Strategic planning. 2. Marketing – Planning. 3. Business networks.
  I. Title.
  HD30.28.N4813 2012
  658.4′012–dc23   2012006427

ISBN13: 978-0-415-62639-2 (pbk)

Typeset in Times New Roman
by HWA Text and Data Management, London

Contents

Figures

Tables

Foreword

The world we live in is increasingly complex. Although countries are still physically as far away as ever, the psychological distance has diminished with advances in communication and travel. Internationalization – facilitated by deregulation and motivated by the recognition that the best prospects for profitable growth may lie in non-traditional rather than historic markets – has brought myriad opportunities to firms in all corners of the globe. Yet the door is also open to new competitors, including those from economically and culturally diverse backgrounds, that are driven by an urgency and hunger forgotten by well-established firms.

At the same time, falling prices for automation and other advances in manufacturing and information technologies allow for rapid changes in product design and the possibility of low-cost customization of products. A host of novel communication channels, including the exploding adoption of social media across all age groups, allows information to flow up and down the chain and around the world at the speed of light. The rapid and free flow of information heralds a new era of consumer empowerment, and provides both a blessing and a curse for business leaders, planners, and marketers who must keep up.

Value creation in this new environment is more and more based on knowledge, responsiveness, and flexibility rather than physical assets, patents, or scale. Successful firms of the future will be those that can harness their far-flung human resources – as well as the resources of their partners and possibly even their competitors – to effectively connect, create, produce, and deliver the products and services wanted by ever more demanding customers.

How can firms succeed in this complex, dynamic, and global market? Importantly, how can business leaders sift through the many interwoven layers of issues and alternatives and make the right choices?

This book brings together into one volume a comprehensive and integrated approach to strategic planning. Marcos Fava Neves presents a new perspective on this critical topic based on three main points: strongly demand driven decisions; a vision of a company as an integrated network, full of relationships that deserve planning; and the introduction of "collective-action" thinking, which raises the prospect for co-opetition between competitors. These ideas are presented in rich detail in the chapters ahead. By following this roadmap, firms of every size can navigate today's complex environment and enhance their prospects of success.

Mary Shelman
Director, Harvard Business School
President, International Food and
Agribusiness Management Association

Acknowledgments

The Steps behind *Demand Driven Strategic Planning*

This book results from almost 15 years of work in the field. Starting as class material, it evolved to a more dense method of strategic planning and management with a strong marketing orientation year after year.

Since the beginning, this method has probably been applied in more than 300 companies. It is used by myself and Markestrat research and project centre in consultancy work, also used as a final dissertation method for undergraduate students on the business course of the School of Economics and Business of the University of São Paulo at the Ribeirao Preto campus and for more than 15 MBA in marketing groups at USP, each of them with around 25 students.

This version includes several revisions throughout the book, and also includes contributions from more recent research in the field. I must acknowledge all these companies, which are not named here.

I would like to acknowledge marketing researchers from the European Marketing Academy, Wageningen University (Netherlands), Industrial Marketing and Purchasing (IMP) Group, International Food and Agribusiness Management Association (IFAMA) who contributed when this method was presented in European and North American conferences and at other other occasions. A special thank you for the wonderful preface from Mary Shelman (Director in Harvard Business School) and the testimonies from other colleagues found at the back cover page.

Also I'd like to acknowledge researchers and friends from Brazilian universities who gave wonderful contributions from the beginning. Dirceu Tornavoi de Carvalho, Marcos Cortez Campomar, Geraldo Luciano Toledo, Ana Akemi Ikeda, Roberto Fava Scare, Luciano Thomé e Castro, Matheus Alberto Consoli, Frederico Fonseca Lopes, Ricardo Rossi, Carla Martoni and specially, to the essential Leandro Angotti Guissoni, a PhD candidate who worked hard helping me in the last two years to try to finalize this project. Thank you to all Markestrat team.

My acknowledgments to the University of São Paulo which gives us a wonderful working environment, the FEARP School of Economics and Business and the FUNDACE Foundation.

I acknowledge my parents Evaristo and Ivani, my sister Flavia, and all my friends for the incentives and good moments.

To my wife Camila, and our daughters Beatriz, Julia, and Cecilia, more than a continuous acknowledgment for all the support and pleasure of life, I dedicate this book with my love.

Marcos Fava Neves
School of Economics and Business
University of São Paulo, Brazil

1 The Company as an Integrated Network

Before proceeding to the main objective of this book and beginning our discussion of demand driven strategic planning (DDSP) it is important to discuss the fundamental concepts that will be used in the development of planning and of the tools that will aid this work and facilitate the implementation of planning efforts, always directing the company towards the market.

Thus, the following points are considered in order to begin DDSP:

- understanding the marketing concept and its importance to the company;
- the company's network vision under the marketing lens;
- the importance of collective actions in marketing (joint efforts);
- the importance of strategic marketing planning, their advantages and general vision;
- beginning the planning process: understanding the company and its history.

What is Marketing?

McCarthy and Perreault (1997) state that if the majority of people, including managers, were forced to define marketing they would say it means "sales" or "advertising." This answer is not completely true; sales and advertising are part of what is known as marketing, which includes several other activities, as we will see later. Thus, marketing is defined as "a social and managerial process by which individuals and groups obtain what they need and want through the creation, offer and trade of products and values with others" (Kotler, 1997: 9); in other words, it is a process that aims at satisfying the needs of both parties through trade.

Marketing is used to understand which are the needs of the final consumers and intermediaries (industries, distributors) through a research process, analyzing the behavior of these consumers, and the market, making it easier to see which segments of consumers may be satisfied, which target market the company will act on, what type of differentiation can be offered, how to generate and adapt products, brands and packages to satisfy these needs, the correct pricing strategies for these products, how to make them available to consumers through distribution channels; and, communicate through advertising, publicity and other tools.

Originally marketing in the USA was seen as a branch of applied economics, with studies about distribution channels in times of product scarcity after World War II. A time when the focus was aimed at production, a time in which everything that was produced was in great demand. Until the first half of the 1950s it was considered an administrative function of sales activities. In the 1960s, with the development of the American economy, many "offering" companies appeared, competition increased, and marketing began to be considered an applied behavioral science subject, concerned with understanding the systems involving transactions of products and services between buyers and sellers.

Thus, a new orientation appeared, seeking to fully satisfy a particular group of consumers, offering them what they wanted, in a better way than the competition. In other words, an inverse process. Instead of producing what one knew, in an environment with little competition and afterwards letting the sales staff create and stimulate the demand, stocking the distribution channels and pushing products to the consumers, through research, companies began to perceive what the consumers were demanding, and began to launch products that completely satisfied their customers. This is the thought process in marketing: a thought process that has been reversed, as shown in Figure 1.1.

In a similar way, Czinkota (2010) describes the evolution of marketing, highlighting the *production era* in which the business philosophy was focused on manufacturing efficiency, the *sales era* in which the business philosophy was focused on the sale of the existing products, and the *marketing era* in which the philosophy focused on the customer's needs and desires. The company offers value to its customers through configuration (the act of "designing" the object – the product), valuation (establishing the trade terms for the object – the price), symbolization (association to certain meanings through advertising) and lastly through facilitation (altering the object's accessibility – point of sale) (Kotler, 1997).

The target market of marketing activities is composed by the final consumers, industrial consumers (anywhere in the world), governments, suppliers, employees, agents, competitors and others. The organization is seen as a unit converting the resources of shareholders, directors, employees and suppliers into products that will go directly to consumers or indirectly to them through agents. Government, competitors and other parties watch this activity with the power to sanction or restrict it. All these parties are a target for the organization's marketing, through the impact they have on the efficiency of the conversion

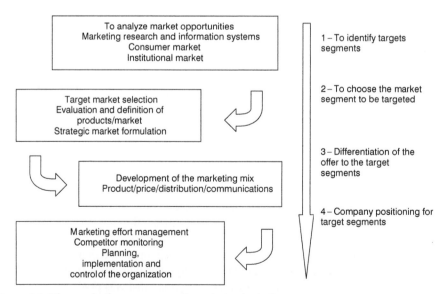

Figure 1.1 The marketing process and market orientation
Source: adapted from Kotler (1997)

of resources. This broad definition of the target market already demonstrates the coherence of an adoption of a network approach in marketing, which will be discussed next.

Moreover, efforts have been made by companies in order to adapt more to a new marketing perspective, where consumers are no longer considered as isolated individuals, since they are now connected with one another by new technology and social media in a way that has never occurred before.

Therefore, there is an increasingly collective power of consumers, and companies must collaborate with their consumers to succeed in their business as "the centrality of marketing in creating growth and shareholder value suggests a new role for marketing" (Doyle, 2000: 29).

In this sense, according to Kotler *et al.* (2010) marketing has now shifted to inviting consumers, creating conditions for them to participate in the company's development of products, communications and so on. In other words, these changes enable creating value through co-creation efforts with consumers.

These changes, along with technology, also makes the process easier in which companies gather market insights – for example, by means of mining social networking data – which in turn makes it possible to improve their understanding of the market's needs. Thus creating, communicating and delivering offers that have value for both the market and the company's shareholders.

A demand driven perspective is both important and challenging within organizations. However, this perspective is very important and can affect company performance and, "as a resource, market orientation is a deeply embedded cultural resource which positively influences the development of marketing capabilities" (Trainor *et al.*, 2011: 165).

The following are some of the relevant characteristics of demand driven organizations. This is the "Demand Driven Tool."

- Their executives and workers listen to and pay attention to the marketplace. This is a major characteristic, since paying attention is difficult – and it is incredible that we deal daily with companies which are closed to information.
- They don't fear being evaluated. In many organizations we see that there is an avoidance of establishing formal and informal evaluations procedures because people will be pressured.
- They dedicate time to thinking. Time to think nowadays is rare as it is costly. We have to pursue financial, sales targets and all this massive communication is disturbing, since when you are thinking you are disturbed by a new email arriving or a mobile phone ringing. Technology made us much more accessible to people, but the obverse is the continual interruption in thinking processes.
- They analyze and model macro environmental changes. They are keen to see what is happening in differing scenarios: socio-cultural, technological, economic, and political and legal. Demand driven organizations analyze how these trends and movements affect them.
- They do mental simulations of possible future changes and their impacts, anticipating movements and reactions. It is the "what if?" question. They model these questions of possible future changes and their impact.
- They establish closer linkage and connection between stakeholders (consumers, customers, suppliers, distributors, government, shareholders, banks, etc.) via strategies such as open lines of communication, own stores, consumer labs, front-line people empowerment and digital platforms.

- They share a sense that they are owned by the consumer. The value of the organization is the value given by the consumer; having a clear understanding of customer problems and how the organization can solve them. This requires a change of mindset in employees.
- They don't fear change. Some companies face an accommodation process. People won't change their indifferent attitude, they think nothing is possible, nothing works. This behavior must be changed by stimulus, "If people don't change, let's change the people."
- They show entrepreneurial and innovation behavior – we see demand driven companies always bringing new concepts and solutions to society.
- They also share the discipline to make things happen. They take note and take action.

The "Demand Driven Tool" can be used by any company by transforming all these topics in questions related to "how can we improve."

Every Company Builds a Network

Marketing is more often seen as a facilitator for transactions that may occur between companies. Companies are more and more interdependent and related to each other, literally forming networks. Whenever a company analyzes itself, it needs to construct a network to be used for research, or to work out segmentation, differentiation, product, price, distribution channels or communications. All companies must understand that they are not isolated anymore. They operate in a complex network, interacting with suppliers, buyers, consumers, competitors, the government and other agents.

Therefore a theoretical model of the company network can be defined as the group of supplier and distributor companies for the focus company. As stated by Alderson and Halbert (1971), companies participate in traditional flows of products, services, communication, information, orders and payments necessary to connect the suppliers of raw materials used for production to the final consumers of their products or products processed from the original products.

The concept of networks varies according to how closely we focus. In this book, we work with a focus on the company under analysis, in other words, the "network of that company." In this sense it is a process of analyzing a company and its group of suppliers and distributors, the existing relations between them and relations with its environment. It is in essence an approach which looks at interactions and relationships. This concept is used by the Industrial Marketing and Purchasing Group (IMP), known as the IMP method or approach (Gemünden *et al.*, 1997; Bridgewater and Egan, 2002; Ford, 1998; Hakansson and Snehota, 1993; Gadde and Hakansson, 2001).

The importance of a company's network has been investigated by several researchers. In general it is considered that a company's network of alliances can affect the value the company creates.

In this sense, Swaminathan and Moorman (2009: 65) stated "networks are key strategic resources that can yield substantial firm value." From the analysis of 230 announcements of marketing alliances in the software industry, they have concluded that "firm's ability to manage a network of previous marketing alliances, has a positive impact on value creation" (ibid: 52); thus supporting previous approaches that networks are an important company resource (Gulati *et al.*, 2000).

What are the advantages of looking at the company as a network, besides the potential contribution to a company value creation?

1   Instead of seeing the selling company as the active party and the purchasing company as the reactive party, the network perspective views companies as belonging to a network of businesses made of a large number of active and heterogeneous companies that interact among themselves and seek solutions for their different problems.
2   Companies are interdependent in sales, purchases, information, technology development and to access other companies in the network.
3   Instead of seeing the company as holder of all resources, abilities and technologies necessary to select and develop its strategies, the network perspective implies that no company has all necessary resources, abilities and technologies, but depends on interaction with suppliers, customers, distributors, partners and even competitors. Thus the importance of collective actions and the understanding of the "network focus" are important for the planning process.

Analyzing the network of a company also allows the addition of facilitator companies (for example, freight forwarders, insurance companies, communications agencies, certification companies, warehousing, logistics operators and others), interfaces with other networks (whether obtaining raw materials or by-products), the inverse of the network (common in cases of recycling or returning via recall, which demands the participation of the distributors) and the impacts brought by the uncontrollable variables (social and cultural, technological, economic, and political and legal/institutional environments) which will be discussed in Chapter 2.

Furthermore, placing competitors in the company's network also allows thinking about collective actions which companies can pursue in marketing (examples range from the participation in sectoral associations to creating an export joint venture between competitors). An example to illustrate the design of a network of a focus company is shown in Figure 1.2.

Figure 1.2 shows that in order to map out the company's network and establish strategies, two support references, among others, constitute important theoretical components for its coordination. The first component is distribution channels, defined by Stern *et al.* (1996: 1) as: "a group of interdependent organizations involved in the process of making the product or service of the company available for consumption or use." The second component is the company's supply chain, which is the opposite of the first component; in other words, the organizations involved in the supply of all materials the company needs to produce and sell. In this way, marketing considers that which goes from the company to the market. Logically, factors such as material quality, scarcity, supplier's brands and other aspects of the company's supply chain have an enormous impact on its marketing, and need to be monitored closely.

Marketing variables are divided into product, communications, distribution, sales force and price, with the objective of making their understanding and planning easier. However, marketing actions must be totally integrated and coherent. Marketing errors happen precisely because of the lack of integration in these areas. It is common to have exaggerated communications, not corresponding to the true attributes of the product, or to lack products at the point of sale when doing specific advertising, or even a sales force which is not prepared to offer a product with high technical specifications.

In the network illustrated in Figure 1.2, the role of the marketing professional is to manage the relations between the company and consumer market. There are other professionals in the company who, in conjunction and obeying marketing principles, work on supply chain management; in other words, managing the relationship with the company's suppliers. In summary, the role of the marketing professional is to manage what I call the sales equation.

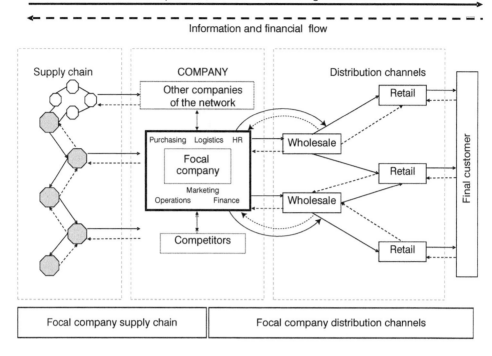

Figure 1.2 Company network theoretical model
Source: adapted from Neves (2003)

The company's sales equation is shown below. It is an attempt at placing all the possible sales and organization variables in an equation.

Sales = f (STEP, competition, products, communication, distribution channels, sales force, price)

where the STEP variable is social and cultural, technological, economic and natural, and political and legal factors.

Therefore, the sales of an organization are influenced by *uncontrollable factors*: the macro environmental factors (social and cultural, technological, economic and natural, and political and legal variables) and competition factors.

Sales are influenced also by *controllable factors*, or by marketing decisions – products, communication, distribution channels, prices and sales force.

In the next section this equation is transformed into a table that tries to summarize an organization's marketing activity, placing under each variable some changes that are happening, or which are the main tools available.

Why Should We Think About Joint Strategy Actions?

With the changes brought by the globalization of markets, companies and their marketing functions have expanded their scope.

Markets in some cases don't have borders, and companies specializing in their core business need international contractual relations to obtain raw materials or distribute their products and services. Real networks are being developed focusing on relationships, and continuous and sustainable development. Cooperative marketing actions are getting more attention and are increasingly studied by marketing executives and academics. Cooperation within a network can be vertical (between agents from distinct technical stages – e. g.: suppliers and distributors), as well as horizontal, involving competitors and companies that have complementary products within the same market. The DDSP method tries to encourage a company vision with partnerships of common strategies, using this sort of analysis in every stage of the method.

Juttner *et al.* (2007: 377), in their study, argued for "demand chain management as a new business model combining the strengths of marketing and supply chain competencies." They stated that demand chain management involves managing the interactions between demand and supply processes for each customer segment, also managing the working relationships between these areas. According to them, "despite these strong arguments for an integrated approach, in many businesses, the supply side still seems to be disconnected from the demand side" (Juttner *et al.*, 2007: 379). The following are some important strategies that can help companies to compete in coming years, the "network era."

1   The first strategy an executive can employ is to develop a diagram of this complex network, and share it with all employees of the company to help them understand that they are not in isolation. What occurs in the external environment will affect the company; if something happens to a buyer or a supplier, the company will also be affected. Therefore, they must keep paying attention and trying to anticipate what will happen and how their company will be affected.
2   The second strategy is in regard to supply chain optimization. Companies need to look at their supply chain continuously to try to reduce costs, to buy from the best available sources from all over the globe. They should always try to find substitute products or ingredients and test their qualities and adaptability to see if they fit. Idle inventory also causes unnecessary loss. There is a need to build a safe and secure continuous supply chain to try to reduce transaction costs, and minimize inventory and losses caused by inefficiency and redundancy. Companies need to think of packaging rationalization and always search for alternatives. Always ask yourself: "how can we do this better?"
3   In terms of reduced margins and the global competition, the third tranche of strategies concerns marketing. Companies have to do what is known as "value re-engineering" by looking at their product line and thinking about how to capture more value. They should ask themselves what could be reduced in terms of content, changing of ingredients, packaging modification. When launching new products, companies should have a clear target, a message easy to understand, and research as much as possible to avoid the risk of failure. Today, there are no longer margins that allow them to keep failing in new product launches. The profit of existing products cannot anymore be wasted in supporting the failure of new launches.

In marketing, the word "simplicity" is also for the new era. Companies should simplify market segments, pay more attention to the cash-generating products and focus on consumers. Communications (advertising and others) should be done with a deep understanding of their costs and impacts. There is no time anymore for media exposure with an unclear understanding of value return.

It is a new era of understanding the customer behavior and, more than this, understanding that the consumer does not want to pay for inefficiencies in the supply chain or marketing activities.

Table 1.1 Organization sales matrix

Uncontrollable variables

Social and cultural values	Technological	Economic and natural	Political and legal	Competitors
• working women • urbanization • demography • ethnicity/race • time shortage • ageing population • individuality • family shopping behavior • security • convenience • leisure • social mobility • income distribution • behavior in workplace • changes in life style • safe food • family size • life cycle of the family • values and habits of consumption • religion • enviroment • green movements • new media • others	• new technological solutions • digital sales (web) • "scanners" • computerized stock control • "just-in-time" delivery • EDI – electronic exchange of data • point of sales data • electronic transfers • technological transfers • ECR • mobile phones • new ways of communication • distance learning • GPS • QR codes • nano-technology • GMOs • others	• changes in income • interest rates • unemployment levels • education levels • exchange rates • economic integration • costs of services • supplier concentration • buyer concentration • product life cycles • trends in GDP • availability of capital and finance • inflation • availability of energy • restrictions of inputs to the natural environment (water, air) • tourism spending • availability of partners and facilitating companies • emerging economies • others	• access to closed markets (protectionism) • packaging recycling legislation • antitrust policy • economic integration (trading blocs) • labeling • types of communication restrictions • labor laws • stability of the government • policy on subsidies • certification of products/process • competition control legislation • international standards and certification • marketing to children • instablities • others	• number and size of competitors • company and competitors' market participation • main strengths and threats for competitors • substitute products • possibility of new entrants into the market • national and international competitors • possibility of mergers and acquisitions • price wars • competitors' retaliation • others

Strategies

Products	Communications	Channels	Sales force	Price
• product and product line analyses	• target market identification	• channel design and description	• current situation and goals	• selection of price goals
• complementary product lines (expansion decisions)	• establishment of the goals of communications	• environmental analysis and impacts for the channels	• evaluation of the adequacy of the sales process	• determination of demand
• launch of new products and services	• definition of the communication mix (advertising, promotion of sales, personal sales and direct marketing)	• specific asset analysis	• determining strategy and structure of sales force	• estimate costs
• branding decisions analysis	• establishment of the communication budget	• definition of distribution strategies (intensive, selective, exclusive)	• analysis of amount and forms of remuneration	• costs, prices and competitor offers analysis
• packaging decisions analysis	• measurement of the results of the communications	• analysis of the flow of marketing and of the functions of the intermediate channel	• performance, supervision, motivation and training	• selection of price establishment method
• others	• details of global communications	• recruitment, selection and motivation of the channel members	• evaluation and budgeting	• selection of final prices
	• strategies to adapt international communications	• value and profitability of channel agents analysis	• others	• price adaptation
	• institutional campaigns versus collective or joint-action campaigns using a network persepective	• development of new channels and alternative channels		• initiatives and responses to changing prices
	• brand communications versus institutional communications	• definition of investments in channels		• others
	• others	• others		

Demand Driven Strategic Planning and Management: What is the Purpose?

Strategic marketing planning is related to the definition of the marketing objectives for a period of three to five years (Gilligan and Wilson, 2003). The authors state that even with the criticism that planning processes have been receiving – such as rapid change in the company environment, lack of creativity, lack of realism, inflexibility – they are important because they test the company's thinking capacity and vision of the future. The process of planning is as important as the plan itself. By planning, we learn and get to know ourselves.

Planning must be oriented to the market; in other words, one must know to what extent a focus on the consumer pervades the organization, along with a commitment to:

- value delivery;
- identification and development of distinct competencies;
- creation of strategic partnerships;
- development of strong relations with important strategic consumers;
- emphasis on market segmentation;
- selection of the target market and positioning;
- use of information about consumers as a strategic asset;
- focus on the benefits and services delivered to the consumer;
- improvements and continuous innovation;
- definition of quality based on the customer's expectations;
- obtaining the best information technology available.

According to Day (1994), the characteristics of an organization that is aimed at the market can be briefly described as a culture externally oriented that emphasizes the customer's superior value, distinct capacities to "feel" the market – the way to forecast the future and the existence of structures that respond to changes in the market's and consumers' demands. Greenley (in Gilligan and Wilson, 2003: 56) laid out distinctions between strategic planning (seen as something with a long-term nature) and marketing planning (seen as an annual exercise), including those listed in Table 1.2.

Table 1.2 Differences between strategic planning and marketing planning

Strategic planning	Marketing planning
General concern with the organization's long-term direction	Concerned with performance and day-to-day results
Provides a long-term structure for the organization	Represents only a stage of the organization's development
General orientation necessary to match the organization and its development	Functional and professional orientation tends to be predominant
Objectives and strategies are evaluated through a general perspective	Objectives are subdivided into specific goals
The relevance of the objectives and strategies is evident only in the long term	The relevance of the objectives and strategies is evident immediately

Source: Greenley (1986)

The planning environment can be considered as a "satellite" and must be in the DNA of each company to provide better preparation for a turbulent future. I call this the "15 Ps Strategic Planning Tool."

Here are the 15 Ps of strategic planning:

- *Prevision*: we must increase our capacity to foresee macro environmental changes and impacts before they happen. A company should cause the surprise, and not "be surprised."
- *Public policy:* there will be an increasing role of public policy and government regulation over companies in the future. We must follow them, negoitate using trade associations, and be prepared to face them. Examples range from marketing to children to global financial regulations.
- *Planet:* The growth in the importance of environment and planet-related issues must be included in a company's planning topics.
- *People:* In the same way, the growth of importance of corporate social responsibility and employee relations. There is growing consumer and press interest in these subjects.
- *Productivity:* There is pressure for better use of scarce resources, and to deliver more at even lower costs. This movement shows companies the need for improved productivity.
- *Profit:* Globally connected shareholders requiring and comparing value delivery have options for investment. So profitability will drive capacity to finance which is crucial for planning.
- *Partners:* The company is an integrated network, a cluster of contracts, with alliances and joint ventures. We must have the best partners in our business models.
- *Proactiveness*: Planning without implemention doesn't work. We must develop an internal culture and behavior to ensure plans are implemented, and to that end people and the company need to be proactive.
- *Providers*: There is a continuous need to reorganize supply chain and service providers to include value, and small farmers and suppliers. Inclusion is one of the most important

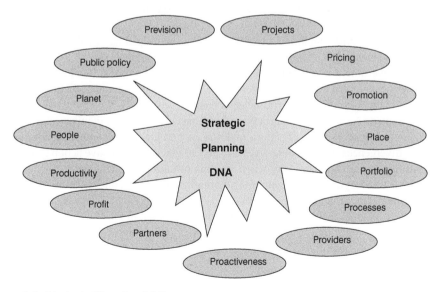

Figure 1.3 Strategic Planning 15 Ps

topics for the future, and companies will be valued by their capacity to promote inclusion of small farms and small suppliers.

- *Processes:* In planning activities, we must review all procedures/processes to find simpler ways of doing things, saving time, resources and promoting simplicity.
- *Portfolio:* From a marketing point of view, we, as companies, must offer products and services from an approach of providing a "solution of customers' problems," and have an adequate and appropriate portfolio of products and businesses.
- *Place:* Amplifying the traditional approach of marketing channels, becoming points of contact and sales with consumers, promoting convenience, exchange of information and experiences.
- *Promotion:* With new generations and new media, planning should foster integrated communication activities providing a continuous flow of information which should react immediately and rapidly to the market and to consumers.
- *Pricing:* When planning prices, we must have an integrative and creative pricing strategy to, at the same time, increase value for the company and its shareholders and increase consumer satisfaction.
- *Projects:* Finally, in any planning process, we need to organize proactiveness and planning using a project management approach so that things happen in a structured way. Planning and proactiveness without organized projects do not contribute to efficiency.

The "15 Ps Strategic Planning Tools" can be used by transforming each "P" into a question related to "how could we improve in …"

The possible results of planning are: the improvement in the coordination of the company and its network; sensing possible changes in the environment quickly; better understanding of consumers; quicker adaptation; less risk of taking uncoordinated actions; improvements in product, prices, communication, sales force and distribution channels; systematization of work and accounts receivable.

Therefore, it can be inferred that planning has the following advantages:

- it describes the value system, the philosophy of the company and it creates a common vision of the future;
- it explains the initial situation and describes the conditions and evolution which occur in the environment;
- it is an instrument of coordination between various functions; it allows maintaining coherence between objectives when there are conflicts or contradictions; it favors arbitration having objective criteria as its basis;
- it stimulates a cooperative, integrated and enthusiastic focus for organizational problems;
- it facilitates the follow-up of actions undertaken, and it allows an impartial interpretation of the divergences between objectives and performance, so corrective action can be taken;
- it improves company flexibility when reacting to unexpected changes;
- it allows more rigorous management and organization, based on standards, budgets, and schedules, rather than on improvisation;
- it leads to a better position for the organization, helping it to move forward in the chosen direction;
- it leads to more socially and economically useful results.

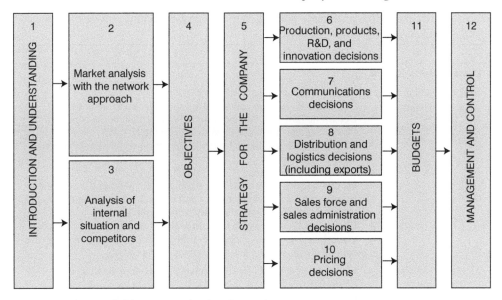

Figure 1.4 Demand driven strategic planning and management structure

To give the reader a general view, the proposed method is shown in Figure 1.4; it is divided into several stages, in accordance with Table 1.3, which is examined in detail in the following chapters.

The DDSP method proposed here has as its point of view that it is necessary to compete, to be fast and that the company is involved in a dynamic system, which includes interaction with competitors, customers, people, resources and other companies.

One of its distinctive features is that it seeks to introduce collective action between companies into the planning process. In other words, in each step of the DDSP there are possible collective actions the organization can paticipate in, whether it is with competitors, other companies that sell to the same group of consumers, or companies that do not have any relation with the company for which the plan is being made. Therefore, collective actions between companies can and must occur. To clarify the planning process, this model tries to format actions the focus company will try to do collectively, emphasizing actions via sector associations which can have a variety of objectives, such as the increase of the whole market, lobbying, tariff protection and others. It also emphasizes actions between specific companies in a sector, for example, two companies sharing sales space, sales force, etc.

The motivation of introducing collective actions and partnerships in the DDSP comes from several studies that demonstrate how cooperation between companies, exchange of information with customers, and partnerships with universities, colleges and research institutes has a strong influence on the technical and economic success of the company product generation process, as well as other marketing activities.

Table 1.3 Demand driven strategic planning and management with a network approach –
detailed sequence of the proposed steps

Step	What Must Be Done

Phase 1 – Introduction

1. Introduction and understanding
   - Understand the company's history.
   - Determine if the organization has existing plans and study them.
   - Determine how the planning process is carried out in the company.
   - Determine which teams will participate in the DDSP.
   - Chose a person within the team who can promote relationships with other companies.
   - Determine cultural aspects.
   - Determine why the process is beginning at this point in time (normally change of management, company professionalization, or, in the case of multinationals, requirements from the head office).
   - Finally, in cases of companies with sophisticated planning processes, verify how DDSP may help the existing model and gradually adapt the company to it, without any unnecessary disruptions.

2. Environmental analysis with a company network approach
   - Map out and understand the company's network in detail as in Figure 1.1.
   - Identify all possible market data in which the company operates (size, growth rates, market participation, life cycle, among others).
   - Identify the threats and opportunities that come from uncontrollable variables (possible changes in the social and cultural, technological, economic and natural, and political and legal environments) in domestic and international markets.
   - Understand existing barriers (tariff and non-tariff) and determine any collective actions to reduce them.
   - Analyze final and intermediary (distributors) consumers' behavior and their purchase decision process.
   - Set up a marketing information system, so the company can always be informed and make structured and well-founded decisions.
   - Determine main domestic and international competitors.
   - Make a proactive list of collective actions that can be carried out jointly with competitors or other companies for all steps listed here (for example, joint market research).

3. Internal situation analysis and competition
   - Determine the strengths and weaknesses of the company.
   - Do the same analysis for the main competitors.
   - Analyze the internal environment and marketing structure.
   - Analyze company value creation, resources and competencies.
   - Analyze the critical success factors.
   - Select companies with the best evaluation (they may be competitors or not) to be benchmarks (sources of good ideas) and in what particular areas.

4. Objectives
   - The main objectives must be defined and quantified (in terms of sales, market participation and market presence, entry in new markets).
   - The level of detail must be high, so the objectives can be monitored throughout the period of the plan.
   - The objectives of network partnerships and alliances must also be included.

5. Strategies to reach the objectives
   - List the main strategies (actions) that will be used to reach the objectives proposed in item 4.
   - Perform market segmentation, selection of target markets, differentiation strategies and positioning, among others.
   - Make a broad summary of the actions foreseen in Phase 2 (this summary must be made after the plan is complete, steps 6 through 10).

Step	What Must Be Done

Phase 2 – Plans for Controllable Marketing Variables

6. Product decisions
- Analyze products and product lines, as well as complementary product lines to enable decisions about expansion.
- Use the concept of networks to verify product opportunities (joint product packages with competitors, complementary product lines with other companies and other actions).
- Find opportunities for launching new products.
- Detail services that are (or will be) offered.
- Make brand decisions (individual branding, family branding, distributor private branding).
- Make decisions in relation to packaging (label, material, design).
- Prepare a budget for products, new products and other actions that are not in this step.

7. Communications decisions
- Identify the target audience which will be the object of communications (company messages).
- Develop the objectives for these communications (brand knowledge, brand memory, persuasion, among others).
- Define the communication mix that will be used; in other words, define plans for advertising, for public relations and publicity, for sales promotion, as well as direct marketing actions.
- Identify actions that can be made jointly with other companies.
- Prepare the budget for communications actions.
- Indicate how the communication results will be measured, so the company can continuously learn how to use the best tools according to its experience.

8. Distribution and logistic decisions
- Analyze the company's product distribution channels and seek new ones, defining the distribution objectives, such as: presence in markets, type and number of points of sale, services offered, market information, product promotion and incentives.
- Define opportunities and threats of the current distribution system.
- Identify possible distributors' and consumers' desires to adjust the services offered.
- Define the way of entering markets, whether it is through franchises, joint ventures or other contracts, or even via vertical integration; creating domestic or international contracts with the distribution channels.
- Determine an annual distribution budget.
- Verify how distribution actions may be made jointly with other companies of the network.

9. Sales force and sales administration decisions
- Produce an analysis of the current sales force situation; in other words, map territories, sales potential, coverage indexes, participations, and define objectives for the next period, based on performance indicators.
- Define the sales force approach to customers (strategy).
- Set boundaries for the sales force's actions, directing their efforts, establishing (or not) a support team in the company.
- Define the ideal size of sales force for the company, and finally, establish how it will be paid.
- Recruit, select, supervise, motivate and train the sales team; these are necessary steps to guarantee continuity of the work.
- Evaluate and monitor reaching of goals, this is part of leading the team to issues raised in earlier steps.
- Also, list network actions, including cooperating with competitors and other companies that are in the same target market.
- Create a budget for the sales force.

continued …

Table 1.3 continued

Step	What Must Be Done
10. Pricing decisions	• Define the company's objectives in relation to pricing. • Analyze domestic and international demand. • Analyze and control production costs. • Analyze costs, prices and offers of the competition. • Choose a method to be used in price setting and decide which types of prices and variations (regional, conjuncture, etc.) will be used. • Develop procedures for how the company reacts to changes in competitors' pricing.
11. Budget	• Budgets for all marketing variables, such as activity related to market and consumer analysis (item 2), products (item 6), communications (item 7), distribution (item 8) and sales force (item 9) must be defined, giving a complete budget for the DDSP, with the aim of reaching the planned goals.
Phase 3 – Monitoring, Follow-up and Plan Management	
12. Execution, control, follow-up and correction	• This phase begins after the plan is finished. It refers to the follow-up, the teams involved and corrective actions; in other words, plan management. The plan (i.e. the document) must be a living document, in constant discussion and constantly updated by the company. It can be divided into several projects.

Chapter Activities: Demand Driven Strategic Planning for your Company

The DDSP that is proposed in this first step has as distinctive features: a strategic approach; joint marketing actions; and a partnerships approach. These features will be present in all of the following chapters. In this first phase, it is recommended the following analyses be made:

- determine how planning is done in the company;
- determine the existing company plans; understand the company's history;
- determine which team will participate in the DDSP, with the objective of making the plan (the document);
- choose from this team one person to act as promoter of relationships with other companies, with a view to the construction of alliances and joint projects; some companies already have a network manager, who is responsible for the company's network, but this is uncommon;
- identify cultural aspects;
- determine why the process is beginning at this point in time (normally change of management, company professionalization, or, in the case of multinationals, requirements from head office);
- perform the "Demand Driven Tool";
- perform the "15 Ps Strategic Planning Tool";
- and finally, determine, in the case of companies with sophisticated planning processes, how DDSP may help existing planning models and gradually adapt the company to DDSP; often models that propose a total change or disruption in the way in which the company is working will face great resistance; therefore, a transition period, or even merging the existing planning process with the one proposed here, will be beneficial.

Now we move on to Step 2, the external analysis of the network the company operates.

Questions

1   Why is a company's network vision under the marketing lens important?
2   Can a company be more competitive by developing collective actions in marketing?
3   What variables should be considered in the sales equation by an organization?
4   How does a company develop its demand driven strategic plan?
5   What must be done in each step of the demand driven strategic plan?
6   How can the 15 Ps of planning be useful for your company?
7   How can the demand driven tool be useful for your company?

2 Analyzing the Company's Environment and Market (External Analysis)

This chapter uses the company network approach to analyze the macro environment in order to have a broader understanding of the threats and opportunities in a context characterized by rapid change. It is recommended that the following analyses are made in this stage:

- map out and understand in detail the company network, as in Figure 2.1;
- gather all possible data on the market in which the company operates (size, growth rate, market participation, life cycle, among others);
- identify threats and opportunities that come from the uncontrollable variables (possible changes in the social and cultural, technological, economic and natural, and political and legal environments) for domestic and international markets;
- analyze the behavior of final and intermediary (distributors) consumers and their purchasing decision process;
- set up an information system so the company can always be informed and make well-supported and well-founded decisions;
- make a proactive list of collective actions that can be undertaken jointly with competitors or other companies for all the steps listed in this chapter.

How to Map Out Your Company's Network

In Chapter 1 we saw what the company network is; here it will be mapped out. The objective of this stage is to describe all agents that have functions in the network, from the initial suppliers to the final consumers, to form a general view of the main industries and organizations that interact with the focal company's network.

The process is progressed by indentifying the agents that have a negotiation function (suppliers, manufacturers, industries, wholesalers, retailers and others) in the overall product flow. Functions (like shipping, for example) and facilitator companies should not be included, as they do not buy products, they only have negotiations related to services (finance, in the case of banks; insurance, in the case of insurance companies; shipping, in the case of shipping companies, etc.).

Figure 2.1 shows a company that is part of a complex system consisting of various agents with distinct characteristics. The fundamental point of this external analysis is to understand and, when possible, to try to predict changes caused by the agents or variables external to the company, whether from the immediate environment (suppliers, competition, distributors and customers) or from the macro environment (social and cultural, technological, economic and natural, and political and legal).

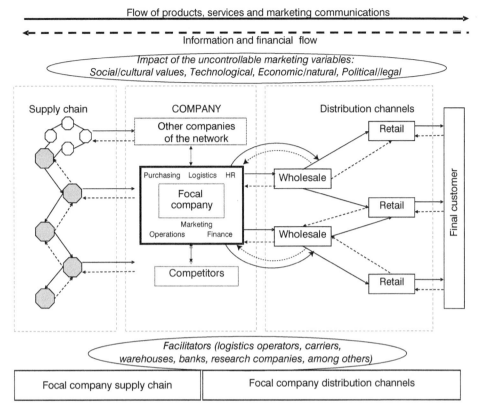

Figure 2.1 Company network and main variables
Source: adapted from Neves (2003)

Evaluating and Quantifying the Market

It is very important to have an information system and Table 2.1 shows some important questions for consideration in this regard.

In this step it is important that the team involved in the planning process is engaged in acquiring information about the history, size and trends in the markets the company is active in. Forecasting demand is among the main management tasks, and is the basis of executive planning. It supplies information to the production area concerning purchase volumes, funding and use of resources for the predicted levels of activity, numbers of people necessary in the organization, and so forth. Demand forecasts are fundamental for almost every decision in the sales area. This information has to be regarded as fundamental in the definition of territories, evaluation of salespeople, setting of quotas, selection of representatives or salespeople.

It is important to make the distinction between potential sales, (i.e. total sales in the sector), and the sales forecast, (what the company hopes to achieve out of this total, taking into consideration the environment and the company's program) as shown in Table 2.2.

In cases where the company has a large geographical coverage, it needs to have an idea of the market size it has in each of its products in all regions where it is active. In this way regional market data can also be evaluated, as in Table 2.3.

Table 2.1 Marketing information systems

What's the information for?	Where does it fit in the planning?	How to see and understand the information needs within the company	Which information is relevant to the company?	Where/how to get the information
• to anticipate change • to make better decisions • to redirect • to prevent • to improve • to plan • to innovate • to renew	*In the internal and external analysis* Chapter 2: STEP/end consumers/ intermediary consumers (organizational/ industrial) Chapter 3: internal (company)/ competitors	• internal research • existing information • past decisions made • which information the company needs and wants • what are the sources • updating • new sources • subjects and events • websites • periodicity	1. internal archives 2. intelligence 3. research *Internal:* • sales • costs • human resources • production *External* • STEP • market • consumers • competitors • costomers • government	• distributors: resales • salespeople: reports • consumers: research • employees • suppliers • companies • competitors • shareholders • government • advisory committee, advisory board: advice/ orientation

Table 2.2 Market evolution

	2013	2014	2015	2016	2017	2018	2019	2020
Amount ($)								
Volume (quantity)								
Average price								
Sales per company								
Company market share								

Table 2.3 Market evolution by region

	2013	2014	2015	2016	2017	2018	2019	2020
Region A								
Region B								
Region C								
Region D								
Region E								
Total								

Finally, the total sales forecast by product can be estimated through forecasts for different sales teams or, conversely, the total sales target for products are allocated to different teams. The underlying philosophy for the construction of the demand forecasts will depend on the demand forecasting policy used by the company.

Demand forecasting is generally done by the marketing department together with the sales department (or the marketing department simply does it when they are not separate departments), but the production department or product managers can also make demand forecasts. As demand forecasting is about future sales, and marketing is responsible for sales, then ideally marketing must be the area responsible for it.

Analyzing Opportunities and Threats

STEP analysis evaluates the social and cultural, technological, economic and natural, and political and legal (institutional) factors. This analysis is well described in the literature as an important tool of the planning process. An "environmental matrix" must be drawn up for each of the four groups of factors. To help understand this process, important aspects relating to drivers and the implications of their effect on company performance should be considered, and if necessary, other groups of factors can also be considered in completing the matrix.

Johnson and Scholes (2008) propose five stages in the analysis of the macro environment:

1   Devise general weighting of environmental influences, with the intention of identifying the different environmental factors that could influence company performance.
2   Evaluate the "nature" of the environment and the degree of uncertainty and existing change. In relatively static environments, historical analysis can be useful. However, if the environment shows signs of instability, a strong emphasis on the future will be necessary.
3   The third stage involves a focus on specific environmental factors (social and cultural, technological, economic and natural, and political and legal).
4   After identifying the company's competitive position, the opportunities and threats coming from the environment must be identified.
5   In the final stage, strategies must be established to utilize the opportunities generated by the environment and also minimize the negative impacts of the threats.

Table 2.4 shows the main influencing factors, in each of the four groups that are part of the macro environment which must be considered at the time of the environmental "audit."

The identification of macro environment factors that affect the organization is not sufficient to create strategies. During the planning process the team needs to transform the information collected into practical actions. In the model proposed in this book, the transformation of information collected into actions is performed by completing Table 2.5.

In the impacts/opportunities column, the implications (threats or opportunities) that come from environmental changes of the four factors (social and cultural, technological, economic and natural, and political and legal) are listed. In the actions column, company executives must outline the action strategies for each environmental change which protect the company from threats and take advantage of opportunities. After this analysis, which should be made for the variables that present the greatest opportunities or present threats to the company, the planning team can group them and propose specific projects in order to use the opportunities and/or neutralize possible threats. Figure 2.2 exemplifies this process.

Table 2.4 The STEP structure for the macro environment audit

Social and cultural factors	Technological factors
• demographics; • life styles; • social mobility; • education levels; • attitudes; • consumerism; • behavior patterns; • women's participation in the labor market; • population concentration in large cities; • races/ethnicity; • time scarcity; • population aging; • personal individuality; • family shopping trips; • search for security; • convenience; • leisure; • wealth distribution; • attitudes at work; • concern with food safety; • family size; • environment; • new media; • others.	• government and industry level of investment in research and development; • speed of technology transfer; • product life cycle; • direction of technology transfer; • change in the cost of technology; • research entities and institutes, and universities that are developing research; • research programs; • life cycle of equipment used; • improvements in the equipment; • sales through mail, telephone, Internet; • scanners, computerized stock control and delivery; • electronic data interchange (EDI); • genetic modification; • satellites; • digitization; • cellular telephones; • nano-technologies; • QR codes; • others.
Economic and natural factors	**Political and legal factors**
• business life cycle; • interest rate; • exchange rate; • credit lines; • inflation rate; • investment levels; • unemployment; • energy costs; • types of financial institutions; • growth trends (GNP); • nature and basis of domestic and international competition; • commercial blocks; • education level; • economic integration; • supplier concentration; • buyer concentration; • energy availability; • restrictions of environmental raw materials (water, air, among others); • tourism expenditure; • others.	• political and legal structure; • alliances and political orientations; • legislative structure; • identification and analysis of the government agencies that legitimate; • antitrust policies; • political and governmental stability; • interest and exchange rates (in their political aspect); • labor legislation; • international commerce regulations; • environmental protection legislation; • pressure groups; • power of the labor unions; • packaging recycling laws; • packaging restrictions; • restrictions on communication types; • tariff barriers; • taxation policies; • agricultural subsidy policies; • product certification and/or processes; • others.

Sources: based on Gilligan and Wilson (2003), Johnson and Scholes (2008), Stern *et al.* (1996), Rosenbloom (1999), Berman (1996), Achrol and Stern (1988) and consulting projects

Table 2.5 Drivers of change and actions that must be implemented

Social/cultural		Technological		Economic/natural		Political/legal	
List of impacts/ opportunities	List of company actions	List of impacts/ opportunities	List of company actions	List of impacts/ opportunities	List of company actions	List of impacts/ opportunities	List of company actions

Threats	List of threats identified in the STEP analysis	List of projects and actions for the company based on the STEP analysis
Oppportunities	List of opportunities identified in the STEP analysis	

Figure 2.2 Consolidation of the project and actions based on the STEP analysis

Analysis of the Company's Industrial Sector

In this section sectoral analysis will be considered in the light of the model proposed by Porter (1997). According to Porter, there are five basic competitive forces that influence an industry's (sector's) potential for profit:

- the threat of new entrants (competitors) in the sector;
- the rivalry intensity among existing competitors;
- the threat of substitute products;
- buyers' bargaining power;
- suppliers.

The threat of new entrants (competitors) is a constant concern for companies. If a certain industry is yielding excessive profitability for the participating companies, new companies will naturally be attracted to this industry. Unless barriers to entry are established, the "invasion" of new entrants will tend to reduce the general profitability of that industry. Wright *et al.* (2000) and Grant (2002) suggest some ways of establishing entry barriers: demand economies of scale, product differentiation, demand for capital, high exit costs, access to distribution channels and the retaliation that can be made by existing companies in the market against the new entrant.

The price that consumers are willing to pay for a product depends, in part, on the availability of substitute products. Because of negotiating advantages, the bargaining power of buyers in a sector can reduce the profitability of selling companies. For Wright *et al.* (2000) the concentration of buyers, relevance of the acquired products in relation to the total company cost, differentiation of products, costs of change, profit margin, possibility of backwards vertical integration and availability of information are factors that influence the bargaining power of the focal company's buyers.

The analysis of the power determinants between a company and its suppliers is analogous to the previous analysis. The key issue in the relationship between the company and its suppliers is the degree of difficulty the producers have to change suppliers. Wright *et al.* (2000) suggest the suppliers have power in the following circumstances:

- the supplying sector is dominated by few companies and is more concentrated than the sector to which it sells;
- there are no substitute products;

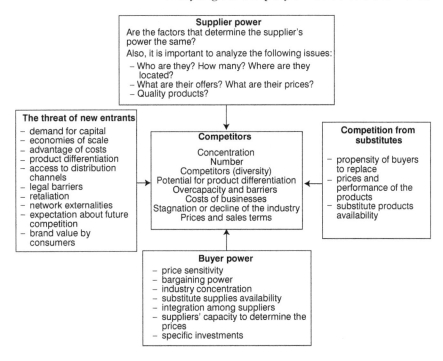

Figure 2.3 Determinants of the competition's intensity – the five forces model
Source: adapted from Porter (1980) and Grant (2002)

- the sector that is buying is not an important customer for the suppliers;
- the suppliers' products are important inputs for the buyer's business;
- the suppliers' products are differentiated or have high change costs built-in to its costs;
- the suppliers can make a forward vertical integration, entering the company's market.

Finally, the degree of rivalry among existing companies in the sector is the main determining factor of the degree of competition and profitability in an industry. The intensity of the competition between companies in an industry will depend on various factors, such as the number of existing companies in the sector, the sector's growth rate, high fixed or inventory costs, the absence of differentiation or change costs, high exit barriers, among others. More details about the company's relationship with its competitors will be presented in the next section. Figure 2.3 attempts to show a summary of the sector analysis.

It is suggested that, in this step of the planning process, an analysis for your company be done using data and information about the sector in which it operates.

Analyzing Your Consumer

As highlighted by Abell (1980), knowledge of consumer purchasing behavior is a key factor in the definition of a company's business. The analysis of the consumer must include the following factors:

- analysis of the purchase decision process;
- analysis of the final and intermediate consumer's behavior;

Table 2.6 The consumer's purchase decision process

Step of the process	How the step happens	What ideas can be used	Which questions must be asked
Recognition of the purchase need	Personal values and necessities associated with external influences, mainly coming from social interaction, make the current state different from the desired, thus giving rise to a need.	• Apply the most frequent and efficient stimulus in order to stimulate this need; for example, advertising showing the benefits.	• Which need is fulfilled when consuming this product? • Are these needs evident? • How much is the target public involved with the product?
Search for information	The search is made through internal sources (memory, knowledge) and in external sources (market and through personal contacts).	• Identify how much the consumer searches for information and the sources he most uses. This helps the company improve the product's pricing, its distribution strategy and mainly the communications/ advertising plan. It needs to work with the sources that most influence the consumer.	• Which product or brand does the consumer remember? • Is the consumer motivated to look for external sources? Which are those sources? • Which are the product attributes that are most researched?
Evaluation of the alternatives	The consumer will choose an alternative that is the strongest in the criteria that he values most.	• The company should, through research, identify what the consumer values (attributes) and be competitive in these attributes. Reposition in the attributes analyzed, reposition competitors, change the weight in the consumer's criterion of analysis.	• Does the consumer evaluate and compare alternatives? • What are the alternatives and criteria of choice? Can it be altered? • What is the result of the evaluation of alternatives? • Are they truly different? Can this be proved?
Purchase decision	At this point purchase decisions are taken; in other words where to buy, when to buy, what to buy and how to pay.	• A strong effort must be made at the point of sale (in food purchases, two-thirds of decisions are made here). • Observe the growth of purchases by mail, e-mail, telephone and catalogs.	• Will the consumer spend time and energy until the best alternative is found? • Where do you prefer to buy the product (channel) and at what moment in your day?
Post-purchase behavior	Comparison between product expectations and its performance. The consequences go from extreme satisfaction and positive word-of-mouth or even filing a lawsuit against the company.	• Maintain an effective and timely toll-free number or e-mail address. • Do surveys to monitor the consumer's satisfaction. • Remember that only 5 percent of unsatisfied consumers complain. The rest simply stop buying.	• Is the consumer satisfied with the product or service? • What are the reasons for the satisfaction/ dissatisfaction? Does he comment on this to other people? • Is there an intention of repeating the purchase? Why?

Source: based on Engel (1995)

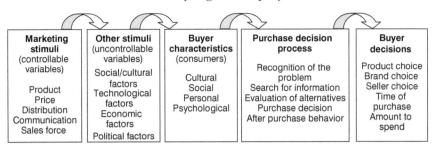

Marketing stimuli (controllable variables) Product Price Distribution Communication Sales force	Other stimuli (uncontrollable variables) Social/cultural factors Technological factors Economic factors Political factors	Buyer characteristics (consumers) Cultural Social Personal Psychological	Purchase decision process Recognition of the problem Search for information Evaluation of alternatives Purchase decision After purchase behavior	Buyer decisions Product choice Brand choice Seller choice Time of purchase Amount to spend

Figure 2.4 Purchase behavior model
Source: Kotler (1997)

- what is the internal and external relevant consumer information for marketing;
- where is the relevant consumer information.

It is of fundamental importance that companies focus on their consumers and remain market-oriented. There is a tendency that market driven companies can obtain better returns on their investments, higher success level in the introduction of new products and a high level of market performance.

In order to get this orientation then, we start from the analysis of the consumer's/customer's purchasing behavior. What will influence the consumer's purchase decision process are the marketing incentives introduced by companies through product characteristics, price, communications (promotion, advertising) and distribution strategy, in addition to the environment incentives, which are the economical, technological, political and cultural factors, plus the cultural, social, personal and psychological characteristics of this buyer. These three factors influencing the purchase decision process will result in the buyer's decisions, as shown in Figure 2.4.

The consumer's purchase decision process that composes the model previously shown can be analyzed in more detail. At the same time that the process steps are explained, it is sought to show how these tools can be used by companies and which questions they ask their consumers, in the form of research and even in daily company routine, in order to identify their preferences and deliver the best offer possible. The model is seen in Table 2.6.

In this step of the planning, the planning team completes a table similar to Table 2.7 to analyze the customer's/consumer's purchase decision process. Table 2.7 can be completed for each type of customer; in other words, distributors, wholesalers, retailers and final consumers.

Table 2.7 Analyzing the purchase decision process of your customers/consumers

Step of the purchase process	Describe how the process is done	What opportunities are there for your company?
		List of opportunities

The Consumer's Kingdom

When analyzing the purchase decision process of consumers, it is relevant for the companies to consider changes that have happened in the marketing behavior of companies over the past 30 years. First, the so-called wild view of marketing, that dominated the 1970s, 1980s and in some markets even the 1990s. The era of the wild view of marketing has ended in most industries, although in some, even today, these "dinosaurs" still exist. This "wild view" used to view marketing as the architect pushing consumption, full of advertising, sales and aggressive selling. New products were designed for sales, mass consumption and profit, with short-term goals. From this "wild view" perspective, marketing is seen as manipulative and companies are not market orientated, causing lack of measurement and spreading problematic relationships with the market. Most companies did not listen at all to consumers. All organizational structure was designed for selling, short-term results and short-term relationships.

At the end of the 1980s and the beginning of 1990s, several environmental changes ocurred in most countries and markets. I consider the most important to be the widening of markets and internationalization, the fast rate of technology change and progress, market deregulation, increase in global competition, with some markets having more offers than demand.

Another bundle of important changes came from the information and communication process, with technology, the internet and World Wide Web, increasing the speed of socio-cultural changes in consumers. We can also point the consumerist movement, the growth of ethics in citizens' behavior and the emergence of societal marketing movement (inclusion) as important changes in the last 20 years.

These changes have brought us to an era of consumer sovereignty, or an era of the consumer taking over production chains, that should now be redesigned towards the satisfaction of this new king with professional purchasing behaviors and new and growing expectations. This new era made companies understand that consumers value their time, want well-being, good experiences and rewards, and exercise free choice in an individual way. For companies with poor behavior, we had the emergence of consumer nonprofit organizations (NPOs) (bringing countervailing power) and wide public attention to consumer rights. The risks for companies increased at an incredible pace with fast communication processes, discussion groups, web-based complaints and new media.

The sovereignty of consumers led companies which want to conquer markets and competition to a new strategic behavior. In essence, they needed to be demand driven. This behavior is based on paying attention to and collecting information about consumers, competitors and the environment, and having a deep analysis and rapid reaction of environmental changes.

Companies switched to a long-term approach, valuing satisfaction and well-being of buyers. It is a new integrated network organization, dynamic and aligned, decentralized with delegation and now designed with a problem-solving approach. This problem-solving approach is "from trying to sell to helping to buy." There is a continuous search for new ways to solve existing needs, launching added value solutions that take account of and value corporate social responsibility, having a smooth and collaborative network with suppliers, distributors and service providers, with a strong focus on smart market segmentation, knowledge generation and dissemination, and measurable/accountable marketing.

With this behavior, there are several success stories of companies with performance contributing to growth of demand, democracy and inclusion. The target is to have very satisfied consumers with repeat purchases – what is called the "lock in" strategy. Companies build relationships and informal contracts with consumers that can even blind them towards competitors, increase their cost of changing to another company, building a sustainable competitive advantage, with growth and profitability.

Consumers' Risk Analysis

Do companies have contracts with consumers? First of all, contracts are relationships, and are either formal (written and signed) or informal (such as oral contracts based on trust); in many societies informal contracts have a greater value than written and formal agreements.

The difference between consumers' expectations and what is received when a product is purchased – dissonance or gap – has the subject of much study in marketing. Companies are facing an era of high expectations and these bring extra responsibilities. They would like to have loyal consumers buying what is offered, and giving returns. But can this be achieved and these contracts established?

Traditional analysis would say that companies should have a quality product, attractive price, responsive service, good communications, marketing channels, sales processes, etc. But we can look at it in a different way, studying risks and looking at the offer through the consumer's lens.

The focus should be to look in the opposite direction, from the consumer's perspective, analyzing possible risks that consumers are trying to avoid when buying, to start a relationship and build a sustainable contract. What are these risks? How could we modify our strategy to avoid them? Here is a list of 10 questions to consider:

1   What are the risks of poor performance (the product will not fulfill consumers' needs completely)? We need to understand what consumers expect in terms of quality, conformity and other criteria used to measure performance. For example, some companies make the economic benefits of using their products clear to the market. When new products using new technology are launched, most consumers are hesitant to buy and even early adopters are sometimes hesitant.
2   What are the risks of the purchasing process taking more time or being more inconvenient? Consumers need simple purchase experiences, so all the processes (credit, delivery, showrooms, and internet, among others) should be mapped and analyzed from the consumers' point of view so as to be quick and simple. Losing time nowadays is almost a crime!
3   What are the risks of a perception of the offer being of poor value? We need to understand how the consumer is putting value on our offer and what really is being offered. If there is a gap, probably the company is mistaken in its advertising or other marketing activity.
4   What are the risks of being seen as not belonging or not giving pleasure, comfort and well-being in the community? Some products are purchased based on opinions, and will be used in situations where consumers will face the opinions of others, friends, family, neighbors, colleagues and others. Consumers are searching for acceptance and sometimes buy a product or service to fulfill a sense of belonging, of "taking part."
5   What are the health or security risks associated with the product? If it is a food or beverage, for example, is there a perceived health risk, and is there any value in terms of certifications or other associations.
6   What are the payment or finance risks to the consumer? Will the consumer be able to pay, should payment be facilitated by offering credit or by other means?

7   What are the risks of not coinciding with consumers' views as regards society, the environment, employment or other values? Production processes, marketing and other aspects of the company should be linked to what is valued by the buyer.

8   What are the risks not being able the resell the product in the case of durable goods that are used and then sold on (cars, for instance)?

9   What are the risks of the consumer not understanding the product or service? These risks are sometimes neglected, but consumers want simple solutions and products that are easy to use and to understand?

10   What are the risks to the consumer in terms of maintenance, servicing, or other post-sales factors – such as costs relating to insurance, maintenance, energy consumption and other variables.

Successful consumer relationships today focus on experiences. To be successful means performing better than the competition in avoiding consumer risks and delivering benefits.

This will bring about a relationship with consumers who tend to be loyal if we keep searching to offer better value. When consumers perceive that a brand is not offering the best value, they may transfer to a competitor.

External Analysis and Collective Actions

After the external analysis is completed, the company can define its own individual action plan with the objective of taking advantage of opportunities and minimizing negative impacts from changes in the external environment. On many occasions, these actions can be implemented jointly with other agents in the network, reducing costs and improving quality. A company can participate in collective actions with suppliers, producers, distribution channels or facilitator companies. In the process of defining collective actions, plans which are of common interest and which can be implemented jointly must be evaluated, taking into account the relevance of these actions to the company. Table 2.8 presents a matrix that can be completed with the objective of identifying the potential of initiating collective actions with the members of the focal company's network (the company where DDSP is being implemented).

From this starting point, executives will be able to place actions in a hierarchy by level of importance. Whether joint implementation for these actions is possible, and whether companies will be interested in collaborating in them will be evaluated later. The actions which are capable of collective implementation, and which do not cause problems for an individual company's strategies, will have priority. Then, these proposed actions will be considered in the light of the topics of Chapters 4 and 5, establishing objectives and proposing strategies to reach them.

In Chapter 3, the third part of the DDSP method, the process of internal analysis of the company will be described. Internal analysis must be carried out simultaneously with external analysis, since they complement each other in finding out the real situation in which the company exists. The information from the internal and external analyses will support the definition of the company's objectives and strategies.

Table 2.8 Matrix of collective actions between the members of a network

Ideas for collective actions with suppliers	Ideas for collective actions with distribution channels	Ideas for collective actions with facilitator companies (freight carriers, banks, logistics operators, etc.)	Ideas for collective actions with its competitors
Action 1	Action 5	Action 7	Action 9
Action 2	Action 6	Action 8	Action 10
. . .	. .	. . .	. . .

Activities to Analyze Your Company's Environment and Market

At this stage of the plan it is important to undertake the following activities with the planning team:

- map out a detailed network of your company (in accordance with Figure 2.1);
- make tables from the data survey of the market in which the company operates and forecast future sales (by product, product lines, by region, etc.) (Tables 2.3 and 2.4);
- complete the STEP analysis table details and the projects which are to be developed (Tables 2.4 and 2.5 and Figure 2.2);
- complete the analysis of the five environmental competition forces (Figure 2.3);
- identify ideas to take advantage of opportunities as regards customers'/suppliers' behavior (Figure 2.4, Tables 2.6 and 2.7);
- Answer the questions in the "Consumers' Risk Analyis" tool;
- identify ideas for partnership actions with companies within your network (Table 2.8).

Questions

1   How does a company map out its network?
2   What is STEP analysis and what variables should be considered when undertaking it?
3   Other than STEP analysis, what are the types of external analysis an organization should do in this stage of the DDSP?
4   How can the collective actions be integrated in the external analysis process?
5   How is consumers' risk analysis performed?

3 Analyzing the Company and its Competition (Internal Analysis)

This chapter presents the major steps to be undertaken in DDSP to analyze the company's internal situation and to analyze its competitors. Since this analysis has the objective of detailing the company's internal situation, it is important that it is carried out using comparisons with competitors. The company's advantages and disadvantages, and strong and weak points should be seen in the light of comparison with other companies, with industry standards or even with other industries.

In this way, the following analyses can then be undertaken:

- internal environment and company structure analysis;
- analysis of the company's strong and weak points vis-à-vis competitors;
- internal analysis versus the performance of the main competitors;
- value creation, resources and company competencies analysis;
- analysis of critical success factors.

The analysis in Chapter 2 gave the company information regarding the opportunities and threats of the environment, which need to be maximized in the case of opportunities, or minimized in the case of threats. This internal analysis focuses mainly on the identification of the company's competencies and their interaction with the external environment and the competition.

Analysis of the Internal Environment and Structure

The marketing efforts of an organization are molded by the internal forces that are known and controlled by the company. These internal influences include the activities of production, finance and human resources. Other forces are, for example, company location, research and development, and the image the company projects to its public. The location of the factory determines geographical limits of the company's market, especially if shipping costs are high or if products are perishable. The research and development factor can determine if the company will lead or follow other companies in its area of activity (Etzel *et al.*, 2001).

Kotler (1997) comments that if a business is not doing well, it is not because its departments lack necessary forces, but because they are not sufficiently integrated. Some recent research has investigated the use of Internet and various information technologies to facilitate interactions among the departments and between the company with its customers (Trainor *et al.*, 2011) in a way that contributes to the execution of business processes, creating a competitive advantage for the company.

Therefore, it is very important to evaluate interdepartmental relationships as part of the internal audit. Such issues are directly related to the type of organization structure adopted by the company. In the DDSP of a company, the main decisions taken are under the responsibility of the strategic marketing function, in a close relationship with the areas of R&D and production, finance and administration. Specifically, this means that strategic marketing orients the product policy and makes decisions in relation to the economic viability of launching new products.

In order to complete the initial phase of the internal analysis it is important that the company evaluates to what degree it is market oriented (or demand driven), allowing an evaluation of how the departments are oriented to the customers' needs. This analysis can be conducted through questionnaires to those responsible for the various departments, about the departments' focus when meeting the customers' needs. Table 3.1 presents a list of questions to be answered in this evaluation of the company's orientation in relation to the customer; the grades range from 0 (no development is made in relation to this activity) to 10 (makes great effort in these activities) for the factors and activities listed. Using an intranet to carry this out will make it easier to quantify and analzye the results.

Analysis of the Company's Strong and Weak Points

The analysis of a business's strengths and weaknesses, generally, allows one to state that it is not necessary to correct all of the company's weaknesses, nor to give much emphasis to all its strengths. The important factor for analysis is whether the business is limited in its opportunities or whether it should acquire strengths to explore better opportunities (McDonald, 2002; Kotler, 1997).

Gilligan and Wilson (2003) present a form to analyze competition that involves the selection of the main competitors to be evaluated, the definition of the necessary information to be gathered, the definition of those responsible for executing research, the allocation of resources for such a process, the development of reports with the analyses and the compilation of the results as a part of the planning. Figure 3.1 synthesizes the main phases of the analysis of the competition, its results and information sources.

The analysis of the strong and weak points demands substantial use of search resources, selection and analysis of information about competitors. Such types of information can be (1) easy to obtain or low cost, or (2) hard to obtain or high cost, or be anywhere within these extremes. The sources and types of information and the degree of difficulty in obtaining these pieces of information are presented in Figure 3.2.

Although it is difficult to develop an exhaustive list of all the information that needs to be collected for the development of intelligence on the competition, it can be divided into ten areas that should seek information and update them constantly. Table 3.2 lists the types of information that companies should seek regarding their competitors.

Competition rivalry refers to the battle between companies for market share. In this context, the analysis of competition must begin by the definition of the company's market (Porter, 1992; Grant, 2002; Gilligan and Wilson, 2003). In competition situations, companies can compete on a range of factors that may or may not involve prices. Price competition erodes profits through margin reduction. Non-price competition erodes profits by raising the fixed costs (for example, development of new products, R&D, etc.) and marginal costs (for example, product improvements, investments in communications, etc.). The way in which the company can pass on the cost increase to the customer is by raising prices, therefore

Table 3.1 Evaluation of the company's customer orientation

Are these activities carried out?	Grade 0 to 10
Research and development Is alert to global innovations, via web and others. Dedicates time to meet customers and listen to their problems. Accepts involvement of marketing and production areas, among others, in each new project. Tests and evaluates the competition's products. Seeks to know the customers' reactions and asks for suggestions. Continually improves and perfects the product, based on the market feedback.	
Purchasing and production Stimulates the suppliers' continuous innovation, not allowing them to grow complacent. Proactively seeks the best suppliers, instead of choosing only from those that approach the company. Reduces transaction costs seeking long-term relationships with a smaller number of reliable and high quality suppliers. Does not make concessions to quality in order to save on price. Invites customers to visit and get to know the facilities. Visits the customers' facilities and verifies how they use the company's products. Continuously seeks to manufacture goods faster and/or at a lower cost. Continuously improves product quality, trying to reach a zero defects measure. Satisfies the customers' demands for "customization," when this can be done in a profitable way.	
Marketing Listens and studies the customers' needs and desires in well-defined market segments. Allocates marketing efforts according to the potential of long-term profit of the target segments. Creates winning offers for the target segment. Continually evaluates the company's image and customers' satisfaction. Continually collects and evaluates ideas of new products and how to improve existing products and services in order to satisfy the customers' needs. Influences all company departments and employees so that they consider the customer in all they think and do. Has specialized knowledge of the customer's sectors of activity. Endeavors to offer the customer "the best solution." Only makes promises that it can keep. Transmits the customers' needs and ideas to the people responsible for product development. Serves the same customers for a long period of time. Establishes a high standard for customer servicing, capable of answering their questions, answering their complaints and solving their problems in a quick and satisfactory way. Publishes favorable news about the company and "controls the damage" of the unfavorable news. Acts as an internal customer and an advocate of the public with the intention of improving the company's policies and practices.	
Accounting and finance Periodically prepares "profitability" reports by product, market segment, geographical areas (regions, sales territories), order size and individual customers. Prepares invoices suitable to the customers' requirements and answers their inquiries quickly and with courtesy. Understands and supports marketing investments (i.e. institutional advertising) that yield the customers' preference and loyalty in the long term. Makes financial packages that are adequate to the customers' financial needs. Makes quick decisions regarding the customers' capacity of honoring their financial obligations.	
Other employees that have contact with customers Are competent, attentive, pleasant, reliable and receptive.	

Source: adapted from Cooper and Lane (1997), Las Casas (1999), Jain (2000), McDonald (2002) and Lambin (2000)

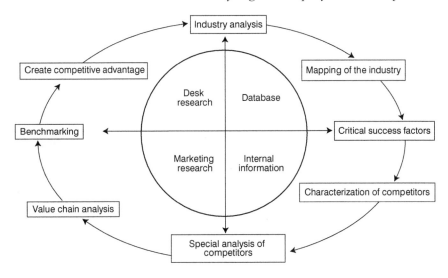

Figure 3.1 Approaches for the analysis of the competition
Source: Gilligan and Wilson (2003)

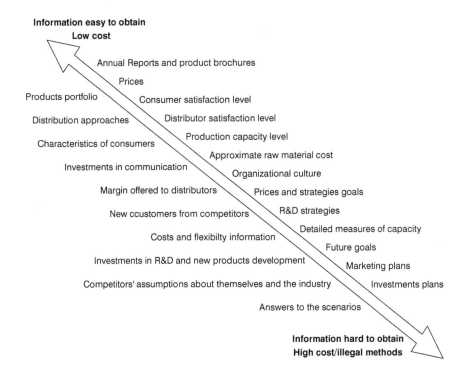

Figure 3.2 Management information needs for competitive intelligence
Source: Gillian and Wilson (2003)

Table 3.2 What should companies try to know about their competitors?

1. Market • number of units sold; • sales by product line; • tendency of sales; • market share; • trends in market share. 2. Buyers • customer profile; • purchase motives; • standard product use; • new customers; • lost customers; • proportion of repeat purchases; • loyalty to the brand; • identity and image among the customers; • level of product satisfaction, performance, quality and reliability; • existence of special relationships. 3. Products, services, brands and packaging • amplitude and depth of the product lines; • level of product performance; • new products policy; • investments in R&D; • modification and introduction of new products; • quality level; • style, design; • name, brands and packaging; • warranty and support services; • lead-times; • patents. 4. Communications • level of investments and standards; • effectiveness of the promotional actions;	• fliers and product catalogs; • sales promotions; • publicity and advertising; • media plans and schedules; • public relations. 5. Distribution channels • programs for customer return or loyalty; • types of distribution channels used; • relationships and power balance; • shipping structure; • costs structure; • flexibility; • existence of contracts; • dealer objectives; • level of distributor performance; • capacity and level of dealer support; • inventory level; • shelf space; • warehouse location; • profit margins of intermediaries. 6. Sales force/HR • size, capacity and experience; • geographical and customer coverage; • level of assistance available; • salaries and commissions; • post-sales service; • customer support philosophy; • sales territory; • competency, courtesy, presentation, friendliness and knowledge; • governance form. 7. Prices • cost level; • cost structure; • price list and discount table;	• credit and payment conditions; • special terms; • product return operations. 8. Finance • performance level, margins and profitability; • availability of financial resources and flexibility; • structure of capital; • financial flexibility. 9. Management • main executives; • objectives (short- and long-term); • philosophy and culture; • expectations; • attitudes towards risk; • special abilities; • competitive strategies; • strategic commitment; • organizational structure; • investment plans; • critical success factors. 10. Others (production, environment, etc.) • actions related to the environment; • ISO norms; • certifications; • labeling; • sales per employee; • capacity utilization; • types of equipment used; • methods of acquisition of raw material; • main suppliers; • degree of vertical/ horizontal integration; • commitment to market sectors; • efficiency/quickness; • work environment; • developing technological innovations.

Source: based on Gilligan and Wilson (2003), Neves (2003), McDonald (2002), Grant (2002), Lambin (2000), Las Casas (1999), Cooper and Lane (1997) and Kotler (1997)

Table 3.3 Description of the company's main competitors

	Competitor 1	Competitor 2	Competitor 3	Competitor n
Main characteristics				
Main suppliers				
Main segments				
Infrastructure				
Invoicing				
Sales force and compensation				
Strategic movements				
Others				

Source: Gilligan and Wilson (2003)

non-price competition is less likely to affect profits than the price competition (Porter, 1992; Besanko *et al.*, 2000).

An initial descriptive analysis of the competition can be made (as in Table 3.3) followed by a detailed comparative analysis of the competition. This process involves the attribution of scores to structural factors and marketing mix for the company and its main competitors. The score ranges from 0 to 10, where 0 indicates the company is very poor and 10 indicates the company is excellent (the best). In this way a ranking is obtained with ratings that evaluate in which factors the company is better or worse than its competitors, thus facilitating the development of actions and strategies. This analysis can be undertaken based on the layout of Table 3.4.

Conducting complete and regular marketing audits in a structured way will supply the company, in time, with knowledge about the business, market trends and how the competition adds its value, serving as a basis of the definition of company objectives and strategies.

Company Value Creation, Resources and Competencies

Competitive positioning based on value creation has been considered the foundation for the success in marketing (Hooley *et al.*, 2004a). The competitive positioning that a company chooses is a combination of the market choices and the differential advantage that it is seeking to create as a way to guarantee its market. Although each department can dominate a target competency, the challenge is to develop a superior competitive capacity to manage these processes. Stalk *et al.* (1992) call these competition processes "based on capacities."

The value is created as products move up the vertical chain of the company, the "value chain." The value chain represents the aggregation of value created by the company activity, for example: production, marketing and logistics. Each activity in the value chain can, potentially, increase the benefits that consumers obtain from a certain product, but can also add costs to the company producing and selling such products (Porter, 1992; Besanko *et al.*, 2000).

By moving through the vertical chain, the products gain economic value (value added). A producer, in each stage of the chain, combines products and services produced in the prior stages with capital and work to create a product of more value to his customers than the materials used to produce it. The benefit perceived in the product (*B*) represents the value the consumer attributes to the product. The cost (*C*) represents what is sacrificed when the components are converted into final products. The value created is the difference

Table 3.4 Internal analysis versus competition

Evaluation factor	Grade from 1 to 10			
	Company	Competitor 1	Competitor 2	Competitor n
Product				
Quality				
Style				
Brands, packages				
Warranty and support services				
Cost				
Lead time				
Price				
Price level				
Discount policy				
Credit conditions				
Payment conditions				
Special payment terms				
Communications				
Publicity				
Personal sales				
Promotion				
Advertising				
Distribution				
Distribution channels				
Channel coverage				
Location				
Transport system				
…				
Human resources				
…				
Production process				
Quickness				
Efficiency				
Capacity utilization				
…				
Others				
…				
Total				

Sources: based on Gilligan and Wilson (2003), Neves (2003), McDonald (2002), Grant (2002), Lambin (2000), Las Casas (1999), Cooper and Lane (1997) and Kotler (1997)

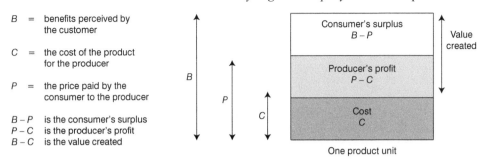

Figure 3.3 Components of the created value
Source: adapted from Besanko *et al.* (2000: 396)

between the value attributed to the product and the value of the components used to produce it.

In this way, Besanko *et al.* (2000) state that to reach a competitive advantage, with a performance superior to that of the competitors, the company must not seek only to create positive value, but also to create more value than its competitors, as shown in Figure 3.3.

Thus, companies whose product and price characteristics offer the consumer more surplus will have more competitive advantage. As the value created, $B - C$, is the sum of the consumer's surplus, $(B - P)$, and of the profit, $(P - C)$, the companies that create more value than their competitors will be able to overcome the competition's surplus offer to the consumer and attract their customers, reaching a higher profitability than its rivals (Besanko *et al.*, 2000).

The value chain identifies activities that create value for the company. However, the company will only create more value than its competitors if it performs better in some or all of these activities. In order to do this, the company must have resources and competencies that its competitors do not have, otherwise any strategy could be copied to create a similar value (Besanko *et al.*, 2000; Prahalad and Hamel, 1990).

What are Company Resources?

A company's vision based on resources has great impact on understanding the conceptualization of strategies. When the main strategic interest was to choose an industry and position for cost and differentiation advantages, the tendency was for companies to adopt similar strategies. The vision based on resources emphasizes individuality and unique characteristics of each company and suggests that the key to profitability is not to do the same thing other companies do, but explore differences, explore new avenues, explore more creative ways of satisfying needs.

Grant (2002) comments that it is important to distinguish company resources from company competencies. According to Grant, the basic units of analysis are company resources: capital, equipment, human resources, intellectual capital, etc. But on most occasions these resources alone do not create value for the company. In order to establish a competitive advantage, resources must be organized and used to create organizational competencies. These competencies and critical success factors are the basis for the development of strategies that will determine the company's competitive advantage. Figure 3.4 demonstrates these relationships.

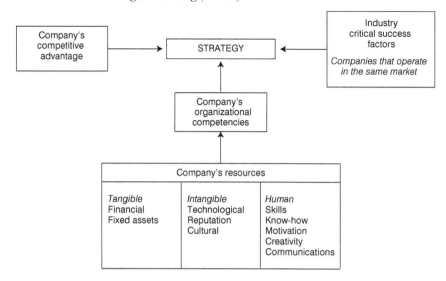

Figure 3.4 Relationship between resources, competencies and competitive advantage
Source: Grant (2002: 139)

Day (1994) suggests a distinction between resources and competencies, in which the assets are resources the company has accumulated (investments, plant, location, brand value), while the competencies represent the "glue" that bonds these resources enabling them to be employed as advantages. A starting point in identifying the resources of the company and its competitors is to classify the resources as tangible, intangible and human, as detailed in Table 3.5, and from this classification the company can compare its resources with the resources of its competitors.

Tangible resources are the easiest to identify and evaluate, for example, financial resources and fixed assets that can be evaluated through financial statements. Grant (2002) comments that in order to identify how to create value from tangible resources the company must answer two main questions:

- What are the opportunities for savings related to the use of financial resources, produced goods and fixed assets?
- What are the possibilities to employ the existing assets in a more profitable way?

Intangible resources, for many companies, contribute much more to the total value of the assets than tangible resources. Among the most important intangible resources are brands, which together with names and history make up reputation assets, the value of which is in the trust customers have in them. Like reputation, technology is an asset that is not evident in the company's earnings statements. Intellectual property, patents, copyrights and business secrets include technological and artistic resources, whose property is protected by law (Grant, 2002).

Human resources are the productive services that employees offer the company, in terms of abilities, knowledge, reasoning and decision making abilities. The ability of the employees to coordinate their efforts and integrate the different abilities does not depend only on their interpersonal abilities, but also on the organizational context. The way in which

Table 3.5 Classification of the company resources

Tangible resources	Relevant characteristics	Key indicators	Company evaluation versus competition
Financial resources	Company's capacity for funding. Equity capital. Investment capacity.	Net equity. Cash flow. Credit rate.	
Physical resources	Group of production possibilities and the impact in the company's cost position. Key characteristics. Size, location, technique, plant sophistication and flexibility and equipments. Location and alternative uses for the land and facilities. Raw material reserves.	Market value of the fixed assets. Equipment depreciation. Production scale of the factories. Flexibility of the fixed assets. Use of strategic alliances in production.	
Intangible resources			
Technological Resources	Intellectual property, patent portfolio, copyrights, commercial secrets. Innovation resources: research, technicians and scientists.	Number and importance of patents. Income from patent licensing and copyrights. R&D teams. Number and location of the research resources.	
Reputation	Brand reputation with consumers. Reputation of the company in relation to quality and reliability of its products and services. Reputation with the suppliers, governmental agencies, banks and community.	Brand recognition. Brand value. Percentage of repeat purchases. Objective measures of performance of comparative products. Research the organization's reputation.	
Culture	Values, traditions and social norms.	Organizational climate.	
Human resources			
HR	Education, training and employee experience. Abilities available to the company. Employee adaptability and contribution for the flexibility of the organizational strategy. Collaborative and social abilities of the employees. Employee commitment and loyalty.	Educational, technical and professional qualifications of the employees. Wages in relation to the industry. Percentage of days lost with work suspension or industrial disputes. Absenteeism rates. Employee turnover rate. Way they speak of, admire and have affection for the company.	
Creativity	Product innovation, processes and ways of working.	R&D advances. Number of innovations and product launches.	

Source: adapted from Grant (2002: 140)

this context affects the internal collaboration is determined by the key intangible resource, the organizational culture (Barney, 1986 cited in Grant, 2002).

Analysis of the Company's Competencies

The company's competencies differ from the company's resources: they are the activities the company does especially well when compared with other companies. One must have in mind that the resources are like "nouns" (things that companies own) and competencies are like "verbs" (things that companies do). Competencies reside within specific business functions or in the company's capacity in managing relations between elements in the value chain or in coordinating activities between them (Besanko *et al.*, 2000).

Prahalad and Hamel (1990) made important contributions to the concept of essential competencies, making a distinction between the fundamental competencies for the company performance and strategy, which bring a disproportionate contribution in order to maximize the value given to the customer or the efficiency with which the value is delivered, and supply the basis for entering new markets. These competencies are differentiated, for independently from their basis, they have some common characteristics, such as the fact of being valuable for multiple products and markets, being part of organizational routines (implying that the competencies can persist even when people leave the company), and are tacit, i.e. are hard to be reduced to simple algorithms or procedure manuals.

This way, resources, competencies and critical success factors are determining conditions for a company's profitability. The ability to manage resources, competencies and critical success factors, also, are of great importance for the company, given that competencies are generally tacit and it is difficult to replicate them in other companies, which supports the company's competitive advantage.

Analysis of Critical Success Factors

The understanding of the market and the analysis of the external environment that was made in Chapter 2, combined with competition analysis, allows an evaluation of an industry's potential profitability. However, it is important to understand how profits are shared among the companies that compete in that industry. So, analyses of an industry seek to make explicit the sources of competitive advantages within it. Then, it is sought to identify the factors within the industry's environment that determine its capacity for surviving and prospering. These are the so-called critical success factors.

This concept was initially developed by Hofer and Schendel (1977) who defined the critical success factors as variables that a company's management can influence with its decisions and that may affect significantly the company's competitive position in an industry. Within a specific industry, they derive from the interaction of two groups of variables, the economic and technological characteristics of the industry, and the competitive weapons, with which companies of several industries have developed their strategies.

Grant (2002) mentions that in order to survive and prosper in an industry, a company must satisfy two criteria: first, it must supply what the customers want to purchase, and, second, it must survive competition intensity. Thus, the analysis must begin by asking two questions:

- What do the customers need?
- What does the company need to continue competing?

In order to answer the first question it is necessary to analyze consumers in detail, which involves identifying them, knowing their needs and establishing the basis on which they choose the offer of one supplier instead of another. The second question requires the company to examine the basis of competition in the industry, its intensity and forms of competitive advantages (Grant, 2002). These analyses were initially discussed in Chapter 2, but they complement the development of the plan as a way to identify the critical success factors and compare them with those of the competition. Figure 3.5 and the Table 3.6 outline this analysis and its comparisons.

Finally, a list of critical success factors can be made, weighting them in accordance with criteria defined by the company, and then comparing them with the competitors' critical success factors, based on judgment or company information. It should be emphasized that the company must seek to choose at least three and no more than ten critical success factors for a good analysis (Grant, 2002).

Thus, after defining the critical success factors (for example, has access to distribution channels, or produces on a large scale), weights are allocated (totalling 100) for each factor;

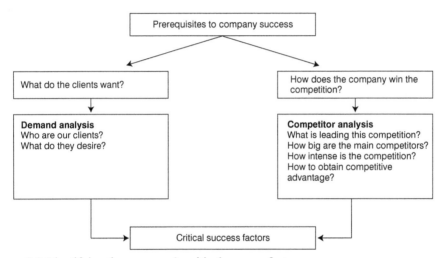

Figure 3.5 Identifying the company's critical success factors
Source: adapted from Grant (2002: 97)

Table 3.6 Comparison and weighting of the critical success factors

Critical success factors		Focus company		Competitor 1		Competitor 2	
CSF description	Weight	Grade	Weight × grade	Grade	Weight × grade	Grade	Weight × grade
Access to the channels	50	6	300	7	350	6	300
Produces on a large scale	30	8	240	7	210	9	270
. . .	. . .	. . .	. . .	. . .	. . .	. . .	. . .
Qualified team	20	9	180	6	120	8	160
Total (P × N)	100		720		680		730

Source: developed from Grant (2002) and McDonald (2002)

Strengths	List of strengths identified in the competitor analysis	List of projects and actions related to these points to be improved by the company
Weaknesses	List of weaknesses identified in the competitor analysis	

Figure 3.6 Consolidation of the project and actions based on the competition analysis

next the planning team can allocate scores from 0 (the company is very poor in this factor) to 10 (the company is excellent in this factor), weighting each factor with the coefficient. Subsequently, these values can be summed and the "total grade" of each company can be calculated.

In this way, based on the example of Table 3.4, it can be seen that the focal company has a score for the critical success factors similar to "Company 2," and as the access to the channels and large-scale production are the most important critical factors, these must be the focus of actions, improvements and investments, when the DDSP objectives and strategies are defined.

The final result of the analysis of the company and its competition can be presented according to Figure 3.6, where the company's main strong points are listed, as well as its weak points and the actions and projects that must be developed to take advantage of the company's strong points in relation to its competitors and seek to minimize its weak points.

Activities that You Must Undertake to Analyze Your Company and the Competition

At this stage of the plan, according to what has been discussed in the preceding sections, it is important that you undertake the following activities with the planning team:

- complete the market orientation table and evaluate it, scoring your company, as in Table 3.1;
- perform a complete analysis of the competition, seeking information available in websites, newspapers, magazines, publications and sales force, to complete Figure 3.3 and Table 3.3;
- perform a critical analysis of the company's resources (tangible and intangible), completing Table 3.4 and answering the questions listed in it;
- perform an analysis of the critical success factors and compare the company and its competitors, following the example in Table 3.5;
- consolidate actions and projects based on these analyses, as in Figure 3.6.

Questions

1   What company's activities should be analyzed in the internal analysis as regards customer orientation?
2   Why is it important to evaluate competitors within the internal analysis?
3   What are the approaches in the analysis of the competition?
4   How can companies have more competitive advantage in the market?
5   Identifying the company's critical success factors is important for a company to compare itself with competitors. How does a company identify its critical success factors?

4 Establishing Company Objectives

In any planning process, objectives and goals must be carefully established. Starting from the proposed objectives and goals, the strategies to reach them will be outlined in Chapter 5. The lack of clarity of the proposed objectives can compromise the whole DDSP sequence. According to Oliveira (2002), the objectives serve the following company purposes:

- provide people with the feeling of a specific and adequate role in the company;
- give consistency to decision making among a large number of different executives;
- encourage dedication and fulfillment based on expected results; and
- supply a base for corrective actions and control.

For Thompson and Strickland (1990) the establishment of long-term objectives directs current actions by having in view future results, besides stimulating the managers' consideration of future implications of the actions made in the present time. And the short-term objectives have the purpose of reaching a specific target, in a narrow time frame.

Gilligan and Wilson (2003) state that three main aspects of the company should be covered, answering these questions:

1   The nature of the current business (what business *are* we in?)
2   Where it should go (what business *should* we be in?)
3   How should we get there?

According to Oliveira (2002: 160), an objective is "the quantified target or point, with established fulfillment time frame and responsible people, that is intended to be reached through an extra effort." The expanded definition of the term objective inserts an element of "challenge" at the moment of establishing the objectives. Thus, at the moment of defining objectives, executives must presuppose an alteration of the status quo, defining a time frame and also the people responsible for achieving the proposed objectives.

Bateman and Snell (1998) distinguish simple objectives from strategic objectives. For these authors, strategic objectives are aimed at long-term results, at the value and growth of organizations. This way in the planning process the long-term objectives (or strategic) must be differentiated from the short-term objectives. Wright et al. (2000) differentiate these two groups of objectives into general and specific.

The general objectives are more generic and seek to translate the long-term "wishes" of the company's administration. The specific objectives, in turn, are restricted and quantifiable versions of the general objectives. For example, a company can have the general objective of being the largest in the market. Some specific objectives to reach the general objective could be: increase sales to classes "A" and "B" by 10 percent per year for at least the next five years; increase market share in classes "C" and "D" at a rate of 7 percent per year (for the next five years).

The terms objective and goal are routinely used as synonyms. And in fact the use of these terms as similar or not varies from author to author. To Kotler (1997), the term goal is used to describe the objectives in terms of magnitude and period; in other words, goal is the quantification of the objective. Thus, for this author the general objectives can simply be called "objectives" and the specific objectives can be called "goals." Oliveira (2002) comments that a goal is a specific type of objective; the goal is an objective that, while being realistic, challenges the members of the company. For this reason, companies constantly establish increasingly audacious goals for their teams, seeking to motivate the achievement of a maximum standard of performance, even in adverse situations. For the purposes of this book, the terms objectives and goals are being used as synonyms.

The first step to establish adequate objectives or goals in the DDSP is to define which are the company's greater objectives. It is emphasized that the objectives established must be consistent with the company's capacities (in accordance with what was presented in Chapter 1). It is also fundamental to make the objectives consistent with the external (Chapter 2) and internal (Chapter 3) contexts in which the company is placed; in other words, this stage of the DDSP must be undertaken based on the analysis of all the information collected in earlier stages. It is for this reason objectives and goals only now appear in this book.

Objectives can be quantitative (increase sales by 10 percent) or qualitative (improve the company image). They may also be determined in the short, medium and long term.

Table 4.1 Characteristics of the objectives

Characteristic	*Description*
Hierarchical	The objectives must be arranged in hierarchy, showing which have priority. It would also be interesting to clarify how the priorities were established.
Numbers must appear	Where possible, objectives must be quantifiable, allowing analysis of results over time.
Realistic	The objectives must be obtained from an analysis of opportunities and threats in the environment and from the strengths and weaknesses of the company, as well as the company's resources; and not from the personal ambitions or opinions of executives or employees.
Consistent	A company may have several objectives and important challenges simultaneously; but they must be consistent with each other.
Clear	The objectives must be clear, simple to understand, and understood by all involved in the process; and they should be in written form.
Communicated	The purpose and the content of the objectives must be communicated, directly or indirectly, to all staff involved.
Separated into functional objectives	The corporate objectives of the company must be divided into specific objectives for each functional area of the company (marketing, human resources, finance, and production, etc.).
Motivators	They must motivate staff to develop and implement strategies in order to fulfill the objectives.

Source: based on Oliveira (2002) with contributions from Kotler (1997).

While the company is progressing, the plan will be revised, the strategy will be regularly modified, and when appropriate, objectives will be redefined. The risk with establishing non-measurable objectives is that following up results is difficult, resulting a consequent loss of interest in the plan. Some parameters are easily measured, such as company revenue. Table 4.1 summarizes the main characteristics of the objectives.

Table 4.2 is a worksheet which can be used to develop the main marketing objectives and expected results for a set time frame (in the example, four years).

Other objectives can be developed from those listed in Table 4.2, targeting products, business units, the external market and sales areas, as illustrated in Table 4.3. Equally, the same level of detail can be applied to product lines (Table 4.4) and to target segments (Table 4.5).

The objectives that are the basis for the preparation of strategies or action plans vary between companies and also depend on the context in which they are being defined.

Table 4.2 Worksheet showing the main DDSP objectives of a company

Criteria	2013	2014	2015	2016
Income ($)				
Profit				
Sales margin				
Market share				
. . .				

Table 4.3 Worksheet showing geographical distribution of sales objectives

	2013	2014	2015	2016
Business unit 1				
Business unit 2				
Business unit 3				
External market				

Table 4.4 Worksheet showing main product line sales objectives

	2013	2014	2015	2016
Line 1				
Line 2				
Line 3				

Table 4.5 Worksheet showing major growth rate objectives by target segment

	2013	2014	2015	2016
Target segment 1				
Target segment 2				
Target segment 3				

Activities to Establish Objectives

In summary, the following factors must be considered at this stage of establishing DDSP objectives:

- the main objectives must be defined and quantified (in terms of sales, share and presence in markets, entry in new markets);
- the level of detail must be significant, so they can be monitored throughout the period and at the end of the plan;
- network objectives (partnerships, joint and collective action objectives) must be included.

After the objectives have been defined, the next stage of the DDSP is the development of the strategies to reach the proposed objectives. This strategy development stage is the subject of Chapter 5.

Questions

1   What are the main DDSP objectives of a company?
2   Besides the main DDSP objectives of a company, what other objectives should a company have?
3   What characteristics should a company analyze in order to establish its objectives?

5 Strategies to Reach the Objectives

In this chapter, the main strategy concepts and the role of strategic marketing will be presented. Subsequently the following topics will be examined in more detail:

- generic business strategies;
- definition of the market in which the company operates – segmentation;
- action strategies – differentiation and positioning;
- strategies for growth and diversification;
- portfolio analyses;
- strategies aimed at establishing competitive advantage;
- ways of sustaining competitive advantage.

Strategy

Despite the variety of definitions and concepts of strategy, Besanko *et al.* (2000) state that many use common phrases like "long-term goals," "policies," that suggest strategy is related to decisions the company makes and consequent success or failure. In developing the concept of strategy and its connection with the concept of objectives, Ansoff (1965) differentiates between them, commenting that the objective is seen as a point where one wants to arrive, and the strategy is the means to reach this objective.

One of the most important aims of strategy is how to connect a company with its environment so as to maximize the results of this interaction. For Mintzberg and Quinn (1996), corporate strategy is the standard of decisions in a company that determines and reveals its objectives, purposes or goals, produces the main policies and plans for the fulfillment of those goals, and defines the amplitude of businesses the company will own, the type of economic and human organization that it is or intends to be, and the nature of the economic and non-economic contributions that it intends to make for shareholders, employees, customers and the community.

Based on the development of strategies, marketing relies on the analysis of the needs of individuals and companies. From the point of view of marketing, buyers seek a solution for a problem, which may be obtained in different technologies. The function of strategic marketing is to follow the evolution of the reference market and identify the different current or potential product markets and segments, having as its basis the analysis of the needs that it intends to satisfy. Thus, the function of strategic marketing is to direct the company to existing attractive opportunities or create attractive opportunities which are well adapted to

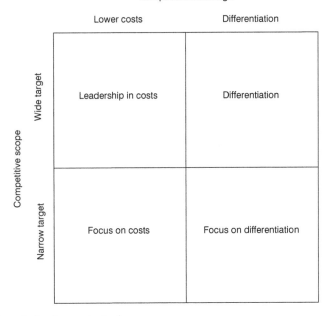

Figure 5.1 Generic business strategies
Source: Porter (1992)

its resources and know-how, and which offer potential for growth and profitability (Lambin, 2000; Toledo, 1973).

A company has a competitive advantage when it has a differential that allows it to maintain a superior position in relation to its competitors. In this sense, there are several ways to obtain a competitive advantage, such as: manufacturing products with more quality than the competition; offering better services to consumers; having lower costs than the competition; having a more convenient geographical location; creating products that perform a specific function in a superior way to rival brands; manufacturing a more durable and reliable product than the competition, and delivering more value to consumers.

In fact, all of the suggestions above can be summarized as being a combination of good quality, good service and acceptable prices. In a wider sense, these three generic strategies can be applied in isolation or in combination. Although, according to Porter (1992), when considering types of strategies, the following are found: leadership in costs, differentiation, and focus (in costs and in differentiation), as shown in Figure 5.1.

According to Porter (1992), competitive advantage is in the core of any strategy, and in order to obtain it a company must make a choice about the type of competitive advantage it seeks to obtain and how it will reach it. Table 5.1 summarizes the main characteristics of these generic strategies.

Table 5.2 suggests how to use the concept of strategies, by studying what the company currently uses and what it can use in five years.

Table 5.1 Characteristics of generic strategies

	Factors	Possible advantages	Possible disadvantages
Cost	• Economies of scale. • Economies of scope. • Capacity utilization. • Experience curve. • Industry concentration. • Raw material and component prices. • Location. • Process efficiency. • Purchase process. • Lean logistics. • Organization/ coordination of the vertical chain. • Efficiency of the agents.	• Can keep company profitability even with price wars. • Uses the buyer's capacity of reducing prices. • Increases entry barriers, given economies of scale or the nature of the cost advantage. • Positions the company favorably in relation to its competitors and substitute products.	• Changes in technology can eliminate the advantage. • Competitors and new entrants can gain experience, copy or invest in state-of-the-art production processes. • Emphasis on cost reduction to the point where changes in the product or market are not met. • Unexpected increases in costs that reduce the price advantage necessary to fight competitors with the differentiation strategy.
Differentiation	• Product. • Services. • Human resources. • Image.	• Can isolate the company from the competition, reducing consumers' price sensitivity. • Creates an entry barrier. • Can result in better margins. • Buyers are less sensitive to price, as comparison of alternative products is diminished. • With the customers' loyalty, the company is better positioned than its competitors and substitute products.	• Differentiation costs can become too high to maintain brand loyalty. • Differentiation factors can change from consumer to consumer. • Imitation reduces differentiation, mainly in mature industries. • Competitors are quick to imitate actions that are successful.
Focus	• Distinct from others focusing on a specific segment.	• Allows meeting specific needs of a segment, group of buyers, product line or geographical region in a more efficient way than the competition. • Can use characteristics of the latter two strategies, but with a reduced target public.	• The extension of the cost differential among competitors of a wide market and a focused company eliminates the cost advantage of serving a reduced target or compensates for differentiation reached by the focus. • The difference between desired product, focus segment and market can get narrow. • Competitors can find submarkets and eliminate the focus advantage.

Source: based on completed consulting projects and on Porter (1992), Moore (1992), Besanko *et al.* (2000) and Grant (2002)

Table 5.2 Matrix of strategic alternatives

Type of leadership the company seeks today	Advantages for the company by using this strategy alternative today
Which would be the alternative today?	Why is the alternative not viable at first?
What would be the alternative five years from now?	What are the advantages in using a certain strategy alternative within five years?

Value Creation and Capture Trilogy: the VCC model

Value capture is one of the most important strategies for companies nowadays and can be provided using the characteristics of generic strategies. Value capture entails a complete understanding of the network of the company being analyzed and the redesign of activities to attempt to increase margins and thus have more value. In this book we call this the "value creation and capture trilogy," and companies have three main possible ways of undertaking this strategy.

The first of these ways of capturing value is in costs. Trying to reduce the costs (1) of the company to increase margins and value. Good ideas and creativity are the focus here. The second way is via differentiation strategies (2), with activities that will try to increase margins via prices, since the value given by consumers is increased because of the actions by the company. Finally, the third set of activities relates to collective actions (3) that may be undertaken by the company.

Value Creation and Capture Trilogy: Costs

How can cost be reduced to capture more margin? Basically, there are two major components of costs where there is a possibility of improvement: internal costs, and costs of inputs and services purchased (supply chain costs). Internal costs will be considered first.

A company should look at all the activities it performs and try to see how to improve them. These activities are those relating to production. First, a company should always focus on exploring its core competencies. Second is the question of how to better use resources and assets (b) of the company by analyzing which resources (assets) a company has and how could these assets be better used. This is a simple question of how to use assets more and better. Third is the search for scale strategies (c); what is the production level that will bring economies of scale? Another possible way of capturing value is through the quality and cost of materials (d); new materials and components may offer better solutions. Labor efficiency (e) is also important, making the best possible use of human resources and minimizing overhead costs. Simplicity is the watch-word here.

A continuous redesigning of operations (f) towards "cellular" control of costs is another way of reducing costs. Every activity must be seen and analyzed as though it were a cell in terms of how it could be done better. Technology (research and development) (g) and financial architecture (h) – reducing the cost of capital and finding funding sources with more competitive rates – completes the list of the internal factors the company can use to control costs and capture value.

The second set of activities involved in the cost approach of our value creation and capture trilogy (cost, differentiation and collective actions) are related to the supply chain of a company (buying processes and relationships with suppliers).

A company should try to reduce the bargaining power of sellers (i), working with strategies related to promoting competition within a group of reliable suppliers and to have a continuous assessment of substitutes/alternative inputs (even if imported). This will increase the company's negotiating power, thus increasing margins. Another possible way is in purchasing (j); if a seller has periods in the year when their demand is lower, a buying company with a good capital structure can purchase more effectively in these periods.

Another strategy is contractual governance aimed at reducing transaction costs (k). Efficient processes which take advantage of information systems and technology will help reduce these costs.

Value Capture Trilogy: Differentiation

How does differentiation capture more margins? The differentiation approach has five major possibilities, each with its own tools and ideas:

a. an integrated relationship approach;
b. products/solutions;
c. services/people;
d. packaging;
e. brand/image.

In an integrated relationship approach (a), a company, as the first option to be considered, should search for closeness with its customers, establishing "lock in" strategies, where it offers a complete package for customers, and increases their costs of switching to a different offer or company. In such a relationship, it is also important to offer performance to the buyer (who is value driven) and a unique solution which simplifies the buyer's decision process and costs.

Turning to products/solutions (b), there are products with improved ingredients or nutrition attributes. Launching innovative products for booming markets should be considered. Another opportunity is linked to innovations and products that expand the size of markets. Some companies, when targeting young people, offer toys or other gifts together with their products to increase value and consumption. Products which provide new buying experiences are experiencing growth in the market. Another opportunity is to take advantage of special dates (Christmas, Valentine's Day, Olympic Games). There is the growing appeal with consumers of "home-made" and fresh, locally produced products. Legal protection, such as patents for innovative products, is also a strategy for value creation and capture.

Services and people (c): a company should search for quicker, more reliable, "just in time" delivery and another opportunity to look at the buyer's decision process, offering services that may reduce the possibility of customers asking for discounts, showing the benefits to customers of this product rather than that from a competitor. In services, a company may try to set standards for the industry, and this may act as an entry barrier for competitors. Having the best and most well-trained staff gives an advantage in several businesses. Channel-related strategies also have a place here, such as being in convenient locations, being present at the point of sale and offering new distribution formats for emerging segments and other types of buyers.

Packaging (d) offers several possibilities and techniques, using different materials and factors such as attractiveness, practicality, recyclability, transparency, shelf life, sustainability programs (packaging recycling initiatives), packaging with sounds and smells, offering supply chain (traceability) information on packaging, information on how to use the product, social and life style issues (slimming, fitness).

There are also well-known brand and image (e) strategies to increase value via improvements in the general brand and image of the company. By applying traditional integrated communications strategies to manage brand and image in the best way possible a company establishes permanent "loyalty contracts" with buyers, and receives added value through the recognition given by consumers to the brand and image.

Value Creation and Capture Trilogy: Collective Actions

Continuing the proposed trilogy on value creation and capture, the third set of activities relate to collective actions, a central part of this book. Joint or collective actions are defined as activities that a company performs with another company, or even more than one company. The companies may be competitors, non-competing companies which operate with the same markets, or even totally unrelated companies. The advantages of working together are so huge that companies need to explore them much more in the near future to counter increases in competition, compressed margins, and to control costs.

Collective actions be divided into to seven areas:

a. supply chain
b. internal management
c. products/brands/packaging/services
d. communications
e. marketing channels and sales
f. pricing
g. horizontal and vertical collective associations.

Starting with joint and collective actions within the supply chain (a) (here considered to be all the suppliers of the company), the most common activities are buying inputs together with other companies, so increasing bargaining power with suppliers. Another is to create a common purchasing structure shared with other companies, to provide scale economies and reduce redundant purchases.

With internal management (b), the idea is to invest in projects with other companies for issues related to quality, traceability, information systems, human resources management (sharing training, structures, etc.), financing and accountancy (using collective tools, sharing accountancy), lawyers and other areas. Here an analysis of what assets the company has, and how these assets can be better used by sharing with others, is an important part of the analysis.

Joint or collective actions in products/brands/packaging/services (c) may also contribute to capturing value. Examples are: complementing the product portfolio with other companys' products, to have a more complete offer; jointly creating new products and technologies (reducing individual investment); facilitating the adoption of new technologies and defining dominant standards; using other companys' brands to enter new markets (brand licensing); sharing customer service structures, for example, related to the guarantees, maintenance, recall of products; and finally, using the same packaging infrastructure. This will be covered in Chapter 6.

Joint or collective actions in marketing channels and sales (d) could also be undertaken to capture value. Examples are: companies with interests in the same market segments sharing channels to increase sales; combining efforts to open up international markets; salespeople from different companies complementing their product portfolio with products from another company; sharing costs of training on customer characteristics (knowledge about customer features) between two or more companies; increasing exchange of information between salespeople (about sales and potential sales in their market); and joint market studies increasing knowledge of sales areas, to determine number of salespeople, alignment of areas and to determine quotas. This will be covered in Chapters 8 and 9.

In pricing (e), joint and collective actions are also possible. Examples include: offering packages of products and services with more value and convenience, for example combining agricultural inputs. There is a significant chance that the customer's price sensitivity is reduced as a consequence, allowing the company to charge more for the package compared with separate products. Companies also can share discounts (through loyalty cards, for example) and other pricing strategies. This will be detailed in Chapter 10

There are examples of capturing value through collective actions via communications (f): conducting joint advertising with companies of the same industry or with companies which have the same target market; making joint investments to increase consumption of the industry's generic product, creating knowledge of the product and encouraging favorable public opinion about it, to the benefit of all participants; sharing public relations infrastructure; sharing stands, and having common exhibition and demonstration areas and other promotional activities.More information on this subject will be presented in Chapter 7.

The last topic for value creation and capture is via horizontal and vertical collective associations (g). These include participation in associations, cooperatives, pools of producers, joint ventures, alliances and other collective forms. The benefits of participating in cooperatives are clear, and strong industry associations also help activities such as lobbying, market protection, tax reduction and other activities to protect margins.

To use the value creation and capture (VCC) model, a company can investigate these topics in internal workshops to discover what ideas could be developed.

What is the Company's Position in the Market Place?

Markets consist of buyers that differ among themselves in terms of wishes, purchasing power, geographical location, attitudes and purchase practices. According to Hax and Majluf (1991), segmentation is the key to business analysis, strategic positioning, resource allocation and portfolio management. Segmentation makes it clearer as to where the company will employ competitive actions and how it will compete, by helping the company visualize these groups of consumers.

As stated by David (2001), market segmentation is an important variable in strategy implementation, for three reasons. First, market development strategies, product development, market penetration and diversification require increase in sales through new markets and products. To implement these strategies with success, identification of market segments is necessary. Second, market segmentation allows the company to operate with limited resources given that production, distribution and mass advertising are not required. This allows small companies to compete with larger companies. Finally, segmentation decisions directly affect product, distribution, communication and price variables.

Table 5.3 presents a delineation of the main segmentation variables (bases). In this way, in order to evaluate the potential of market segments, strategists are required to understand consumers' characteristics and needs, analyze their similarities and differences, and develop profiles of the consumer groupings.

Thus, a company can use one or more segmentation bases to identify in its market, and current and potential consumers who have similar characteristics. Take, for example, a company that works with consumer products. It can use demographic variables to define its target segment, for example, customers that are in the southeast region (geographical). The company can use other variables to specify its segment in more detail, i.e. consumers of the

Table 5.3 Main segmentation variables

Segmentation variables for consumer markets ("B2C")	Segmentation variables for the industrial markets ("B2B")
Geographical: • region • size of the municipality • size of the city or metropolitan area • concentration • climate.	*Demographics:* • industrial sector • company size • location.
Demographics: • age • gender • family size • family life cycle • income • occupation • religion • race • nationality.	*Operational:* • technology • user status • customer capacity. *Purchase approaches:* • organization of the purchasing function in the company • power structure • nature of existing relationships • general purchasing policy • purchasing criteria.
Psychographics: • social class • life style • personality.	*Situational factors:* • urgency • order size • specific application.
Behavioral: • occasions • benefits • user condition • rate of usage • degree of loyalty • aptitude stage • attitude in relation to product.	*Personal characteristics:* • similarities between buyers and sellers • attitude in relation to risk • loyalty.

Source: adapted from Bonoma and Shapiro (1983), Kotler (1997) and Gilligan and Wilson (2003)

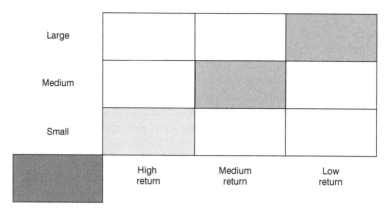

Figure 5.2 Segmentation matrix

southeast region, who are men aged between 18 and 25, and who consume the product at parties and night clubs (geographic + demographic + behavioral).

A brand concept map, using mapping methods to manage brand identity and brand knowledge, can also be used to segment the market. This is a new approach (Brandt *et al.*, 2010) that considers the influences of brand experience and brand awareness on brand perception to analyze further the different subgroups of consumers who may have different brand perceptions. In this case, "a segmentation technique that uses brand perceptions as its main criteria" should be applied (Brandt *et al.*, 2010: 188).

At this stage of the DDSP, matrices with quadrants which represent the company's target market segments should be made. Figure 5.2 can be used as a model, grouping the variables from Table 5.3, and defining segments for the company.

A customer value map can be made by discussing at this stage of the DDSP criteria of customer groups important to the company: sales volume, contribution to margin, customers the company "cannot leave out," customers to be attracted from competitor companies, etc.

Creating Differentiation and Positioning

Discussion of differentiation and positioning has already been started in the section on the value creation and capture model, and it will be continued here due to the importance of differentiation and positioning for the success of a business.

Modern strategies centre on these activities: market segmentation, as discussed in the previous section, differentiation and offer positioning. The adoption of a target market approach entails the following stages. The first stage is market segmentation. The second stage is choosing the target market and selecting one or more market segments to work with. The third stage is market positioning, the act of establishing and communicating the main benefits of the product to the market.

Some studies suggest that an organization distinguishes itself in a market in relation to its competitors through the differentiation of its offer (products or services), as shown in Table 5.4. In this way, a company can evaluate the main forms of differentiation, whether through products, service, image or human resources, that can best be used when planning. Table 5.5 offers the opportunity to consider how the company can be different and what are the opportunities for improvement.

Table 5.4 Differentiation options for companies

Type of differentiation strategy	Definition
Products/quality	Product characteristics that make it better – not fundamentally different, just better. The product performs with more initial reliability, has long-term durability or superior performance.
Design	Offer something that is truly different, that escapes from the "dominant standard" giving unique characteristics. This process includes product design, process, visual symbols, architecture, company identification.
Image	An image is created for the product (Mintzberg and Quinn, 1996). This can also include differences in a product that do not involve intrinsic improvements in performance.
Service	Supplying services also offers a strong possibility of differentiation (Mintzberg and Quinn, 1996)
Human resources	Through hiring and training staff more qualified than the competition, and improving their competencies, courtesy, credibility, reliability, responsibility and communication.

Source: based on Porter (1997), Mintzberg and Quinn (1996) and Kotler (1997)

Positioning of the Offer

Positioning is the act of developing the company's offer so that it occupies a specific place of value in the mind of target consumers. This requires the company to decide how many differences it will promote with these consumers. In a general way, it is worthwhile establishing a difference while satisfying criteria of importance, distinctiveness, superiority, communicativeness, predictability, availability and profitability. Positioning is a fundamental element in DDSP, hence the positioning decision has an immediate effect and implications in the whole marketing mix. Positioning will depend greatly on the analyses of the market segments, competition dynamics and the company's strengths and weaknesses (Porter, 1997; Mintzberg and Quinn, 1996; Kotler, 1997). In defining its market positioning, an organization can strive to achieve some long-term positions, listed below (based on Andreasen and Kotler, 1996):

- *Market leader:* if a company has an excellent offer, has recognition, has superior distribution, has resources and the competition is relatively weak, then it can choose to maintain or improve its leadership position. In mature markets, generally there is one leader that sets price changes, develops innovations and sets the rules. In order to keep this position, the company must find ways to expand total demand, must protect its current participation through defensive products and offensive actions aimed at competitors, and try to expand its market share even more, even if it remains constant, by gaining the competitions' share.
- *Market challenger*: if the organization is not the leader and the leader has long-term advantages, the company must not give in, but challenge the leader and the other industry participants, and even attack companies of the same size that have an inferior offer, or smaller participants that have financial difficulties.
- *Market follower (of the leader)*: there are many reasons to adopt this strategy: when the leader is strong and/or has substantial resources that can make the challenger strategy

Table 5.5 How can the company be different?

Differentiation strategies		
	Differentiation variables	*Opportunities for improvement*
Product	Standardization Style Durability Maintenance Attributes Economy Performance Cost Reliability Ease of use Packaging	
Service	Delivery Easy to buy and support Installation Assistance/care Training Offer and maintenance quality Return Credit Digital	
Human resources	Courtesy Competence Credibility Character Commitment Communication Charisma Proactive approach Flexibility Appearance	
Image	Brand Identity Tradition Denominated region Concept Process Culture Craft Inclusion	

Complete the table below with ideas from the improvement opportunities above

Differentiation oppotunities ranking			
Ideas list	Implementation cost	Return	Balance
1 2 3 4 ...			

too expensive; when imitating an innovative leader can lead to satisfactory results; or when this strategy is part of a general portfolio of strategies. The market follower needs to know how to keep current customers and to maintain low costs and high quality.

- *Market niche taker:* almost all industries have companies that are specialists in parts of the market, avoiding conflicts with more powerful competitors. This final strategy is one where the organization finds a group of target consumers whose needs are not well met by other participants and dedicates itself to this segment. These companies occupy market niches, in which they operate efficiently, by specializing in products or services that other competitors neglect or ignore. Specialization is the key for the niche idea. Companies have to specialize in market, customers, products or their marketing mix. They should try to seek market niches that are safe and profitable (Kotler, 1997).

Starting from the strategy concept proposed by Ansoff (1965), which separates objectives from strategy; because of the current company strategy and structure, there can be scenarios where actual sales are less than projected sales. In this case, the difference is a planning gap that can be reduced or eliminated with growth strategies. The following strategies relate to the type of growth the company aims to have.

Company Strategies: Growth and Diversification

Within these strategies, the company can: (1) identify opportunities to grow with its current business (intensive growth), or (2) identify opportunities to purchase other businesses related to the current business (integrated growth), or (3) identify opportunities to add attractive businesses not related with the current business (diversified growth). Table 5.6 summarizes these growth opportunities.

The company can develop its products within the same market, develop the market via new segments, channels or geographic area, or simply promote the same products in a more vigorous way in the same market. Such strategies can be better seen in Ansoff's matrix (1965) sketched in Figure 5.3.

Where penetration strategies are not sufficient to leverage company sales, the company can choose growth through integration. It can incorporate one or more of its suppliers (vertical integration backwards), buy distributors (vertical integration forwards), or even incorporate competitors (in cases where there are no legal restrictions) (horizontal integration).

Table 5.7 makes an analysis of the growth strategy types, demonstrating how it can be achieved by the company and has a column on the right for ideas to be raised within the focal company of the DDSP.

The main advances in diversification happened from the 1950s until the 1990s, it being an important source of growth for companies, with the development of management techniques, portfolio analyses and a greater orientation of companies towards growth and the maximization of shareholder profitability and return. Recently diversification has been questioned, due to the greater need for focus on companies' end activities (resulting from

Table 5.6 Main growth opportunities

Intensive growth	Integrated growth	Diversified growth
Market penetration	Backward integration	Concentric diversification
Market development	Forward integration	Horizontal diversification
Product development	Horizontal integration	Conglomerate diversification

Source: adapted from Ansoff (1965), Rumelt (1986), Salter and Weinhold (1979) and Kotler (1997)

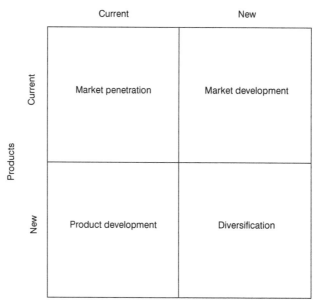

Figure 5.3 Growth strategies (product/market expansion grid)
Source: Ansoff (1965: 109)

market pressure for increasing value delivered to shareholders) and due to the current turbulence and ideas about company boundaries based on resources and competencies (Besanko *et al.*, 2000; Grant, 2002).

Diversification can be characterized in three groups: concentric, horizontal and conglomerate (Ansoff, 1965; Rumelt, 1986; Salter and Weinhold, 1979; Galbraith and Kajzanjian, 1987; Kotler, 1997).

Given the above comments regarding development of diversification strategies, some limitations of the main forms of diversification are presented in Table 5.8, which is an attempt to summarize the main motives that lead a company to diversify, the way it can be done and alternative suggestions that could be feasible to diversification.

Portfolio Analysis

As companies develop in their markets, the main questions that are posed for the DDSP are: In what business is the company? In what businesses should it be? In what businesses should it not be?

To answer these questions, portfolio analysis was developed, the main concerns of which are: the extension of the portfolio (acquisitions, mergers, new businesses and entry into markets); elimination of businesses from the portfolio; and changes in the balance of the portfolio through the allocation and reallocation of investments and other resources. According to Hamermesh (1986a), portfolio planning can be defined as being analytical techniques that help in the business classification of a company, the allocation of resources and the choosing of a competitive strategy based on the potential growth of each business and of the financial resources that will be both consumed and produced by these business units. In what follows, two tools for portfolio analysis will be presented.

Table 5.7 Summary matrix of growth strategies

Type of growth strategy	How can it be achieved?	Possibilities for the company
Larger market share of the current market	Stimulate current consumers to buy larger quantities of the product; communicate and publicize the product's benefits; attract the competition's consumers; stimulate change of brands and convert non-users into users.	Idea 1 Idea 2
Developing new markets	New markets for existing products, whether in new groups of potential customers in its area, or in other distribution channels in current markets, or expanding its operational area to other regions not yet explored.	
Developing the product	New products for markets in which the company already operates, creating different models, differentiated level of quality, versions or innovations.	
Concentric diversification	A strategy where the company seeks new products or opportunities that have synergy in terms of technology and marketing with current products, even if these products meet needs of different customers.	
Horizontal diversification	In this case, the company can seek new and different products that serve the same segment of consumers it currently serves, whose products are not related technologically with current product lines.	
Conglomerate diversification	This is the situation where the company seeks or develops new businesses that are not related to its current technology, products and markets.	
Vertical integration backwards	The company buys out a supplier as a supply strategy	
Vertical integration forwards	The company buys out a distributor or the next stage of production as a strategy of advancing in the chain.	
Horizontal integration	The company grows by buying out competitors.	

Source: based on Ansoff (1965), Rumelt (1986), Salter and Weinhold (1979), Kotler (1997), Besanko *et al.* (2000)

BCG Growth–Share Matrix

Developed by Bruce Henderson from his experience as founder of the Boston Consulting Group and studies made at the Harvard Business School, the structuring of the BCG matrix uses simple variables on each axis: industry attractiveness, which is measured in terms of market growth; and relative market share. The four quadrants of the BCG matrix suggest profit and cash flow standards and recommend appropriate strategies for each situation (Henderson, 1984; Grant, 2002). Figure 5.4 illustrates the model of the BCG matrix.

The BCG classification characterizes businesses in the following way (Henderson, 1984):

Table 5.8 Motives for diversification and alternatives to diversification

Motives for diversification	Means or incentives	Alternatives to diversification
Managerial factors	• Executives' search for status/ prestige and increase in salaries through the organization's growth	• Focus on obtaining status and higher salary level through the pursuit of market leadership or innovation
Risk reduction	• The company seeks to reduce its risks through diversification. This can happen when companies have cash flows coming from different sources, and can transfer resources to avoid insolvency	• Shareholders diversify their stock portfolio in other companies • Resources can be cheaper from other sources
Profitability	• Diversification because of attractiveness of a new business with high rates of return	• By reaching economies of scale it will be possible to have higher levels of profit
Market power	• Diversification can bring predatory prices, dumping, crossed subsidies • Reciprocal purchases between companies • Arrangements between company conglomerates, with one buying from another	• Other forms of vertical coordination, such as contracts, joint ventures, licensing, strategic alliances, franchises • Other forms of horizontal coordination, such as collective actions, as well as initiatives through participation in associations
Economies of scope	• Increase savings producing different products or in different businesses • Tangibles: share information systems, distribution channels, sales force, research laboratories, centralization of administrative services, R&D • Intangibles: share the brand, corporate image, technology, organizational competencies at the corporate level	• Other forms of vertical coordination, such as contracts, joint ventures, licensing, strategic alliances, franchises • Other forms of horizontal coordination, such as collective actions as well as initiatives through participation in associations
Synergies between business units	• In supply purchases • Joint administration • Create a service market • Information sharing • Learning–experience curve • Share legal, human resources, accountancy services • Fiscal planning	• Outsourcing can be more efficient than maintaining internal activities

- "star" businesses are self-sufficient in terms of cash; with time they become bigger and also better cash generators;
- "cash cow" businesses that generate more cash than they consume;
- "dog" businesses generate little cash; as part of profits are reinvested, they are "cash traps";
- "question mark" businesses that require more cash than they generate, resulting in a loss for the company.

Market share

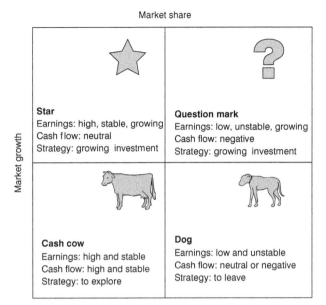

Figure 5.4 BCG Growth–Share Matrix
Source: adapted from Henderson (1984) and Grant (2002)

The BCG matrix is simpler than the GE/McKinsey matrix described in the following section, and is useful for preliminary analyses. Indeed, the BCG matrix has been widely used by companies due to simplicity (Grant, 2002).

The GE/McKinsey Matrix of Market Attractiveness and Competitive Position

In his study, Hamermesh (1986a) had the objective of explaining how the strategy is planned and implemented in large and diversified companies and criticizing executives of these companies for the way they used portfolio planning. With the development of his matrix, Hamermesh had the basic idea of representing businesses of a diversified company graphically to help strategic analysis in four areas: resource allocation; formulation of strategies for the business units; analysis of the balance in the portfolio (growth planning and cash flow); and the definition of the performance objectives.

The axes of the GE/McKinsey matrix are the source of superior profitability for a company: the competitive advantage (market position, competitive position, return on investments, etc.) and the industry attractiveness (market size, rate of market growth, industry profitability, cycles, importance of the markets, etc.), as illustrated in Figure 5.5.

Even though the BCG matrix, like the GE/McKinsey model, seeks to classify the company's cashflow position, they have important differences, because the Hamermesh model (1986a) takes into consideration:

• other variables besides market growth: industry size, profitability and price practices;
• other variables besides market share: strategic business unit (SBU) size, profitability and technology.

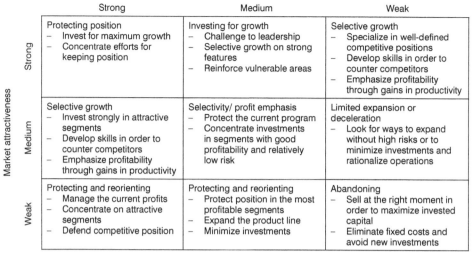

Figure 5.5   GE/McKinsey Market Attractiveness Matrix
Source: adapted from Hamermesh (1986) and Kotler (1997)

In this way the planning team can examine the position of its businesses or products and classify them in portfolio matrices as an analytical and visual tool to support decisions of which businesses or products the company should invest in, withdraw investments from, or whether it should maintain the current strategies.

Strategies that Focus on Establishing and Maintaining the Competitive Advantage

Once the resources and competencies of the company and its competition are defined and identified, it is necessary to understand how they relate to the long-term objectives and company strategies. The profit return that resources and competencies provide ("income") depends on the extent to which the company employs these resources and competencies to establish and maintain competitive advantage. The profits the company receives from resources and competencies depend on three factors: its capacity to establish a competitive advantage; its capacity to maintain this advantage; and its capacity to retain the returns from the competitive advantage (Wernerfelt, 1984; Collis and Montgomery, 1995; Grant, 1991).

For a resource or competency to be able to establish a competitive advantage, two conditions must be present. First, it must be rare – if it is widely available within the industry then it may be essential for companies and not be a sufficient basis for an advantage. Second, it must be relevant – resources and competencies have value only if they are related to one or more critical success factors within an industry.

Competitive advantage is a company's capacity to surpass its industry's performance; in other words, achieving a higher profitability than the industry's average. It is sustainable when the company persists in spite of the competitors' or potential entrants' efforts to affect it or neutralize it.

Ways to Create and Maintain Competitive Advantage

Profits gained with company resources and competencies depend not only on its capacity of establishing competitive advantages, but also the length of time it will be able to maintain them. This depends on the duration of the resources and competencies, if they are difficult for the competition to imitate; in other words, if they are difficult to be replicated (Collis and Montgomery, 1985; Grant, 2002; Specht and Willrodt, 2004). Table 5.9 summarizes some actions for the creation and maintenance of the competitive advantage.

Activities for the Definition of Company Strategies

The strategic dimension of the DDSP was examined in this chapter, with a greater focus on actions that can be made by the company, and decisions for the next three, four, or five years. Several of these strategies can be made in conjunction with other companies of the network, in strategic alliances, joint ventures, outsourcing, etc.

At this stage in the DDSP, the following must be undertaken:

- select the generic strategy the company will adopt, completing Table 5.2;
- the Ansoff matrix completed for the focal company (Figure 5.2);
- the definition of the markets the company will operate in – segmentation – using Figure 5.3;
- answer the possible questions coming from the VCC model that will supply ideas for value creation and capture;
- action strategies – differentiation and positioning strategies, using Table 5.4;
- strategies of growth and diversification, completing Tables 5.7 and 5.8;
- portfolio analyses using the matrices in Figures 5.4 and 5.5 for the company;
- strategies that focus on the establishment, maintenance and appropriation of the competitive advantage, using Table 5.9.

In the next stages of the DDSP, strategies connected with the controllable variables of marketing will be studied, emphasizing products (Chapter 6), communications (Chapter 7), distribution channels (Chapter 8), sales force (Chapter 9), prices (Chapter 10), and finally the budget for the plan (Chapter 11). Many of these decisions have an operational character, but also are strategic. For example, this year's communications plan must be linked to the brand and product positioning strategies for the next five years. The structuring of a franchise project for this year must be in accordance with the strategy for channels the company has for the next five years. As usual, decisions are linked.

Questions

1 How does a company differentiate its products from competitors to gain customer preference?
2 What are the five differentiation (options) tools?
3 Can competitors develop the same differentiation strategy?
4 How can a compy create and capture value?

Table 5.9 Actions to create and maintain a competitive advantage

Ways to create competitive advantage	How to create and maintain this advantage in your company?
Take advantage of the learning curve – a company that has sold much larger volumes than its competitors in the past has moved along its learning curve and reached lower unit costs. Companies with a lot of accumulated experience can offer products at lower prices than their competitors, increasing their volume even more and improving their cost advantages.	
Create network externalities – for some products, the individual benefit of a consumer purchasing a product can increase when a larger number of customers use the product or it is expected that they will come to use it in the future. One can see the externality phenomenon "when an additional consumer enters the user network creating a positive benefit for those who are already part of the network."	
Create reputation – with the growing speed of technological change, the life cycle of the majority of resources, like equipment and technology, is being reduced. Reputation and brands, on the other hand, are resistant to the passage of time. In the case of experience products – whose quality can not be evaluated before the purchase or use – quality reputation can supply a significant advantage to the first established company. This uncertainty combined with reputation makes brands a powerful mechanism of isolation.	
Create legal restrictions – patents, copyrights, as well as governmental controls over the market, such as licensing, concessions, certifications or the interruption of quotas.	
Create superior access – the company can obtain high quality or productivity from inputs, like raw materials and information, in a better way than the competition, thus gaining the capacity to maintain cost and quality advantages. Usually better access to inputs is reached through the control of supply sources (vertical integration), contracts or good long-term relationships. The obverse of this advantage is the superior access to consumers, via more productive and efficient distribution channels.	
Create economies of scale – when the minimum scale is relatively large or the company has an elevated market share, entry barriers are created, discouraging smaller companies to enter the market and limiting the number of companies that can "adjust" to the market.	
Create a cost of change to the customer – the existence of factors that discourage the customer from changing suppliers, such as payment of fees per contract, or the elimination of a service granted in the current model, financially discourage the customer from changing.	

Source: based on Collis and Montgomery (1995), Grant (2002) and Specht and Willrodt (2004)

6 Product, Service, Brand and Packaging Decisions

In this stage of the DDSP, the following tasks must be undertaken:

- analysis of products and product lines, as well as complementary product lines, for expansion decisions;
- use of the concept of networks to identify joint products (e.g creating package products in conjunction with competitors, complementing the product line with other companies' products, and other actions);
- identification of opportunities to launch new products;
- detailing of all services that are currently offered and will be in the future;
- making decisions in relation to brands (individual brands, collective brands, distributors' own brands);
- making decisions in relation to packaging (labels, material, design);
- producing budgets for expenses relating to products, new products and other actions.

Product Decisions

In the marketing mix, the product variable assumes a fundamental role, as it represents the group of attributes, functions and benefits that customers buy. Goods, services and ideas compose a product, forming a company's offer, which meets a need (McCarthy and Perreault, 1997; Kotler, 1997).

According to Garvin (1987), for an offer to be perceived as "high quality" by the consumer, the following factors must be considered:

- *performance*: the product's capacity to do well what it is expected to do;
- *characteristics*: the number and complexity of characteristics that differentiate the product; usually they allow the product to have more functions;
- *reliability*: the possibility of a product failing or not within a certain time frame;
- *conformity*: the degree to which the design and operational characteristics of the product comply with existing standards;
- *durability*: the time frame before it needs to be replaced;
- *services offered*: the development, speed and effectiveness of the services offered before, during and after the purchase;
- *aesthetics*: the more subjective aspects of the product – design, color, taste;
- *quality perception*: the reputation, product or brand perceived image.

To reach the desired quality intended by the company and perceived by the consumer, Lambin (2000) states that a quality program must "establish standards for each of these components and establish indicators that will allow the permanent respect of these standards." Thus, each component of a product's composition is a potential differentiation factor.

Decisions about Product Lines and the Product Life Cycle

Besides individual decisions regarding products offered by the company in the market, a strategic definition of the product mix offered is also necessary. The totality of products sold by a company, organized in lines, constitutes its product mix. The lines are formed by groups of directly related products (of similar function), sold to the same consumers, through the same channels, within a specific price range.

The amplitude, range, or breadth of a product mix is defined by a series of different product lines; the length is the number of products (different brands) within a line and the depth of the line are the types of products inside each brand (Etzel *et al.*, 2001; Kotler, 1997). Companies that offer multiple product lines enjoy numerous benefits; for example, protection against competition and possibly a larger market share. Although this strategy involves an increase in production costs, advertising, distribution channels, among several others, when costs are excessively high it can cause a reduction in the product line length (i.e. the number of different brands within a product line).

As stated by Dowell (2006: 963) "having a complex product line can make it difficult for firms to make adjustments if products are found to be unsuccessful," showing how complex the decisions involving a product line are for a company, and making it important for a company to evaluate its product line.

One of the ways to evaluate a company's product line, in order to facilitate decisions about line lengths or brands or even product elimination, is made through sales data, from which one should evaluate the line or item feasibility. Based on sales data, it is important to establish which products have the best margins and contribute most to company profitability.

This does not mean that items with smaller margins must be eliminated from the product line. Other factors must also be taken in account, such as cross elasticity demand (when the sale of an item – with a low margin – leverages the sale of another with a higher margin) and products that are attractive to the customer, being those "key products" or order openers. Using the example in Figure 6.1, several analyses can be conducted into product lines and decisions about them.

In this way, data from the product lines are used to perform a Pareto analysis (also known as the ABC analysis curve), using several criteria (for example, volume, income and margin). In this case, observe that product "A2" is the main product in terms of volume of income, but in terms of its margin contribution to the company it is one of the lowest. On the other hand, product "B2," whilst having large sales, is the most important in terms of income and profitability for the company. Another example is product "C2," that in spite of low sales volume and income, is excellent for company profitability.

As will be seen in following chapters, these analyses and tools are useful in showing the planning team which items or product lines must be prioritized in the marketing plan in terms of investment, improvements, sales efforts, communications and distribution.

Consequently, a matrix can be constructed (similar to the portfolio analysis discussed in Chapter 5) to define possible actions for product lines. As shown in Figure 6.2, the team can decide, for example, to stimulate the sales volume of products "C1" and "B5," improve margins of product "A2" and remove product "A3" from the line.

Product	Volume	Income (US$)	Gross margin (%)	Margin (US$)
A1	2,200	15,400	12	1,848
A2	11,000	27,500	15	4,125
A3	220	660	30	198
A4	10,000	30,000	40	12,000
A5	3,500	21,000	20	4,200
A6	2,700	13,500	35	4,725
A7	900	10,800	80	8,640
B1	5,300	15,900	28	4,452
B2	7,000	35,000	45	15,750
B3	700	2,800	100	2,800
B4	4,100	8,200	20	1,640
B5	4,000	20,000	70	14,000
C1	1,100	12,100	85	10,285
C2	550	8,250	110	9,075
C3	1,000	7,000	80	5,600
C4	300	1,500	50	750
C5	750	6,750	70	4,725
Total	55,320	236,360	44	104,813

Figure 6.1 Product line analysis

Application of the Concept of Life Cycle to the Product Mix

One of the main and most enduring marketing concepts is that of product life cycle. In the normal cycle, products are created, their sales grow, reach maturity, decline, and finally cease. Products, companies and industries have life cycles (Figure 6.3). According to Grant (2002) the life cycle comprises four phases: introduction, growth, maturity and decline. He highlights that two factors are fundamental: growth of demand and production, and the diffusion of knowledge.

The life cycle and its stages are defined by the market's growth rate. In regard to the creation and diffusion of knowledge, note that new knowledge in the form of product innovation is responsible for the birth of industries, and the knowledge creation and diffusion process shows itself as the main influence in the evolution of the industry (Grant, 2002). According to Grant, during the phases of introduction and growth there can be differences between standards and designs. The result of competing standards is normally convergence to a dominant design, a product architecture that defines the appearance, functionality and production method that will be adopted by all (for example, the videocassette).

The appearance of a new design marks a critical point in an industry's evolution. As the sector grows together with the development of technology, there is a change in the process from radical innovation to an incremental progess, leading the whole sector in a new growth phase in which large-scale standardization reduces the risk for all participants (Grant, 2002).

The concept of product life cycle has one of its main correlations with the learning curve concept. According to Fuller (1983), the costs to operate a process tend to fall as the people involved gain experience. The cost reduction trend can be explained by three factors:

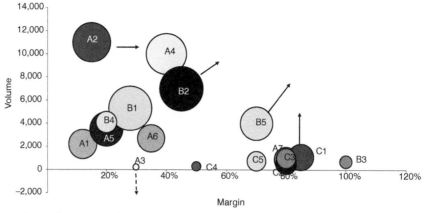

Figure 6.2 Product comparison: volume vs margin vs revenue

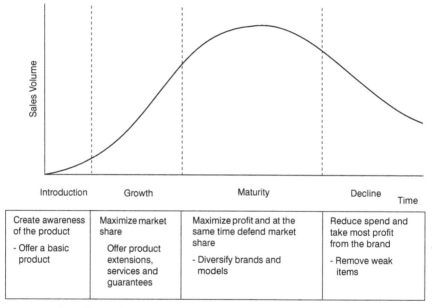

Figure 6.3 Product life cycle and marketing strategies
Source: Kotler (1997)

- as time passes, an industry's production rate tends to accompany the product's life cycle, costs decrease as the consumption rises from the introduction phase to the maturity phase, with larger volumes and gains with economies of scale;
- company costs decrease because raw material costs also decrease;
- costs can decrease due to the experience gained in production.

The Development of New Products and the Innovation Process

The search for success in the current competitive environment requires companies to innovate. A significant challenge is developing products and innovating, seeking a competitive advantage, guaranteeing growth and profitability while also managing risks and growing complexity. An innovation culture is one of the main sources of a competitive advantage, as it supports the development of new products. The new product development (NPD) and launch process, according to Kotler (1997), can be illustrated as follows:

a. Generation of ideas
   - ideas from consumers: from mail, discussions, tests, surveys, descriptions of problems, suggestions and proposals for improvements they are willing to pay for;
   - ideas from competitors: through suppliers, distributors and salespeople, and benchmarking;
   - ideas from research and development in the innovation areas of companies;
   - employees, suppliers, distributors and consumers must be encouraged to supply ideas.
b. Idea triage
   - has the objective of reducing the number of ideas to a few attractive and practicable ones;
   - ideas must be evaluated according to the requirements for success of the product (reputation, brand, R&D, HR, marketing, production, etc.), the relative weight given to each of these items and the level of the company's competency in these areas.
c. Concept development and testing (idea elaboration)
   - who will use the product?
   - what are the main benefits?
   - on what occasions will it be used?
   - what needs will be met?
d. Developing the marketing strategy and commercial analysis
   - size, structure and target market behavior;
   - planned product positioning;
   - product price forecast;
   - distribution strategy;
   - marketing budget;
   - sales and profit goals in the long term;
   - cost and profit estimates (cashflow statements).
e. Product development
   - physical development of the product;
   - functionality tests;
   - consumer/household testing.
f. Market testing
   - how will consumers and dealers react?
   - do a market test for consumer goods based on a test market (how many cities, which cities, how long, information types and actions to be taken?).
g. Commercialization
   - when? (timing choice);
   - where? (geographic strategy);
   - to whom? (target markets);

Table 6.1   New product launch evaluation matrix

Products	Market size	Contribu-tion to margin	Access to channels	Access to raw materials	Level/number of competi-tors	Invest-ment necessary	Total
A							
B							
C							
. . .							
Factor weight							

- how? (market penetration strategy);
- therefore, it can be inferred that in turbulent environments, the rapid development of new products can help companies to compete.

Which new products or services should the company launch? Several factors should be taken into consideration and Table 6.1 shows a suggested analysis. The products must be placed in the first column; next, an analysis must be performed of the factors listed, such as market size, expected contribution to margin, access to channels (scores can be attributed to each item, from zero to ten). In the last row of the table, the factor must be weighted; for example if the access to channels is more important than the number of competitors, it should receive a higher weight, as this factor has a larger impact. Finally, the total column will show the number of points received by each product, and the products ranked by which will receive the most effort from the company in terms of launch priority. Subsequently, each product will have its DDSP launch project.

Creating a Winning Concept, More Than a Product

A more unstable global environment, lower margins, incredible access to new technologies, large amounts of information coming from the digital world, higher risks, complexity and the emergence of new competitors and "copy-etitors" (companies that copy immediately the product) bring a dynamic world of opportunities, challenging management in innovation.

It is difficult to run a company nowadays, and having a strategic plan towards innovation and innovative concepts is even more difficult. Executives suffer from lack of time, pressure for short-term results, a fast-changing environment bringing "surprises every day" which demand attention, difficulties in forecasting and problems of internal company culture related to unsuccessful planning experiences in the past and avoiding taking on more tasks or activities. Sometimes it is difficult to plan because of the entrenched attitude that "this doesn't work here…"

The search for success in the current competitive environment requires companies to innovate. There is the challenge of how to develop an innovation culture supporting the development of new products, guaranteeing growth and profitability. Given this, we should move further than traditional new products, but how?

Innovations can be even more creative and pursue an objective of creating "a concept." It is instructive to analyze examples of companies that launched products or ideas that have become concepts. First of all, let me define a concept. It is more than a product, and involves a complete package of solutions, new behavior patterns, cultures and even communities. It is something new that makes a difference. Take, for example, Starbucks, McDonald's, or the new digital world of Facebook, Twitter, Google and other innovations; when they came to the market, a new idea and a concept came together. How do we create concepts?

The new product development process has well-known and well-established activities (as proposed by Philip Kotler and other marketing academics). What I am trying to do here is adapting these towards a broader inspiration of a "concept behavior creation." We can think of this process in seven steps.

1 *Proposal of concept ideas:* ideas from consumers in chats, emails, letters, discussions, tests, surveys and communities. These may involve descriptions of their problems, suggestions and proposals for improvements. Ideas could also come from suppliers, distributors and sales staff, or from external or internal research and development areas, employees, shareholders or others. All the participants should be encouraged to contribute ideas for concepts for new products, thinking of who might benefit from this concept, what are the benefits related to this concept that might be developed further to become new products, when the product might be used, and what needs will be fulfilled. For this process to evolve it is sometimes useful for the company to talk to consumers and pay attention to changes in the market.

2 *Selection of concept ideas:* reducing the number of concept ideas to a few attractive and practicable ones evaluated in accordance to the likelihood of success (reputation, brand, R&D, HR, marketing, production, etc.) and the company's competence in these areas.

3 *Concept marketing strategy*: plans about the size, structure and target market behavior; the planned concept positioning and details of prices, channels, communications, selling, profit goals in the long term; cost and profit estimates (cashflow statements).

4 *Building an integrated concept network:* designing the concept as an integrated network of contracts, participants, its financial design, partners and others. Who will participate in this innovation? What is the "architecture" of the concept, its participants and tasks?

5 *Physical development and testing of the concept*: involving testing and the approvals needed. At this stage investigating how consumers and other stakeholders will react and performing market tests should be carried out.

6 *Making it happen (the launch of the concept):* this stage is going to the market. Decisions involve questions of when (choice of timing); where (geographic strategy); to whom (target markets) and how (market penetration strategy).

7 *Continual redesign*: a concept, once created, is not forever and must be permanently renewed. A concept must bring value to the consumer, so as to build a "lock-in" strategy (by trying to create disincentives for the consumer to exchange the offer for a competitor's – for example by having support clubs and communities such as miles clubs, cards, culture clubs, among others – having clear communications, superior quality, design and being focused on problem solving. And always thinking about how to improve.

Brand Decisions and Image Construction

Brands and brand creation are vital ingredients, necessary for success in the market. Consumers use brands as sources of information, simplifying choices and reducing acquisition risks. They capture beliefs about the attributes and general image of the product from other consumers. Manufacturers are more and more interested in selling new products under the aegis of well-established brand names which are familiar to consumers, thereby increasing the product's acceptability (Iacobucci, 2001).

For the American Marketing Association (AMA) a brand is a name, term, symbol/sign, or a combination of all these, which is associated with different products or services of a specific company. Essentially, a brand means the promise of delivering a product or a particular "package" of characteristics, benefits and services to consumers (Etzel *et al.*, 1997). It has the role of reducing the transaction cost for the consumer, reducing uncertainties (Farina *et al.*, 1997).

Brands allow consumers an association between functionalities, images and experiences. In a competitive market, products become more uniform, therefore brands evolve to offer a differentiated value for their customers. The success of the brand depends on associations made in consumers' minds.

The big challenge of a brand is to develop an arrangement of ideas associated to its symbol, not only being a name, but a group of meanings. The construction of a brand is oriented by a vision of the desired positioning and implemented by the decisions related to the marketing mix. The brand, in reality, establishes a "contract" with the consumer.

Thus, it can be said that in the current competitive scenario, a company's brand is its main resource for competitive advantage and a valuable strategic asset that should be guaranteed and its inherited value managed as a company asset, Even today, the brand message to the consumers is very frequently weak, confusing, irrelevant, or worse, not differentiable from the competition's offer (Aaker, 1996).

The brand has a value to the organization, for it is a legal entity with market value different from that of the sales that it is capable of generating among consumers (Schultz and Barnes, 2001). This value must be based on the consumer, for it represents the differential effect that brand knowledge has in the customer's reaction. Aaker (1991) defines brand value as being a group of assets or liabilities related to a brand, its name and symbol, which add or subtract value promoted by the product or service. He identifies four main categories through which the brand value can be reached: brand recognition, brand association, perceived quality, and loyalty to the brand. These categories are closely related. Thus the loyalty to the brand depends on its recognition by consumers, on the power of established associations, as well as the quality level perceived.

According to Aaker (1996), the challenge for a brand is to have a clear and distinct image, which matters to the consumer and truly differentiates it from other competitors. For the construction of big brands, the author suggests the company regard its brands not only as a product or service, but also as an organization, a person and a symbol.

The brand as an organization should form associations with people, culture, the company's programs and values. Thus to assign priority to the executive strategy of innovation, market leadership or product quality has direct impact on the perception of the brand. The personality of a brand aims to transform the brand into something more interesting and memorable, and can become a form of identification and expression of the person's, consumer's identity. Finally, a strong symbol can bring cohesion and structure to the brand identity, making it more recognizable and easier to remember. Thus, a more stable contract is made with the consumer.

Brand Decisions

For the construction of opinions about the brand as a consequence of the marketing activities, Kotler (1997) states that the following decision steps should be followed and included in the DDSP at this stage (see Table 6.2):

Note the importance that the strategy of developing retailer private brands has had in the current competitive context, being an important tool for the distributor, with different roles of coordination for the industry and its distribution channels. Private brands are developed and managed by distributors (retailers, wholesalers and the service sector) using their own logos on products and selling them to final consumers (Machado Filho *et al.*, 1996; Toledo *et al.*, 1997).

Table 6.2 Main brand decisions

Brand decisions	Actions (ideas) for the company's offers (products)
Brand use Should a brand be created for a product? To create a brand means investing in packaging, promotion, registration, communications and also being exposed to an image risk. The advantages for the company are: product identification is easier, legal protection, opportunity for loyalty and profits, possibility of market segmentation and, finally, the opportunity for a good image in the market.	
Brand sponsorship Who should sponsor the brand? Retailer private brands can represent several advantages for both sides involved in this relationship.	
The name used Which name (brand) should be printed on the product? • *Individual brands* mean independent names for independent products without an image risk in case of failure; however the product may not benefit from a good corporate image, if it exists. • *Global brands* (company name on all products) allow lower development and promotion costs and should be used when the product line is not too diversified. • *Product family brands* can be used when there are products positioned in the same way.	
Brand strategy Which strategy should be used? • *Product line extension:* the company introduces different versions (new attributes, flavor, color, size) within the same category with the same brand. • *Brand extension:* same brand for another category of product, exploring the image gained in the original product's category. • *Multi-brands:* new brands in the same category to explore different segments and fight competitors. • *New brands:* when the company wants to start a new business and concludes that current brands are not appropriate. • *Combination of brands:* two or more brands can be combined in the same product in a special offer.	
Brand repositioning Creating other meanings in the consumer's mind, new differentials in view of the competition.	

Source: adapted from Kotler (1997)

Package Decisions

If two-thirds of people make decisions at the point of sale, and if convenience and product re-processing issues are gaining importance, then packaging assumes a new era of importance in marketing. The package is "the group of design and production activities of the container or the wrap of a product" (Kotler 1997: 440). According to the author, "the container or wrap is called package and can include up to three types of material. The primary package, or consumption unit, is the product that will be offered to the consumer. This package can be packed into a secondary package (cartridge, display) or not, depending on the product offered. This product is transported in a larger box (dispatch or shipment unit) that contains a dozen, six or however many the producing company decides."

In Table 6.3, Mestriner (2001) stresses the functions and roles of packages in companies and in society nowadays. We can complete the table with an additional column where ideas for the company are suggested, starting from the analysis of the package functions. In other words, what can we improve?

According to Mestriner, the package as a marketing tool must be explored, seeking to make the product more competitive, and an efficient and innovative means of communication. In order to make the product more competitive it is necessary to obtain an advantage at the point of sale, attracting attention visually, emphasizing a product attribute that places it at an advantage, raising the product's perceived value and adding meaning to it, making it more appealing and desirable, so that it offers something the competition is not offering.

In order to be an efficient means of communication it is necessary to work with promotions, discounts and launches; advertise the product itself, the line and even the company; offer combined product kits and be a vehicle of direct marketing, including flyers, coupons, souvenirs and other information within a package. Finally, in order to innovate, new materials, new labeling processes, new ways of opening, dosage and display systems must be sought to obtain a competitive advantage. The reasons to develop new packages are many (Kotler, 1997):

- search for improvement of productivity in the production line;
- loss of market share;
- introduction of a new visual identity program in the company;
- stability of sales for a long period and declining profits;
- radical change in the product;
- plagiarism of package by competitors;
- change in the product's distribution channel;
- search for an identity that is more connected to sales promotion;
- change in the package technology;
- new materials and innovative concepts that increase the product's expiration date;
- change in the consumer's habits;
- recycling;
- and other changes in the regulatory environment of packages.

Service Management

Aggregated services have become increasingly common as an important differentiation factor. When a product is not easily differentiated, offering a service that adds value to the offered product can be interesting. Among the most frequent services are simplicity

Table 6.3 Package amplitude and decisions (ideas) for the company

Dimensions	Function		Points of improvement for the company's packaging
Primary functions	Contain/enclose and protect	Transport	
Economic	Component of the production cost	Raw materials	
Technological	Conditioning system New materials	Product conservation	
Marketing	Call attention Transmit information	Awaken desire to purchase Overcome price barriers	
Conceptual	Build product brand Form concepts about the manufacturer	Add significant value to the product	
Communication	Important opportunity of communicating the product	Support for promotional actions	
Social and cultural	Expression of culture and development of companies and countries		
Environment	An important component of urban waste	Recycling	

Source: Mestriner (2001)

in making orders, the way the product is delivered to the customer (and this includes the customer service and how the product is delivered), equipment installation, training and advice for consumers to maximize the product's usefulness, technical assistance, among several other options. As the author states, there is an inexhaustible number of forms to offer services and benefits to consumers.

According to Zeithaml (1990, cited in Lambin, 2000) there are ten factors that determine the quality of a service:

- *competence*: the service renderer has knowledge, means, know-how and required capacity to supply the service; this refers to the organization's professionalism;
- *reliability*: the organization's performance is always dependable, safe and at a constant level;
- *responsiveness*: each member of the organization strives to respond promptly, in any circumstances, to the customers' requests;
- *access*: physical and psychological, each member of the organization is accessible, easy to contact and pleasant;
- *understanding the customer*: the organization strives to understand the customer's specific needs and adapt to them in the best possible way;
- *communication*: the organization is careful to keep the customers informed of the offer's precise content;

- *credibility*: fame, reputation, guarantee of seriousness and organization honesty;
- *security*: customers are protected from all risks (physical, financial, moral);
- *courtesy*: all personnel maintain cordial, polite relations with the customers;
- *tangibles*: the organization strives to materialize the services offered, creating substitutes to their intangibility.

For companies whose main offer is a service, Iacobucci (2001) lists special circumstances that emerge.

Services are intangible; in other words, they cannot be felt, they are not an object that can be evaluated, and rather, they are an action. The service cannot be evaluated before it is consumed, therefore there should be substantial evidence the service offered will be in accordance with the customer's expectations. Care with the appearance, location and customer service becomes indispensable.

- Services are *inseparable*, for they are consumed and produced simultaneously; this makes the interaction between the consumer and the company fundamental. In this way, the offer becomes limited (by the salesperson's necessary presence), but the choice of the service still has a big chance of having the price becoming secondary, because of the unique characteristics of the person supplying it.
- Services are *variable*, for they are rarely executed in the same way and because of this, investments in standardization, personnel training and research with the consumer to monitor their satisfaction are necessary.
- Last, services are *perishable*, for the service cannot be stocked; it is necessary to constantly manage the offer and demand in a short period of time.

To add to the characteristics mentioned above, Lovelock (1996) lists eight dimensions for service administration. They are: the characteristics of the offered product (when existing); place and time where consumption happens; the process in which the service is offered; productivity and quality of the service rendered; the people involved in the service rendering; promotion and consumer education; physical evidence (establishment appearance); and finally the price. Due to these differentiating characteristics, satisfaction with the rendered service assumes a fundamental role. The customer wants attentiveness during the rendering of the service in order to feel satisfied.

Finally, it is interesting to see the classic model by Parasuraman *et al.* (1985) for service quality evaluation. It is divided into two parts: the consumer's side and the company's side. The meeting point happens in the consumption and in the production, in the rendering of the service itself. However, consumer satisfaction depends on the sequence which will be explained next. Initially, it is necessary to understand the concept of satisfaction proposed by Engel (1995) where the consumer's satisfaction happens when the performance of the product or rendered service is superior to the customer's expectation. If the performance is inferior, they will be dissatisfied, and this is related with the gaps in Figure 6.4.

Consumers construct an expectation for a service. This expectation is shaped through communication between consumers (commentaries and indications from friends and relatives), the consumer's own needs, and from their previous experiences with the company or similar services and the advertising the company has made. From the point of view of a marketing-oriented company a perception regarding the consumer's preferences is developed; in other words, the consumer's needs. The company translates these perceptions into service specifications.

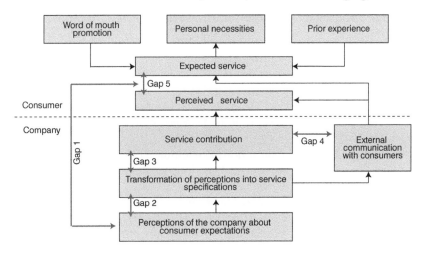

Figure 6.4 Service quality model
Souce: Parasuraman *et al.* (1985)

Once the customer's expectations, and the company's service perceptions and specifications are shaped, the service is then rendered and the consumer has the opportunity to evaluate it. It is from this evaluation that the consumer will be satisfied or not with the company.

If the consumer of a service is dissatisfied, it is because of one or more of the gaps in Figure 6.4. Gap 1 refers to the erroneous interpretation of the company about its consumer's preferences. This myopia is fatal. Gap 2 refers to the company's lack of capacity of transferring the specifications that it correctly interprets as necessary, but that are not implemented for administrative problems. For example, the employees are dissatisfied; the purchase of quality products has failed, among other problems. Gap 3 is related to the rendering of the service itself; there can be problems in customer service quality due to structural problems in the company, such as physical resources or employee qualification. Gap 4 is related to misleading advertising, that elevates the customer's expectation in order to attract him, but does not fulfill what was promised. Last, Gap 5 is related to the consumer's perception, which is inferior to his expectation, leading in the end to dissatisfaction.

Thus a fundamental factor for understanding services is in the fact that "the consumption of a service is a process of consumption, more than the result from consumption." The consumer perceives the service production process as part of the received service and not only as a process result, as in the production of consumer goods. When the competition for offered services is the key to success in almost all markets, and products are defined as being like services, then every business is transformed into a service-rendering business (Grönroos, 2004).

Collective Actions and Partnerships in Products, Services, Brands and Packaging

Among the actions that companies can carry out jointly with others and that are part of the DDSP, those listed in Table 6.4 stand out.

These items must all be introduced into the planning and strategic marketing management process, and appear in the plan, so they can be carried out. In what follows, the marketing communication issue will be approached, which is intrinsically related to products and brands.

Activities for Producing the Plan for Products, Services, Brands, and Packaging

At this stage of the plan the team involved should:

- make product line decisions: completing Figures 6.1 and 6.2 for the company;
- analyze the company's product life cycle, using Figure 6.3;
- analyze new products and services to be launched by the company, filling in the new products matrix;
- discuss with the DDSP team the following questions:
  - What services can be implemented that truly create barriers for the customer's exit (lock-in)?
  - How to improve services offered today by the company according to the "win-win" concept, but that create exit barriers for the customer?
- create a customer "map of exit barriers," giving priority to actions;
- analyze the company brand decisions, building a table of actions in relation to the brand (use the same brand for other products, changes in a brand, launch brand B, among others, completing Table 6.2);
- analyze the company packaging decisions, building a table of actions in relation to packages which are gaining a more important role using Table 6.3;
- analyze the company's services, trying to summarize opportunities for improvements in the services, based on the analysis of Figure 6.4;
- analyze the possibilities of collective actions that can be made with other companies using Table 6.4 for this task.

Questions

1   Which partnerships with other areas (medicine, nutrition) can we use in our products?
2   Which products can be launched, targeting to combat the popular products?
3   Which regional strategies (adapting products to regional preferences) can be adopted in our products?
4   Which traditional or retro factors can be used in our products?
5   How can political and legal restrictions affect our product strategies?
6   Which brands or latent products of other companies are opportunities for us to complete our product line(s)?
7   Are there purchasing opportunities and brand sales?
8   Can changes in our products and product lines bring any risks to our identity?
9   What kind of companies can we create joint ventures with to improve innovation?
10 How can we prevent lack of innovation in the company?
11 Which products can be aggregated in our product line to acheive our objectives (brand, channel, salesforce)?
12 How does our product line compare to our competitors?

Table 6.4 Opportunities for the use of collective actions in products, services, brands and packages

Actions	Description	Ideas for the company
Companies complement their product lines	Companies begin to complement each other's product portfolio with the other company's products. Thus, the offer can be seen as being more complete, adding convenience to the consumer's purchase process. They can be manufactured with the company's brand or a third-party brand.	
Companies develop new products and innovation projects jointly	Companies can create projects for the development of new products and create new technologies in conjunction, substantially reducing individual investment.	
Market development and definition of dominant standards	Companies can invest jointly in the development of markets for new technologies, facilitating their process of adoption and defining a dominant standard that is of the company's interest.	
Companies license other companies brands in non-competing lines	Companies use other companies brands, through payment based on sales or time periods, so that through these brands they can enter markets easily.	
Companies share infrastructure services	Companies can have the same structure to offer services to their customers, for example, related to the maintenance of products, and thereby share costs.	
Same structure of package development	Companies can use the same packaging infrastructure, or use the same outsourced company. They can still work with the same type of input material for packages (for example, plastics, cardboard) in ways to reduce the product cost.	
Share and coordinate quality systems	Companies can invest in a common project for issues related to quality, product traceability and information systems.	
Share product recall projects	Companies can divide return structures and product recalls, mainly in an outsourced form.	

7 Communications Decisions

Concomitant with making decisions regarding product, service, brands, and packaging, it is necessary to develop another stage of the DDSP, which involves communications decisions. Among the controllable variables of the marketing mix, communications, also known as promotion, has the important role of informing target consumers of the existence of a desirable product, with a certain price, available in a certain place. All modern organizations, whether private companies or non-profit entities, use forms of marketing communications to promote their offers and reach their financial and non-financial objectives. The following analyses should be made during this stage of the DDSP:

- identify the target audience that will receive the communication (company messages);
- develop the desired objectives for this communication (brand knowledge, brand memory, persuasion, etc.); try to reach a positioning and unique product message;
- define the communications mix that will be used; in other words, which tools, defining the advertising plan, public relations and publicity plan, sales promotion plan, as well as direct marketing actions;
- identify which actions can be made in conjunction with other companies;
- budget communications activities and possibly determine the expected return for these investments.

Marketing communications consist of efforts made by a company to transmit its information to the other members of the network, seeking to influence attitudes and behaviors. More specifically, communications strive to tell the target public that the right product is available, at the right price, in the right place (McCarthy and Perreault, 1997).

The development of efficient communications involves several steps, from the identification of the target public, from whom it is intended to obtain attention for the product offered, to measuring the results of the actions adopted. By developing a communications mix, companies seek to reach one or more objectives, such as:

- *generate a desire for the product category*: before creating a preference for the brand, companies need to make consumers desire the product's category;
- *create brand consciousness*: make the brand known and associated with factors that are positive and desired by the customers;
- *improve attitudes and influence decisions*: persuade customers to choose the company's offer instead of the competition's;

- *facilitate the purchase*: marketing communication variables help facilitate the purchase and, possibly, overcome obstacles created by the non-promotional variables of the marketing mix (product, price and distribution).

In economic terms, Etzel *et al.* (2001) state that the objective of a communications campaign is, at a certain time, to alter the location and form of a demand curve of a product or service. Thus, a company seeks to influence, positively, the demand curve to the right without changing the price variable, thus increasing the volume sold. Communications efforts seek to influence demand elasticity in the product's favor.

To reach these objectives, marketing communications perform three essential roles: inform, remind and persuade. When a product meets the consumers' needs in a better way than the competitors available in the market, promotion has only to play the role of informing consumers. When consumers already display positive attitudes toward the company's marketing mix, it is up to promotion to constantly remind them of the product. However, if there are competing products in the market and consumers have no favorable attitudes to the brand, promotion needs to use persuasion techniques (McCarthy and Perreault, 1997; Kotler, 1997).

Moreover, regarding the marketing communication concepts, many changes have been proposed in the marketing literature, mainly since the 1980s, proposing the concept of an integrated marketing communications program.

The relevance of an integrated marketing communications (IMC) approach is growing. The concept has been developed intensively since the 1980s, when companies adopted a broader perspective on marketing communications, which has caused a shift in this sector, mainly involving the way that advertisers, media and agencies structure programs of advertising, public relations, sales promotion and direct marketing.

The exploration of the different and integrated forms of marketing communications contributes to companies achieving their expected financial goals. However, a communications strategy should be integrated with other marketing decisions, after all "a firm can spend large sums on advertising or sales promotion, but there is little chance of success if the product is of low quality, if it has an inadequate price or if it lacks an adequate distribution to consumers" (Belch and Belch 2008: 9).

It is interesting that, despite the IMC concept and the possibilities of using new media, there still exists conservatism in resource allocation, or in the allocation of the marketing budget across various marketing vehicles. Corstjens *et al.* (2011) found from the analysis of several companies and industries that there is "overspending on some marketing drivers and underinvestment in alternative marketing vehicles," showing that companies should consider and analyze profitable growth opportunities in alternative marketing communication vehicles instead of, because of conservatism, overspending on traditional vehicles.

These are some of the concepts and challenges that should be considered by marketing managers while making communications decisions. A set of tools is presented in this chapter aimed at contributing to this stage of the DDSP.

Identification of the Target Market to be Reached by the Company with its Communications

Identify the target market of the communications. This is the first step of communicating. Who is to be reached with the message? What group of consumers? What group of distributors (retailers, bakeries, butcher's shops, convenience stores)? What group of food companies? It is fundamental to identify the target before deciding what to say, when, where and to whom.

Table 7.1 Definition of the target market and communications actions

Target market (List all)	Priority (High, medium or low)	Message objectives	Message	Tools

Table 7.2 Establishing communication objectives

Questions	Yes/No	Suggestions for changes in the message/campaign
Does the message used in our communication attract the *attention* of the target public?		
Is the content of the message capable of creating *interest* in the public regarding our products/services?		
Do the structure and form of the message manage to awaken our public's *desire* in relation to our products/services?		
Does the message used by the company have the power to influence the customer's behavior and lead to a purchase *action*?		

Establishing the Objectives

After determining the target market, it is important to determine what is the response expected from the public to which the communication is intended. The objective is to place something in the minds of consumers who do not know the product or company, or it can be to change attitudes and increase knowledge of the product to those who already know it, or to make the consumer act by increasing their preference or helping in the purchase decision. The message created will depend on the objective. To facilitate the work of communications planning, Table 7.2 can be used to help specify objectives and desired response patterns to the message, with questions based on the traditional AIDA model (attention, interest, desire, and action).

The Communications Mix (Tools)

Regarding the communications mix, Kotler (1997) had two important observations. The first is that in a given sector, companies differ considerably as to the allocation of resources among the various tools. The second deals with companies that are always seeking ways to increase efficiency substituting one promotional tool for another. The decision about which tool of the communications mix the company should concentrate its efforts on is one of the main questions for marketing executives.

The choice of the amount of investment in each tool of the promotional mix should take into account factors such as nature of the market, marketing channels and the standard distribution for the product, decision-making units, product life cycle and the characteristics of the products or services (Cobra, 1992). The nature of the market determines which is the most effective promotional means. Table 7.3 relates some of the factors that influence the determination of the communications mix.

According to Etzel *et al.* (2001), marketing executives, when analyzing the target market, should consider factors such as purchase readiness (according to the stage at which the consumer is at in the purchase process, a promotional tool will have more or less influence), the market geographical space (the bigger a market is geographically, the bigger the emphasis on advertising), customer type (the strategy depends on the level of the distribution channel that is desired to reach) and market concentration (the bigger a market is, the bigger the use of mass communications).

For the "customer type" factor, if the company's promotion program is oriented primarily to intermediaries, it is said the company adopts a push strategy, and if the company's promotion program is oriented primarily to end users, it is said the company's strategy is to pull. When the pull strategy is adopted, the customers are motivated to buy products from retailers. Retailers, in turn, will order the product from wholesalers, who will purchase the product from the manufacturer. This strategy demands massive investment in advertising and sales promotion, such as prizes, samples or demonstrations at stores.

On the one hand, the push strategy aims to stimulate the next level of the distribution channel to purchase a product. The push strategy usually involves lots of investment in personal sales and sales promotions, such as competitions among sales personnel and displays at trade fairs (Etzel *et al.*, 2001). Marketing channels and the standard of distribution of the product also influence the communications mix decision. If the product is distributed through large distributors, the company can be forced to spend more resources on commercial promotion. On the other hand, taking into account the product's life cycle, publicity can be more effective in the product's development phase, while in the growth and maturity phases, advertising can be more successful; finally in the saturation and decline phases, sales promotion is more effective (Kotler, 1997; Jain, 2000).

In other words, the decision-maker, whether a domestic or an industrial buyer, has the option of buying a favorite brand or the cheapest brand, depending on the characteristics of the products or services. For mass-consumption goods, the most efficient tool is advertising, followed by sales promotion. For an industrial product, personal sales are more efficient.

Table 7.3 Factors influencing decisions about the communications mix

Product factors:	*Consumer factors:*
• Present attributes	Purchase behavior
• Nature of the products	Final consumers versus industrial consumers
• Risk perceived in the purchase	Number of customers
• Characteristics, attributes and benefits	Influence sources
• Position in the life cycle	Customer concentration
• Average purchase quantity	
• Purchase frequency	*Budgetary factors:*
	• Company financial resources
Market factors:	• Resources allocated by the industry
• Market share	
• Industry concentration	*Marketing mix factors:*
• Intensity of competition	• Price versus relative quality
• Demand perspectives	• Distribution strategy/structure
	• Positioning
	• Segmentation

Source: elaborated from Kotler (1997), Cobra (1992), Etzel *et al.* (2001) and Jain (2000)

In addition to the factors mentioned above, the budget available for communications constitutes an important influencing factor; a reduced budget can limit the options the company has in its promotional efforts. Advertising on national TV, for example, requires high investment which is often incompatible with the company's communication budget (Etzel *et al.*, 2001).

What are the Communications Mix Tools?

The group of communications tools used by companies to reach their objectives is known as the communications mix. The communications mix consists of a combination of communications strategies, in the same way that the marketing mix is a strategic combination of product, price, distribution channels and communication (Semenik and Bamossy, 1995) (see Table 7.4).

Table 7.4 presents a summary of the main actions that can be performed with each tool. The communications mix tools can be divided into those for mass communications and those for personal communications. Mass communications forms are those used by companies to reach a large number of potential buyers. Advertising, sales promotion, direct marketing and public relations are part of this group.

The personal communications form is the one in which information is passed on individually to each consumer. Personal communications, in turn, are represented by the personal sales (Semenik and Bamossy, 1995). Each of the tools which are part of the communications mix will be discussed in more detail.

Table 7.4 Main communications tools

Advertising	Sales promotion	Public relations	Personal sales	Direct Marketing
• Ads (TV, radio)	• Contests, games, and lotteries and raffles	• Press kits	• Presentations and sales	• Catalogs
• Ads (printed and electronic)	• Prizes and presents	• Lectures	• Sales meetings	• Direct mailing
• External packages	• Sampling	• Seminars	• Incentive programs	• Telemarketing
• Package inserts	• Trade fairs	• Annual reports	• Samples	• Electronic sales
• Movies	• Exhibitions	• Donations	• Fairs and expositions	• Sales through television
• Manuals and brochures	• Demonstrations	• Sponsorships		• Direct mailing via fax
• Signs and fliers	• Coupons	• Publications		• Email
• Catalogs	• Partial reimbursements	• Community relations		• Voice mail
• Billboards	• Low-interest financing	• Lobbying		
• Panels	• Exchange concessions	• Media identification		
• Displays at the point of sale	• Loyalty programs	• Company magazine or newspaper		
• Audio-visual material		• Events		
• Symbols and logos				
• Video tapes				
• Web sites				
• New forms of digital media				

Source: adapted from Kotler (1997)

Advertising

Advertising involves all paid forms of impersonal communication made by a sponsor, its role being to inform or persuade the target public. The sponsor can be a private company, non-profit organization or individual which in some way is identified with the advertising message. According to Fill (1999) the purpose of advertising is to supply the means by which appropriate messages will be delivered to the target audience in a way to influence their behavior.

According to Kotler (1997) the following advertising characteristics should be highlighted:

- *public presentation*: the use of mass media by advertising gives the message a public nature, granting more legitimacy and standardization to the offer;
- *penetration*: allows the message to be repeated several times, reaching a higher target market penetration; at the same time it gives the consumer the opportunity of comparing messages of various competitors;
- *increased expressiveness*: the characteristics of the advertising media used allow enhancing the message with the creative use of printing, sound and images;
- *impersonality*: advertising is a monologue; the public does not need to pay attention or reply to it if it does not wish to do so.

Other important characteristics of advertising highlighted by Boonee and Kurtz (1998) are: the ability to reach a large group of potential consumers with a relatively lower individual exposure price, a great ability to control the final message, and, finally, the ability to adapt to mass audiences or specific audience segments. As for the negative characteristics, advertising does not allow a totally precise evaluation of the results. Usually it cannot make sales and, because it is impersonal, it cannot adapt to what the consumer wants to hear; customizing and conducting the message according to the consumer's response is an exclusive advantage of personal sales.

Advertising performs two main functions: an informative function and a marketing function. The informative function ensures that people have knowledge of the product's existence, its characteristics and benefits. The marketing function ensures that the consumer is persuaded to buy a certain brand (Pancrazio, 2000). McCarthy and Perreault (1997) unpack these functions, informative and marketing, in the following specific advertising objectives:

- help introduce new products in specific target markets;
- help position the company's brand or marketing mix, promoting its benefits to the target audience;
- help make products desirable through distribution channels and provide information about where the product can be found;
- provide an opening for the sales force, because product recognition makes the sales process easier;
- help buyers confirm their purchase decisions.

Semenik and Bamossy (1995) add to these objectives by suggesting that the construction of brand loyalty is an important objective for advertising, as they consider it less costly to help loyal customers than attract new ones.

Product advertising seeks to promote a product and/or service to the target public. This type of advertising is classified as: informative, persuasive and reminding. Informative

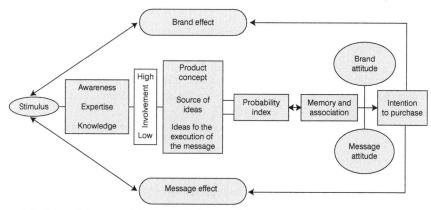

Figure 7.1 Advertising cognitive association model
Source: adapted from Fill (1999)

advertising is used when we want to work on the primary demand for the product, in other words, when one wants to educate the public about the values of the product category. On the other hand, persuasive advertising focuses on the selective demand for a specific brand, seeking to distinguish a brand from the competition. Reminder advertising is used in order to maintain the product's preference in the market and with consumers.

Institutional advertising must have the objective of promoting the image, reputation or ideas of an organization, seeking to facilitate the company's relations with the external and internal environment, including customers, suppliers, banks, employees, shareholders, distributors and society (McCarthy and Perreault, 1997). Finally, direct action advertising seeks a quick response from the target public for the message sent; in other words, the sponsor expects consumers to act as soon as they see the advertising message. Indirect action advertising is projected to stimulate demand over a much longer period of time, and is limited to informing and reminding the consumer of the existence and availability of the product and its benefits (Etzel *et al.*, 2001). In this way, Fill (1999) comments that the various types of advertising involve cognitive associations with the purpose of generating purchase intentions, as detailed in Figure 7.1.

Media Used in Advertising

Following the earlier discussion, one of the essential characteristics of advertising is the ability to reach a large audience. For this purpose, advertising uses mainly mass media as a tool to communicate with its target public. However the lack of selectiveness of traditional media and growing market segmentation have led to mass media fragmentation, creating options that are more focused and that have better cost benefit for companies which advertise.

Decisions regarding the allocation of budget across all possible vehicles have become more challenging because of the importance of new media, including social media and new interactive technologies used in communications.

Traditional media, such as TV and printed media, are expensive and complex, however, "the simple fact is that if there was no stimulus from the traditional media, there might be no material reverberation in the social-media space" (Lapointe, 2011).

The challenge is how companies allocate budget and efforts to develop both traditional and new media; thus, this is more challenging considering the background of a company because "in most industries, there exists a clear hierarchy in terms of the marketing vehicles deployed" (Corstjens *et al.*, 2011). However, conservatism in advertising resource allocation can lead a company to overspend on some media vehicles.

It is important to have in mind that the value or merit of each of the advertising media depends on the advertiser's specific needs and the budget available; in other words, no media will always be the best. The most common are: newspaper (traditional or specialized), mass or specialized magazines, television (national networks, selected market, local or pay-to-view services), radio, outdoor media (billboards, signs at bus stops, giant inflatable figures, advertising in traffic areas, aerial advertising, etc.), Internet, catalogs (yellow pages, industry yearbooks, sectorial lists, etc.), packages, movies, informative fliers, as well as new media. The number of television channels available today shows this fragmentation.

Regarding the message to be conveyed, the AIDA model (create attention, develop interest, stimulate desire, and lead to action) is desirable for the message. The decisions are what to say (message content), how to say it efficiently (message structure), how to say it through symbolization (message format) and who should say it (source). The SCORE model is also used, which means *simplicity* (avoid excessive refinement that disrupts its comprehension), *coherence* (maintain credibility between what is said, who says it and how it is said), *objectivity* (the message should clearly have an objective), *relevance* (the content should be relevant) and *empathy* (identification between form and content of the message and its target segment).

Which are the appeals that would most fit the company's products? Normally, the following appeals are sought (Kotler, 1997):

- content: rational (quality, economy, performance), emotional (unique associations with the consumers, reminding them of some phase of life, humor, desire) and moral (aiming to say what is the right thing to do);
- structure: the order in which the arguments are made;
- format: the expressive use of headings, voice, music, color, photographs, etc.;
- source: depending on the product, the use of people, artists, athletes, experts, who convey trust and add their image to the product or service.

Sales Promotion

A great number of definitions of sales promotion are found in the literature. McCarthy and Perreault (1997) say that there are promotion activities that stimulate interest, the will to experiment or the consumer's purchase. Boonee and Kurtz (1998) refer to sales promotion as short-term incentives that emphasize, assist, supplement, or in some way give support to the communications program. Etzel *et al.* (2001) treat it as temporary incentive activities paid by the sponsor to complement advertising and facilitate personal sales. Kelley (1970) expands the definition as being promotion methods that take a product or a service offered by a sponsor, and give it extra value, calling the target public's attention to the product.

The American Marketing Association (AMA) defines sales promotion as all promotion activities not included within personal sales, advertising and publicity, that are designed to assist mass advertising and personal sales to transfer products from the manufacturer to the consumer.

According to the definitions given above, it can be said that sales promotion:

- stimulates the commercialization of goods or services;
- is directed to all segments that participate in the marketing processes;

- is predominantly short term;
- emphasizes the product or service, placing it in more intimate contact with the audience;
- differs from other promotional tools.

What are the possible advantages of using sales promotion in the DDSP? The following list is based on Kelley (1970), Semenik and Bamossy (1995) and Schultz and Barnes (2001):

- *economies of scale*: a promotional tool can cost relatively little to reach a large portion of the population;
- *effective sales support*: good sales promotion material make the salespeople's efforts more productive by reducing prospecting time;
- *increase the product's acceptance speed*: sales promotion tools, such as free samples, are capable of leading the consumer to try the product;
- *allow sponsors better control*: the sponsor, contrary to what happens in advertising, has the promotional tools under his control and has the freedom to use them both in market segments as well as in national campaigns; and he has control over the budget available, because of the variety of promotional tools and control over their use;
- *possibility of being tested*: almost all sales promotion tools can be tested in smaller market shares, allowing a detailed analysis of their results, before being implemented in the whole target market;
- *attract new users*: sales promotion tools are used to reduce the risk of trying something new; thus they are used a lot when launching a product in the market, an existing product in a market segment that has not yet been reached, or when trying to convert non-users of a product category into users;
- *stimulate repeat purchases*: some sales promotion tools are used to make buyers purchase the product again in subsequent purchases and stay loyal to the brand – discount coupons in the product's package are an example of a promotional tool with this purpose;
- *stimulate larger purchases*: some promotional tools are used to encourage the buyer to take a larger quantity of the product, allowing the company to reduce stocks and increase its cash flow – discounts on prices and products are examples of this tool;
- *increase store traffic*: retailers can increase the store traffic through promotions or special events;
- *stimulate the sales team enthusiasm for a new, improved or mature product*: exciting sales promotions can increase the salesperson's power of persuasion when interacting with buyers;
- *revive sales of a mature brand*: sales promotion can revive sales of a mature product that need an incentive;
- *increase merchandise exposure space on and off the shelf*: commercial promotions allow the manufacturer to temporarily get more shelf space;
- *neutralize competing advertising and sales promotion*;
- *reinforce the advertising*: an advertising campaign can be greatly strengthened by a well-coordinated promotion activity.

At this point of the DDSP it is a good idea to reflect whether these possible advantages are being obtained by the company's sales promotion and how to improve on them.

According to McCarthy and Perreault (1997), use of sales promotion is extensive in mature markets in which there is substantial competition for consumers and attention from intermediaries. In categories of convenience products, as in food, where the market is characterized by the rapid change of brands and the perception of homogeneity between offers, sales promotions also tend to be used more. Sale promotion tends to be used more and more following the growth in power of large retail chains.

As stated by Peattie and Peattie (1994), sales promotion techniques can be classified in two groups: those that increase value and those that add value. The sales promotions that increase value are those that manipulate price and quantity to increase the value perceived by the consumer. Some examples are coupons, price discounts, indirect discounts, etc. Sales promotions that add value are the other tools that, without touching the product's price or quantity, deliver something more to the consumer, for example, games, competitions, web contests, prizes, etc. The authors state that by leaving the price intact and not being subject to the use of coupons, sales promotions that add value avoid financial dangers of price wars or coupon fraud that are common in price promotions.

Sales promotions should be directed at two different types of public: the internal public (the internal sales team and sales representatives) and the external public, (intermediaries, influencers and the target public). Depending on the target public, certain types of sales promotions are used (Pancrazio, 2000).

For the internal public, sales promotion strategies comprise all forms of promotion used on the company's own sales team and on its exclusive commercial representatives. At the same time, promotional activities oriented to the company's sales force, in turn, should encourage the capturing of new consumers, the sale of new products or the sale of a whole company line (McCarthy and Perreault, 1997). In the same way, sales promotion strategies can be developed directed towards intermediaries, also known as commercial promotion, comprising all the promotional tools oriented to the distributor and its sales team. Notice the interface between this part of the DDSP and what will be seen in Chapter 9.

Schultz and Barnes (2001) complement the subject by separating the distribution sales promotion, which consists of activities and incentives directed at wholesalers, retailers and distributors, and the final consumers. In order to implement sales promotion activities, in a similar way to advertising, there is a group of tools that can be used by companies. These tools vary in their objective: they can be used, among other purposes, to attract new consumers, compensate loyal customers and increase repurchase rates of occasional customers. As has already been discussed, sales promotion can be oriented to intermediaries, the company's own sales force, influencers and the final public.

The most common sales promotion tools used by companies are related in Table 7.5.

Public Relations and Publicity

Public relations strategies serve the function of generating in the general public goodwill in relation to the company or organization, and focus on the relationships created between an organization and its various publics (suppliers, members of the distribution channel, employees, shareholders and population in general). Public relations use media to communicate with the public in general, although they differ from advertising as they do not purchase space in printed media or time on electronic media and are not truly controllable. In other words, an important event for the company may not be covered by the media, and worse, can be covered in a negative manner. According to Kotler (1997) the appeals of the public relations activities are based on three distinct characteristics:

*   *high credibility*: articles in newspapers and magazines are more authentic and trustworthy to the readers than ads;

Table 7.5 Sales promotion tools

Oriented to intermediaries:	*Oriented to the final public (industrial market):*
• Rebates (prizes for reaching goals);	• Catalogs;
• Commercial compensation;	• Fairs and demonstrations;
• Concessions;	• Field days;
• Anticipated purchases;	• Seminars, conferences and specialized
• Discounts on merchandise;	courses;
• Special offers;	• Souvenirs;
• Cooperative publicity;	• QR codes.
• Bonuses for space;	
• Fairs, road shows, samples and trade shows;	*Oriented to the final public (consumer market):*
• Repurchase agreements;	• Discount coupons;
• Sales contests;	• Indirect discounts;
• Sales meetings;	• Samples/demonstrations/tastings;
• Point of sale material;	• Tests;
• Promoters;	• Souvenirs;
• Cash incentives.	• Contests, lotteries, souvenirs;
	• Direct discounts;
Oriented to the sales force:	• Fairs;
• Sales contests;	• Discounts/reimbursements;
• Catalogs;	• Special packages;
• Sales manuals;	• Continuity/loyalty programs;
• Rewards.	• QR codes.

Source: Elaborated from Kotler (1997), Schultz and Barnes (2001), McCarthy and Perreault (1997), Semenik and Bamossy (1995) and Pancrazio (2000)

• *possibility of catching buyers unaware*: public relations activities can reach potential customers who prefer to avoid salespeople and ads;
• *dramatization*: with public relations work, the company or product can be more concrete to a potential customer.

Publicity is a sub-function of public relations and its objective is to generate news about the company. Publicity, although it has its costs, is seen as being free and brings a great return over the investment. Publicity can help reach any communication objective. It can be used to advertise new products, inform about new policies, offer acknowledgement to employees, describe advances in research or report financial performance (Etzel *et al.*, 2001). Note that it is not controlled by the company. In other words, it can be positive, neutral or negative.

Many tools can be used by public relations managers, among them are: press kits and news (press releases), photographs, editorial material, company's internal newspaper, sponsorship of events, news hooks, audiovisual material (videotapes and films) about the company, financial reports, company magazines, lectures, seminars and press conferences, advice, technical specifications, relations with the community and government, relations with the market and special events (Schultz and Barnes, 2001).

Normally a company has a permanent advisor for its press function, who develops contacts, writes articles and monitors appearances. This phase of the DDSP evaluates how this activity is being done in the company and suggestions are made for improvement or even new actions.

This activity is absolutely essential nowadays. A company must monitor and be proactive in all new nedia, discussion groups and social relationship sites. In the new world of connectiveness any problem can reach the whole world within hours.

Direct Marketing and Sales Force Communication

The challenge of finding a medium that reaches specific consumers has led many companies to resort to direct marketing. The first efforts through direct marketing focused the advertising through direct mailing lists, in which the target audience was reached through the use of carefully selected lists (McCarthy and Perreault, 1997).

Kotler (1997) raises as characteristics of direct marketing:

- *private*: the message is usually directed at a specific person;
- *personalized*: the message can be prepared so as to reach the person to whom it is addressed;
- *updated*: the message can be prepared quickly;
- *interactive*: the message can be altered, depending on each person's response.

The growing use of the direct marketing can be attributed to extremely high costs of the personal sale visits. Web-based materials, email, telemarketing and direct mailing have been substituted for the sales team in some companies, while in others direct marketing is used to complement the sales team's activities, generating predisposition, creating opportunities and providing openings for salespeople, retaining current customers, inducing them to try products, stimulating change of brands, increasing sales volume or use of the product, and selling through direct responses.

Direct marketing is the use of direct-response advertising, of which direct mailing and telemarketing are the most common. However, since direct-response advertising can involve the use of any media to transmit messages that stimulate the consumers to buy directly from the advertisers, some conventional mass media (newspapers, magazines and television) advertising is a variety of direct-response marketing.

Direct marketing that uses the web and email has had much success. At this point in the DDSP, it would be interesting to research specialized companies in order to find out how the web is being used and evaluate the applicability of these actions for the focal company of the DDSP.

With respect to the sales force, as it is an important variable of the marketing and communications mix, its characteristics, tools and strategies will be examined in more detail in Chapter 9.

Nowadys, the era of connectedness is just beginning, and wonderful opportunities exist to use direct relationships with customers. They want to have a feeling of "taking part," and they need to be recognized as being important to the company.

Establishing the Communications Budget

Establishing a budget is a very difficult task for a company and errors are common, many times a lot less than necessary is spent or the company loses money through excessive communications. The most common methods for generating the budget are: availability of company resources (the company spends the amount it has available); a fixed percentage of sales, perhaps one to five percent of the previous year's sales; competitive parity, the company invests the same amount as the direct competitors; and the objective-and-task method, where the budget is generated based on objectives that are set, what tasks are necessary and how much it is necessary to invest to achieve them. In other words, if the company's objective was to increase market share by five percent in the first year, it can then establish the level of

Table 7.6 Communications budget creation methods

Method	Possible Advantages	Possible Disadvantages
Available resources: based on the resources the company can afford	Simplicity	Ignores the fact that the role of promotion is sales volume; makes long-term planning difficult
Percentage of sales: based on a percentage of the previous year's sales	Expenses are related with the sales movements; relation between cost of promotion, sales price and profit per unit	Circular reasoning; does not consider market opportunities
Competitive parity: spend the same as competitors	Assumption that the company will not "lose ground"	Reputation, resources, opportunities and different objectives
Objective- and task-related: budget is made based on objectives (sales, share, profit)	Allows the use of different tactics; allows thinking and creation; forces collection of data; creates in-company intelligence	It is more complex, as it requires the whole planning process to be completed before tasks can be changed

Source: Based on Kotler (1997)

resources necessary to achieve this target. Table 7.6 compares some methods for establishing the communications budget, pointing out possible advantages and disadvantages

After the budget is set, resources must be allocated among the communication tools, listed in the earlier section on "The Communications Mix (Tools)," depending on the market type, company strategy, product life cycle and consusumers' level of awareness and usage of the product among others. More details about budget forms and tools are presented in Chapter 11.

Table 7.7 presents a simplified model for budgeting and following up communications, showing how much will be paid for each type of communication and when investments will be made.

Measurement of the Communication Mix Results

One of the challenges that affect many marketing managers in companies of various industries is to find and, especially, to select methods that enable them to guide investment in communications.

The results from the marketing communications activities should be monitored, so the company will know if it has reached the set objective. Communications can still represent a big investment for the company. Therefore it should know whether the public remembers or recognizes the message, how many times it has been seen, what they think of the message and finally, what are the past and current attitudes in relation to the product and the company. If they liked it, bought it or spoke of it to other people.

Communications should be evaluated according to their capacity to attract attention, induce attention, awareness, consideration and level of recall of the material, among others. The impact of a sales action, the relation between company spend on advertising, share of this spend on the total for the industry, and market share should be evaluated. Note that one of the ways of measuring the impact on sales is through historical series (correlation between past sales and past advertising spend) and experimental analysis by isolating sales areas and increasing or reducing advertising spend so to evaluate its effect on sales. In terms of public relations, the effect of the number of exposures from a marketing campaign should be established.

Table 7.7 Example communications budget and schedule

| | Year: 2013 | | | | | | |
	January	February	March	April	May	June	Total
Magazine ads – weekly edition	1,500			1,500		1,500	4,500
Newspaper ads – half page Saturdays		2,200	2,200	2,200			6,600
TV channel – 30 × 20-seconds ads			20,000	20,000	2,000	20,000	62,000
Sales promotion – souvenirs	3,500	3,500	3,500	3,500	3,500	3,500	21,000
Participation in events – trade fairs		18,000					18,000
Trade promotion – contests and loyalty programs			4,000	6,000	10,000	10,000	30,000
Public relations							–
Grand total	5,000	23,700	29,700	33,200	15,500	35,000	142,100

The issue of metrics in marketing, when properly applied, also creates conditions to maximize the use of the marketing communications budget, including the amounts spent on agencies. There are several possible indicators that can be used by an organization that wants to evaluate its results in marketing. Some of these are considered from a shareholder perspective according to Doyle (2000) in the value-based communications concept, which examines how marketing communications investments can increase level of cash flow, accelerate cash flow, extend duration of cash flow and reduce risks to cash flow by stimulating the sales growth, enabling premium pricing, creating brand loyalty and allowing faster market penetration by communications activities.

Increasing availability of data because of modern information technology makes it relevant and possible for companies to have a reliable process which allows evaluation of results of the marketing communications plan and gives guidance in marketing-resource allocation.

Box 7.1 presents the ComValor method for the value-based marketing communication measurement.

This is the final and important stage for the company, if it is to continuously improve this process. In other words, all activities should have their results measured, the impact on the audience (how many remembered, saw, took an action) evaluated, the resulting costs and sales analyzed. If a company does this annually it evolves in its capacity of creating good communications plans within the DDSP. Other aspects concering the measurement of marketing actions are examined in detail in Chapters 11 and 12.

Management and Coordination of the Communications Process

In every communications plan there should be actions, people responsible for the plan, deadlines and the integrated use of all available tools, in an organized manner with contingency and course correction plans. Campaigns tend to be more efficient if carried out after marketing research of consumer market behavior characteristics and consumers' image

Box 7.1 The ComValor method

The ComValor method was proposed in 2010 after developing and monitoring a two-year case study for a large beverage company in Brazil and by in-depth interviews with twelve business professionals from five companies in Brazil (Guissoni *et al.*, 2010; Guissoni and Neves, 2011).

A major implication of this method is that the marketing communications performance indicators should be allocated as part of the measurement process instead of being treated separately, making it possible for a company to implement a measurement process and further develop a marketing dashboard. The method consists of five steps:

1   *Campaign management:* it is important to have reliable marketing and communications information. Thus, the communications campaigns should be managed continuously, and the marketing team must also register the metrics that should be used to evaluate each action, along with its goals and possible improvements.

2   *Refinement of results:* it is widely thought that a company cannot attribute its sales or profits results only to its communications activities; refinement of the results means eliminating other internal and external variables that influenced company sales and establishing the impact on sales attributable only to the actions of its communication activities.

3   *Calculation of operational metrics for marketing communication efforts:* to evaluate how successfully the marketing communications activities (for example: sales promotion, advertising, direct marketing, personal sales, public relations and sponsored events) were implemented within a proposed target market for each activity in terms of their execution.

4   *Calculation of financial metrics:* involves indicators to evaluate the financial results from the marketing communications investments, including the return on investment and other indicators which provide analysis from a shareholder perspective.

5   *Classification and presentation of results:* finally, the results attributable only to the communications efforts should be classified as viable or unviable for the company, and subsequently presented to senior management so as to contribute to company marketing communications processes and plans.

of the product. It is also necessary to define the objectives for promotional activity: to create consciousness of product, make it known, improve its image and stimulate purchase. The management and follow-up activities of the strategic marketing plan are described in detail in Chapter 12.

Table 7.8 Collective actions opportunities

Actions	Description	Opportunities (ideas) for the company
Joint advertising	Companies conduct joint advertising. This usually involves retailers and their suppliers, but there are cases involving companies of the same industry, or companies that have the same target market.	
Collective advertising to grow the total market	Companies allocate part of the budget on increasing the consumption of their industry's generic product, to the benefit of all participating companies.	
Promotion of combined sales	Another product from another company or from a group of companies is added the company's own and offered for sale.	
Public relations	Companies share public relations infrastructure and stimulate the development of the market as a whole.	
Development of a lobby	Companies work jointly to create knowledge and favorable public opinion of the product.	
Joint participation in fairs and events	Sharing of stands, common exhibition areas.	
Share sales force	Non-competing companies can share their sales force to sell complementary products and services.	
Others		

Collective Actions and Partnerships in Communication

Communications is one of the most fertile areas for pursuing joint actions with other companies. Table 7.8 shows actions companies can conduct jointly and which should be included in the DDSP.

Activities to Develop the Communications Plan

- Based on the material in this chapter, the communications plan for the company can be developed. For each target public (final consumers, distributors, sales teams, shareholders, journalists, press, society), objectives should be set; where possible they should be quantitative: which tools will be used to reach objectives; how much they will cost; implementation schedule; and how the results will be measured. Table 7.9 is a suggestion of how the process should be carried, using the relevant sections of this chapter to complete the columns. A summary table can be made with all the target publics, and then a specific table for each target public as sufficient information is difficult to fit into a single table.
- Table 7.8 should also be completed giving ideas of actions that can be carried out with other companies.
- Throughout this chapter a series of questions were posed and at this moment the answers can be consolidated.
- How can we use new media and the digital world to communicate and build relationships.

Table 7.9 Definition of the target public and communication actions

Target public (list all the target publics for the company's communications)	Communications objectives	Tools to be used	Budget	Schedule	Measuring results of the actions

Questions

1   How is the communications plan integrated into the DDSP?
2   What is the process of developing the communication plan?
3   List types of objectives which can be achieved by the development of communications strategies.
4   What elements should be used by the company to define the communications mix that will be proposed in the plan?
5   What are the methods of creating the communications budget? What are the challenges?
6   Why is it important for a company to evaluate its communications plan?
7   Which partnerships with other companies can be used in the communications process?
8   What are the most exciting new and digital media forms of communication that could be useful for a company?

8 Distribution Channels Decisions

A fundamental step in the DDSP is to think about how products will be made available to consumers; in other words, how they will be delivered to the target consumers of the marketing strategies developed in Chapter 5. In line with earlier comments, the plan must be well integrated with what is already established in terms of general strategies, product policies, communications, sales and prices; in short, with all the controllable marketing variables.

The topic of distribution is one of the oldest in marketing literature, giving rise to some of its most original theories (Wilkinson, 2001). Some authors regard it in a wider sense, classically calling it "distribution channels" (Neves, 1999).

At this stage of the DDSP, the following must be done:

* analyze existing distribution channels for the company's products, seek new channels and define distribution objectives, such as: market presence, type and number of points of sale, services offered, market information, product promotion and incentives;
* define opportunities and threats of the current distribution system;
* identify possible distributor and consumer needs in order to fulfill service expectations;
* define ways of entering markets: via franchises; joint ventures or other contractual forms; or even via vertical integration;
* explore domestic or international contracts with distribution channels, such as international representation;
* determine the annual distribution budget;
* determine how distribution actions can be done jointly with other companies in the network;
* determine what are the opportunities emerging from web-based marketing and distribution systems.

Channels over the years have always had the power to transform markets, because they are the drivers of consumer access to products and services (Wilson *et al.*, 2008). According to Stern *et al.* (1996), distribution channels are a group of interdependent organizations involved in the process of making the company's product or service available for consumption or use. The emphasis is on how to plan, organize, and control alliances between institutions, agencies and internal relations in companies (or hierarchical relations). It will be noticed, through these definitions, that a connection exists between distribution channels, contracts and transaction costs, although it has been little explored in publications to date.

In this chapter, the presentation of the distribution channel plan will be based on the model proposed by Neves *et al.* (2001). This model is supported by four texts on specific channel planning topics: Stern *et al.* (1996), Rosenbloom (1999), Berman (1996) and Kotler (1997). It takes into account the network focus proposed by this book and consequently includes a focus on transaction costs. The proposal by Neves *et al.* (2001) is also complemented by recent works on distribution channels, but with some adaptation so as to be better incorporated in the DDSP. A summary of this adapted model is presented next:

- description of the company and industry distribution channels;
- revision of the environmental analysis with a network focus, identifying the impact for the current channels;
- analysis of the existing company and industry contracts;
- company objectives for the distribution channels;
- analysis of consumers' needs regarding the distribution channels;
- gap and adjustment analysis;
- selection of the distribution channels;
- construction of contracts;
- administration of the distribution channels.

Describing the Industry's and Company's Channels

The objective of this first step is to describe all the agents that have functions in the channel (i.e. are part of the chain) for the industry which is being analyzed. This allows us to obtain a more accurate view, including the agents and functions they perform. It is important to mention that the distribution channel description used by the company is a detailed description of the company's network performed in Chapter 2 of the DDSP. At this point the channel's functions will be studied in detail, as well as the critical analysis of the capacity for developing extra functions or relocations, as will be shown later in the chapter.

After the analysis at the industry level (where all possible channels are described) the company's channels should be described individually. The company channels can be different from those used in general by the sector; for instance, some possible channels may not be used by the company (for example, sales of products in convenience stores). Sales and financial data must be provided with the objective of understanding which are the most important channels for sales and company profit. Figure 8.1 presents a simple and visual way of understanding the company channels.

Also, a table can be created, such as Table 8.1, for each flow: products and services, communications, information, and payables/financial. The first two flow from the company to the final consumers and the last two flow in the opposite direction. After creating this table, the actors (distributors) should be inserted and an analysis of whether or not they produce the flows should be entered in the second column. The third column should be filled out with possible improvements for the activities in the next period. For example, if a distributor isn't responsible for transporting products but it would be preferable if they were, then in the "proposals for improvements" column the entry would be "try to transfer the transport function to the distributor." This would be an action resulting from the distribution plan. If the company has several distributors (wholesalers, retailers), a column should be added, or possibly a separate table made, for each company that is in the channel of DDSP's focal company.

This table can be filled out for each member of the channel (e.g. Wal-Mart, Kroger, Carrefour), and also for the members aggregated together (e.g. retail industry).

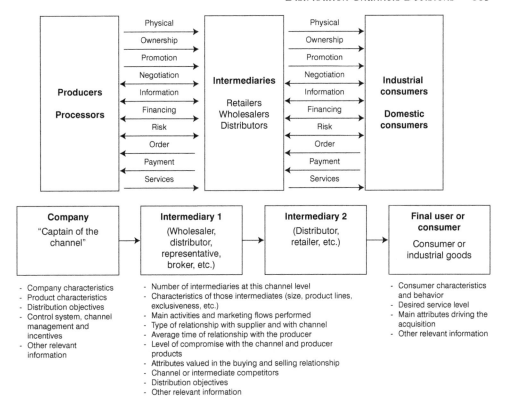

Figure 8.1 Understanding marketing flows and distribution channels
Source: Ansoff (1965: 109)

In order to help completion of the table, some final comments should be added regarding marketing flows performed by the channels. According to Stern *et al.* (1996), there are three basic premises in relation to these functions:

• the participants can be eliminated or substituted in the channels;
• the functions they perform cannot be eliminated;
• when participants are eliminated, their functions are passed on or backwards in the system and taken over by others.

These functions can and should, for the channel's efficiency, be performed by the participants that manage to operate in the most competitive way possible. All are indispensable, and experience, specialization, contacts and scale are fundamental for their exercise. The efficient coordination of the process always involves the sharing of information. The next step is the revision of the external analysis and the identification of its impacts in decisions for the distribution channel.

Table 8.1 Distribution channels flow

Function	Responsibility analysis (who does it and how)	Proposals for improvements in the activities for the next period
Variables in the flow of products and services		
Stock management and stock levels		
Product delivery		
Product modification		
Product lines and variety		
New product evaluation		
Sales volume (performance) forecasts		
User help/installation service		
Post sales service		
Sales service supply (team)		
Training: range and costs		
Product maintenance and repair		
Package/specifications issues		
Unique features present in the contract		
Territorial rights present in the contract		
Market coverage expected		
Export aspects expected		
Time frame (period to carry out the flows)		
Adaptation for specific legislation		
Others		
Variables in the flow of communications		
Execution of advertising (all forms)		
Execution of sales promotion (all)		
Public relation actions (all)		
Direct marketing actions		
Supply information about the products		
Participation in the communication budget		
Communication action with direct sales		
Package information		
Others (fill in)		
Variables in the flow of the information		
Supply information about the consumer market		
Supply information about the competition		
Supply information about changes in the environment		
Participation in the planning process		
Frequency and quality of the information		
Supply information about complaints		
Electronic orders		
Others (fill in)		
Flow of the payments and orders		
Frequency of product orders		
Policies for prices and payments		
Margin analysis		
Commissions (volume and frequency)		
Credit to final consumers		
Billing consumers		
Search for sources of finance		
Price guarantees		
Others (fill in)		

Source: Neves *et al.* (2001)

Table 8.2 Distribution channel impacts.

Trends	Implications for the distribution channels	Possible recommended actions for the channel member or company

Source: adapted from Neves *et al.* (2001)

Performing the Analysis: Identifying the Impacts for Current Channels

At this point it is important to review the external analysis with the DDSP approach on networks, performed earlier in Chapter 2, and identify the specific consequences for the distribution channels. In cases where the impacts for the distribution channels have already been identified in the earlier stage, then development and detailed understanding is necessary here. It is recommended that a matrix be built, as in Table 8.2, highlighting all impacts for the distribution channel coming from changes and trends in the social and cultural, technological, economic and natural, and political and legal environments, and possible actions to neutralize the impacts can be developed throughout the plan (Johnson and Scholes, 2008). For this analysis of STEP variables, the same analysis as that in Chapter 2 can be used, but now applied specifically to channels.

An analysis of the future would be interesting here; the suggestion is to build this table for today and for ten years from now.

Box 8.1 Retailers: the Giants of Chains

At one extreme, a shift in power from manufacturers to retailers has been observed (Planet Retail, 2010) which led to a decrease in the rates of return obtained by manufacturers as the bargaining power of retailers increased (Porter, 1974; Ailawad *et al.*, 1995). An important distinction was made by Ailawad *et al.* (1995) relating to this shift in power; they found that some retailers were gaining power over other retailers and not over manufacturers. However, despite this finding, over time there has been a consolidation of retailers who have become more powerful such as, in Brazil, Wal-Mart, Carrefour and Pão de Açúcar Group (Brazil's leading retailer, jointly owned by a Brazilian group and by the French retailer Groupe Casino) which gives them increasing buying power.

At the other extreme, consumers behave in complex ways, using different channels for different purposes and for different shopping occasions, now there is "a large segment of consumers who are enthusiastic about using multiple channels during their shopping process" (Konus *et al.*, 2008: 410).

In this sense, and considering increasingly empowered customers who exercise their choice in what and where they buy, understanding the multichannel concept is important for reaching the target market. The multichannel concept is the use of multiple channels to provide access to customers for an organization, by describing all the different possibilities and routes in which customers and companies interact, including online and off-line channels (Wilson *et al.*, 2008). In this context, retailers play an important role in channel strategies for the companies.

Retailers have two valuable assets: information about consumers (what, who, when, why they buy), and space for interaction and selling. They are now selling this information to other companies, and offering more space inside stores for communications from other companies; this represents an increasing source of income. Since almost 70 percent of buying decisions are made at the point of sale, this strategy represents an opportunity to win shoppers' preference.

Retailers also face new challenges in operations management. These include permanent reduction of transaction costs, smaller numbers of suppliers (without increasing dependency), and technology (electronic data interchange systems). This also means better product assortment to maximize shelf space.

Convenience services (such as delivery, gift-wrapping presents, offering ready-to-eat meals, bakery, butchery, coffee shops, etc.) are also a trend for some retailers in gaining competitive advantage, There is also a trend toward a "green" movement, saving energy and measuring carbon emissions and being identified as environmentally friendly. Some retailers are adopting a strategy of sustainable initiatives for sourcing, using fair trade and other concepts and increasing the number of small producers as suppliers, even when it means increasing transaction costs.

Internationalization and global sourcing continues to be a trend and retailers face the challenges of different cultures. But this also allows retailers to find the best suppliers from around the world and bring global products to their stores. Retailers are also facing stronger competition from very different formats such as direct sales, online sales, door-to-door distribution systems and an increasing share of consumers' expenditure being spent on food services (restaurants, caterers and other formats).

Last, but not least, is a trend towards joint operations with other retailers, sharing buying structures and centers, stock management, marketing, layout, technology, which may be a first step towards a future merger of the giants in specialized chains.

Box 8.2 The World of Retailers' Brands

Private label (brands developed and managed by distributors, retailers and wholesalers) is one of the most discussed strategy issues and has a major impact on retailers' activities. It has been an important tool for distributors in very competitive sectors and has played differing roles for the food industry, transforming threats into opportunities. The objective of this section is to highlight some important factors for consideration in a relationship to supply products to a distributor's (retailer or wholesaler) private label.

In some countries the share of private label brands at retail has reached over 50 percent of total food sales. Some retailers even sell only their private brands in their stores. The percentage of private label sales within product categories is higher in food and beverages than other product categories.

But what are the possible advantages for food producers when they decide to supply to private labels brands? There are several possible advantages: since communications are done by the retailer, the first is lower costs for the producer. There is also the possibility of increasing sales and obtaining scale gains, since more of the company's factory capacity will be used and purchase of inputs will increase, enhancing negotiation power with suppliers. The producer will occupy greater space on the retailer's shelves (when the same factory is producing both its original brand and the private label brand).

It could also be easier for a producer to obtain credit and funding from banks, since future sales are guaranteed by the supply contract. In product line decisions, it gives the opportunity of alternative product lines with different prices and positioning. It is important to note that private label brands are normally products without technical innovation. Very few new products are launched as private labels. There is improvement in the relationship with the retailer. Another advantage for the company is reputation, since consumers recognize that to be a supplier of a retailer's private brand works as a quality certification. It may also contribute to lower physical distribution costs and producers don't need promotion at the point of sale.

Another point to be considered is that while the company may face a lower market share than the private brand in stores, it has a higher market share for the factory (since it has two brands on the shelves coming from the same factory). The company gains experience, and moreover can supply other retailers, and even other industries. As the retail sector becomes more global, there is the opportunity to be the global supplier in the product category. A final, practical reason to study this proposal is that if one company does not supply the retailer's private label, a competitor will.

What are advantages for the retailer of having private label products? First we need to understand that there are several possible brand formats including: brands under the retailer's name or retail brands, but under another name. There is the advantage of vertical chain coordination, having production without production assets and having lower stocks levels since these will be managed by the producer. The retailer also gets greater bargaining power to negotiate with other suppliers because the flexibility of private label's price positioning. A private label strategy increases the possibility of developing store loyalty (giving identification in the minds of consumers, who will be seeing the brand at home and other places, not just in the store). Private labels normally offer higher margins but they increase pressure on shelf-space, as this limited space is occupied by private label products, reducing space for other brands.

Another possible advantage is the widening of the store's product line. But the retailer has to have very good coordination and careful quality monitoring to maintain the brand image; the reputation of the retailer could be damaged if there are quality problems.

Since retailers are recognized and in some cases approved of by consumers, why not extend their brands to the products sold in the stores? Private labels today are a major concern in marketing. How can the food industry fight against these giants? Private labels increase competition in the food market and enhance retailers' bargaining power. Market leaders are threatened by increasing private label sales even within premium segments of the market, and the second or third brands are threatened from the opposite direction by cheaper private labels.

Analyzing Existing Contracts

It is important to understand how the relationships are "governed" in the distribution channels of the products within the sector in which the company operates, the means of coordination, the general contract practices, and purchasing procedures and processes. The results of this analysis help decide if the company's proposed means of coordination are too difficult to be undertaken and if they will bring high negotiation and learning costs. Asset specificity analysis will help a company to establish contractual arrangements that will protect it from possible risks emanating from these specificities.

Placing Company Objectives Within the Channels

These objectives must be in accordance with the DDSP, in a way that is consistent with the price, product, communications and sales force strategies. The objectives must be set in relation to several variables, each related to the type of channel, including: physical volume and monetary value, profit, sales margins, stock turnover, market share, consumer satisfaction, sales expenses, return on investments in channels, general service offered to the consumer, volumes sold by product type, among other measures.

In terms of behavior-based measures, the most important to be considered are: the customer service department, return process, installation, sales force bonus plan, coverage area, product knowledge and the sales team abilities, financial plan, business plan, advertising and promotion programs, number of complaints by consumers, consumer credit management, sales forecast precision, total sales visits, number of product demos, among others. In this stage the company will create several tables, forecasts and other types of tools to establish the objectives. Useful ideas can be found in Berman (1996), Stern *et al.* (1996), Rosenbloom (1999) and Gattorna and Walters (1996).

Analysis of Consumer Needs in Terms of Distribution Channels

This step is related to market research with final consumers and intermediaries to obtain insights about the distribution system from the consumer's point of view, so that their needs can be fully met. It is very important to build distribution systems that are consumer-oriented (Stern *et al.*, 1996). At the end of this stage you will have a list of the channels' and consumers' needs in relation to this marketing variable.

Gap Analysis and Quick Adjustments

At this point in the plan, companies will have established their intentions as regards distribution channels. On the other hand, they should have a good understanding of the consumer desires regarding marketing channels. These objectives and consumer desires must now be aligned. Quick adjustments refer to a stage, described by Stern *et al.* (1996), where companies don't need to wait for the completion of the plan, but can implement changes in existing channels immediately if these changes show clear advantages. In other words, the company need not wait until the completion of the DDSP; adjustments which in the company's view bring immediate returns can be applied immediately.

Selection of Distribution Channels

Once objectives are established, if the necessary flexibility exists, the company can select the distribution channel structure and channel members. This depends on the availability of the agents in the channel, the type of relationship that will be built, as well other factors identified in earlier stages. Several techniques are available for the negotiation process, and a model for conducting successful negotiations can be found in Lynch (1993) and Martinelli (2002).

Rosenbloom (1999) presents a useful list of criteria to be employed in this selection and suggests how to evaluate these variables through questionnaires and research. The most important criteria to be considered by manufacturers in the selection of the channel are given in Table 8.3.

Table 8.3 Criteria for the selection of channel members

Selection criteria	Commentary
Financial conditions and credit	Financial capacity, credit, guarantees, background, restrictive information
Sales force	Qualification and size of the sales team available, frquency of visits and customer support
Sales performance	Historical information of volume, invoicing per area, salesperson, customers, etc.
Product lines	Aspects about the extension of the product lines; existence of competing, compatible and complementary products
Reputation	Reputation from the point of view of suppliers, customers and consumers. Involves image, character and company history
Market coverage	Size of the operating area, number of customers and possible overlap with other regions
Attitudes	Criterion that takes into consideration aggressiveness, enthusiasm, initiative and predisposition to make partnerships
Size	In general, size is related to sales volume, financial capacity, better equipment, more employees, etc. It is a criterion that should be evaluated with caution
Experience	Indicates if the member of the channel has knowledge and experience of the market, product lines and other companies the member has worked with in the past
Managerial factors	Involves managerial capacity, organization, cost structure, planning, etc.
Support services	Capacity to offer support services for distribution and differentials from local competitors
Market information	Information available and that can be shared with the company regarding the market, products, competitors, trends, etc.
Structure	Adapt the administrative structure, logistics and warehousing for the company and products
Coordination	Capacity and interest in performing marketing functions that will be allocated between the members of the channel
Control	Involves the determination of the control level the company will have over resources and activities in the channel

Source: compiled from Berman (1996: 500), Pelton *et al.* (1997: 326), Rosenbloom (1999: 242)

Table 8.4 Advantages and disadvantages of coordination via the market

Advantages	Disadvantages
• market companies (independent distributors) find more competition, therefore produce more efficiently and develop more innovation capacity (incentives); • outsourced distribution companies develop good market knowledge in general; • market contracts generate powerful incentives – each part of the contract is primarily interested in maximizing its own results; • focus on the company's core competence; • there is high flexibility and change possibility; • motivation: the external parts have powerful incentives to do well because they are independent companies, that accept risks in return for prospects of rewards; • survival of the most economically apt: if the specialists do not perform their functions better than their competitors, they will not survive.	• possible existence of transaction costs in making changes, such as: getting information about products, raw materials, prices, buyers, salespeople, knowledge of the partner, selection of alternatives, negotiation, monitoring, enforcement, renegotiations, settlement of disputes, etc.; • few chances to differentiate; • if the market structure is concentrated, it increases the distributors' bargaining power and reduces the advantages of operating in the market (number of companies); • little control of the distribution and the prices for the final consumer; • difficulty in the coordination of information flow; • difficulty in the coordination of the production flow.

The coordination (governance) via the market consists simply of selling the products in market transactions. All information is contained in the price. As motivating factors for this, there is efficiency, as there are many companies competing in the market, distributing intensely, giving the consumer convenience, and high flexibility and possibilities of change. However, it presents disadvantages of little control and as a consequence few chances of differentiation. A more detailed analysis on the advantages and limitations of this option are shown in Table 8.4.

Another form of coordination of the channel is joint ventures, which are a type of strategic alliance where a third company is created, without the original companies ceasing to exist. It is a contractual form and intermediate between the extremes of vertical integration and coordination via the market. If the company in the DDSP is considering establishing a joint venture, then the possible advantages and risks outlined in Table 8.5 arise.

A company can also use the franchise format for channels. Franchising, which is also a contractual form, and is therefore intermediate between vertical integration and coordination via the market, is "the contract through which a franchiser transfers to a franchisee the right of producing or selling products or services. In exchange, the franchiser receives the revenue flow of each unit, which can become a fixed fee (franchise fee) and/or variable (such as royalties and advertising). In addition to this, the franchisee can contribute with assets, such as capital, management ability or knowledge about local markets. This way, there is a network that shares a brand, a way of doing business and the knowledge that is gained in that activity" (Azevedo, 1996).

The advantages and possible risks of franchising are detailed in Table 8.6.

As mentioned earlier, vertical integration can be summarized as having the distribution function (as part of the company) and assuming functions of the distribution channel (Coughlan *et al.*, 2002). There are several factors to be considered. The possible risks presented for this option are summarized in Table 8.7.

Another additional factor to be considered in selecting distribution channels is the use of multiple channels, which is increasingly common as the segmentation of markets increases

Table 8.5 Advantages and risks in strategic alliances (joint ventures)

Advantages	Risks
• can increase access to critical resources such as marketing, technology, raw materials and components, financial assets, managerial experience, including in a complementary form; • it is a form to get around legal and economic entry barriers in several countries; • gain more market force; • better market coverage (scale); • spread risks; • acquire experience and contact network; • avoid supplier and/or distributor power; • access to distribution channels; • guarantee of operation and access to specific markets; • decrease in stocks, logistic coordination, increasing turnover; • idle capacity utilization; • high adaptation capacity in local markets; • lower cultural risk to enter new markets; • increase R&D creativity; • explore synergies; • unite efforts to reach common objectives; • there is interest in profit sharing; • increase in trust between the partners; • easier to solve conflicts in the channel.	• conflicts between the participating companies; • the construction of the administrative team is a delicate process; • creating its own identity, independently from associated organizations, is critical; • joint ventures can present instabilities in the command structure, in which the governance positions can change, or one of the partners can solely assume control; • technology transfer without any compensation; • yield markets (knowledge of the brand) with benefits in exchange; • each side can face many exit barriers to leave the relationship; • risk of a relationship with unbalanced power in which the more powerful organization controls the weaker ones; • hold-up risk (contract breach) when only one of the parts makes investments in specific assets; • partners can disagree about the division of the investments, marketing or other policies; • cultural difference between companies, such as commercialization and administration barriers; • high expenditure for the company due to control and coordination issues; • a dynamic partner in a joint venture can become a strong competitor; • risk of choosing the wrong partner.

and distribution formats multiply. For example, in Brazil door-to-door distribution has grown recently.

According to Friedman and Furey (2000) the use of multiple channels is positive when this decision increases consumers' range of options, or when new channels allow companies to reach consumers that were not reachable before. However, it is necessary to think about conflicts that may appear if one format "steals" the other format's consumers. A common conflict is direct sales (made easier today with direct communications channels such as the internet and telemarketing) with independent distributors. Several authors have considered the issue of using multiple channels and the conflicts that appear including Webb, 2002; Easingwood and Coelho, 2003 and Wiertz *et al.*, 2004.

Therefore at this point in the DDSP an evaluation should be made about the other channel forms (franchises, joint ventures, own stores), and whether these can be used – for this evaluation, Tables 8.5 to 8.7 may help.

Table 8.6 Advantages and risks in franchises

Advantages	Risks
For the franchiser:	*For the franchiser:*
• it is midway between market and integration to combine advantages from both;	• lack of concern with the network integration process and participation from the franchisees in strategies and new developments;
• long-term strategic relationship between franchiser and franchisee;	
• the company can use information on cost and profitability of the internal channels to negotiate contracts with franchisees;	• the so called "franchise brokers" and "franchisee cooperatives" (where franchisees meet to increase their bargain power with the franchiser) can threaten the system;
• expands distribution channels without demanding high levels of investment. in reality, it uses third party capital which are the franchisees;	• store concentration in the hands of few franchisees can make the negotiation process unequal between the parts;
• Ease of brand management due to larger control;	• there are labor aspects on the franchisee's behalf that could result in law suits for the franchiser;
• More flexibility than vertical integration;	
• gains in scale for marketing and technology (advertising, new product development, administrative procedures);	• there can be brand value loss due to the offering of products below the specified standards by free-riding franchisees; spreading of knowledge gained by ex-franchisees;
• the franchisee can still have local knowledge;	
• exploits the entrepreneurial spirit of the franchisee;	*For the franchisee:*
• the franchisee has the necessary incentive to perform his activities the best way possible, because he will be benefited with residual profit.	• can earn less than expected due to existing expenses in the system;
	• geographical concentration of franchisees in the same area generating competition within the franchise system;
For the franchisee:	• franchiser may not invest in a qualitative form and in a quantitatively sufficient way in advertising and development of new products;
• receive marketing support;	
• predefined location for the venture;	
• efficiency in supplies;	
• market research;	• can limit creativity and innovation of entrepreneurs or franchisers;
• project and layout;	
• counseling on ongoing negotiations;	• the payment system can be discouraging: initial fixed fee plus part of the economic result (royalties) and contributions for communication;
• financial counseling;	
• operational manuals;	
• administrative training;	
• employee training;	• mandatory purchase of inputs from the franchiser, these inputs can be overpriced.
• knowledge already acquired from the franchiser's experience;	
• consolidated brands in the market.	

Building Contracts

This step involves designing written and other types of contracts (for example, verbal agreements) with the partners in the channel, depending on the forms of coordination suggested in earlier steps. Other aspects include escape clauses to counter opportunism in the channel, means of enforcement, adapting to change, construction of exit barriers, design of incentives and monitoring. An analysis of the market's specific institutional environment – e.g. the country – where the company is operating should also be developed to determine whether the most common distribution tactics used are possible in a specific market. For this step the planning team should consult with specialists – lawyers – who can contribute to the analysis and evaluation.

Table 8.7 Factors to consider and risks in the vertical integration

Factors to consider in vertical integration	Risks in vertical integration
• the existence of asset specificity in the relationship with the distribution channels, combined with environmental uncertainty and risk of opportunistic actions, can lead the company to integrate vertically in order to increase control and reduce the risks; • the operation of a channel can guarantee access to market information, which guarantees a competitive advantage, besides reducing the lack of information symmetry regarding performance standards; • decrease of the quality inspection costs, for there is control over the channels; • protection from market oscillations; • on the other hand, there will be "agency" costs in activities that were internalized as a result of different interests in the organization; • integrated tax planning in the chain (transfer of tax benefits) can generate cost advantages; • complete control of the channels and ease in influencing the mission or changing objectives of channels' commercial strategy in a timely manner; • differentiation opportunity in view of the competition, offering products with more value added to the customers in the channels; • access to the distribution channels and increase in the negotiation power with other distributors, if these are used in conjunction with their own channels; • the investment requirement makes access of new entrants difficult, when the company has a large market share and "dominates" access to the channels; • there is a clear gain of power through the growth of the business as a whole; • protection against the closing of the market, for the company has its own access to it.	• the cost to change channels becomes too high; • in the case of integrating, often the costs and expenses associated with the integration are higher than the revenue gained considering the distribution channel's margins; • it can be disadvantageous not to have enough flexibility to accompany the need for development of new markets; • larger exit barriers; • may reduce and limit the innovation rate; • cost of opportunity in investing in a business that offers a lower profitability than other market options; • investments required; • customers may become competitors; • optimum production scale differences between the stages of the chain (complexity of products and processes); • substantial differences among businesses do not generate administrative synergy; • distance from the company's core business; • problems in one production stage threaten production and profitability of all other stages; • occasional closing of the access to research of other distribution alternatives; • the activities at the beginning of the chain are very different and are subject to different financial models.

When writing contracts, the parties should consider possible sources of conflict, establish means of minimizing these sources, and plan actions to be taken if these conflicts appear. According to Berman (1996), conflicts are created when there is incongruity in the roles, differences in perception, incompatibility of objectives, communication difficulties and resource scarcity. The author suggests several methods of conflict resolution: training, shared tasks, establishing common objectives, and distribution channels and commercialization committees.

If the company chooses a franchise format, contract models can be found in the distribution channel books mentioned earlier. If the company decides to enter into a strategic alliance (joint venture) or other type of relationship, Lynch (1993), Gattorna and Walters (1996) and the extensive literature on alliances and networks can be consulted.

Products + services + communications

→

	Industry/ Producer	Intermediary 1	Intermediary 2	Consumer/end user
Activities	• Produces • Delivers • Promotes the brand • Incentivates the channel • Defines distribution politics	• Divides • Reassembles/ repacks • Adds informative materials • Delivers	• Communicates product attributes to consumers • Delivers	• Buy with regularity • Stores products in the proper way • Communicates with other consumers
Transactions	• Prepares contracts • Evaluates and gives payment credit and time	• Gives payment terms • Passes on discount politics and commercial actions	• Gives terms • Makes collections • Programs future orders	• Pays on time • Anticipates acquisitions
Relationship	• Develops training • Performs promotional activities	• Sells/rents distribution structure • Establishes areas of action and sales objectives • Implements incentive actions	• Knows consumption behavior • Develops trust and relationships • Offers other product lines	• Maintains contacts with the company • Demonstrates expectations • Indicates company/channel to other persons

← Information + orders + payment

Figure 8.2   Example of description of activities for the writing of contracts in a door-to-door channel for consumer products
Source: adapted from Consoli *et al.* (2004)

A way of making the writing of a contract easy is to evaluate the channel as a whole and specify the activities that should be performed in particular by each member of the channel. This allows a detailed view of what should be included in the contract in terms of rights and obligations of each member in the channel. An example of this description of activities for writing contracts can be seen in Figure 8.2.

Distribution Channel Management

The last phase of the process is distribution channel management. The literature on distribution channels is vast and suggests several techniques and administrative capabilities. Some aspects relating to the construction of successful and trustworthy partnerships, which are of fundamental importance, are highlighted here. References and tools from relationship marketing theory use commitment and trust to ease the management of the channels (Morgan and Hunt, 1994; Amato Neto, 2000; Gonzalez and Trespalacios, 2004). These topics will be considered in the management plan.

In this phase of the plan, the company should continuously identify actions that will allow the channel to remain motivated, in a win–win relation, such as return policies, prizes, and incentives.

Collective Actions in Distribution

Distribution channels are an extremely appropriate area for the development of joint actions between companies, as they are sources that offer differentiation, and because they can make products available more easily to consumers. In addition to customer services, companies

Table 8.8 Distribution channel network approach

Why the network approach and distribution channel joint actions can be used	Description and examples	Ideas for the company
Access to different market segments with complementary offers.	Two companies that have complementary interests in relation to market segments can share channels and both can increase sales with a lot less effort rather than if each one had to develop its own channel independently for the new market segment.	
Strengthening of the channels of an individual company.	Two companies can make their channels much more attractive to the consumer when combining complementary offers.	
Combined efforts of competing companies to operate in little known markets.	Two competing companies that do not have scale and experience in international markets can combine efforts to open international markets, with well planned joint ventures.	
Blocking of distribution channels to competing companies.	Company distributions can act jointly in order to make the new entrant's access more difficult.	
Economy of scale gains by competitors by better exploring assets of the distribution function.	Two competing companies can decide they gain more by combining distribution efforts but will compete over other marketing variables, such as product or communication.	
Joint events	Companies can group channels for joint events.	

can share distribution channels together in order to complement their markets, and to reach new market segments. Table 8.8 presents ways of rethinking the distribution channel with a company network approach.

Activities for Distribution Decisions

In this stage of the DDSP, you should do the following actions:

- describe the company channels in diagrammatic form;
- perform function analysis and how to improve: think about Table 8.1 for each channel, making a list of improvements to be proposed for the channel, aiming at improving the flows; the list should come automatically from completing the column on the right;
- analyze the macro environmental impacts (uncontrollable variables) for the company channels, having as a result filled out Table 8.2; from there, think of channel project alternatives to take advantage of opportunities; perform an analysis of the distribution channel's future in ten years;
- establish the company objectives with each channel;
- analyze the distributor purchasing decision process, based on what was worked on in Chapter 2, in order to identify existing opportunities for the company; also, the necessary adjustments should be analyzed to align the company objectives with those of buyers;

- coordination forms: see if there are opportunities for joint venture projects, franchises, strategic alliances or even vertical integration in the company channels and, if so, use Tables 8.4 to 8.7 to plan these projects;
- develop a list of motivation actions for the channel and its budget;
- verify which ideas for collective actions can be made in the channels, thinking in terms of Table 8.8 when applied to the company;
- see the new and specific opportunities that arise with the web and digital interactions between companies and consumers.

Analyzing the distribution channel issue is fundamental, mainly in industrial sectors, to analyze sales force issues which appear in distribution channels, whether in direct sales channels or distributor sales forces. Sales force management will be examined in Chapter 9. Once more note that Chapters 6 to 10 must be worked on concurrently.

Questions

1   Which method can be used for a company to develop its distribution plans?
2   How can a company be more competitive using distribution strategies?
3   What are the marketing flows for the distribution channels?
4   Describe some criteria to select channel members.
5   What forms can a company develop to establish its coordination in the channel?
6   What variables should be considered for a company to develop its distribution contracts?
7   Which partnerships with other companies could be used in the distribution plans?
8   How can we use web and digital interaction as a marketing channel for a company?

9 Sales Force Decisions

In this chapter, first the relationship between sales, marketing strategy and business strategy will be discussed. Once this role is understood, the rest of the chapter is organized according to decisions necessary for sales planning and sales organization. These decisions are: establishing criteria for operation of the sales force in the market, implementation of the sales force, which will be referenced as "human resources in sales" topics, how to acquire and maintain a well-prepared and motivated sales team and, finally, the ways of controlling sales. In summary, the following analyses should be undertaken when making a company sales plan:

- analyze the current sales force situation and define the objectives for the next period, both based on performance indicators;
- define the way in which salespeople will approach customers (strategy);
- outline the limits of the sales forces' actions, directing their efforts, and whether to establish a support team for the company;
- define the ideal number of salespeople for the company (size), and establish how they should be compensated (wages);
- recruiting, selecting, supervising, motivating, and training the sales team are necessary to guarantee work continuity;
- undertake evaluation and monitoring in order to reach objectives, which includes following up issues identified in earlier steps;
- network actions, in cooperation with competitors and other companies that operate in the same target market, can also be undertaken;
- a sales force budget should be developed.

A sales force needs to be totally integrated with other marketing elements to produce the greatest impact possible, because a coordinated marketing mix has a greater power over consumers (Rogers, 1993; Churchill *et al.*, 2000).

The sales force has an immense potential for increasing company sales, but on the other hand, it can ruin the whole marketing strategy (Zoltners *et al.*, 2001).

Business Strategy, Marketing Strategy and Sales Force Management

This section presents two major considerations. The first is related to the importance the sales force has within the company. The second, since it is an important function, is which considerations are in the literature regarding integration of company and marketing strategy and sales management.

According to Churchill *et al.* (2000) the more complex the offer, the more support services are necessary and the more scarce the available promotion resources are, then more importance will be given to a variable sales force in the company. When push distribution strategy is used (sales efforts are placed with distributors) there is also a greater importance of the sales force than when a pull strategy is used (sales efforts are towards the stimulation of final consumption). The larger the number of consumers, the smaller is the importance of the sales force. Also, the greater the need for information during the purchasing process, the greater is the need for salespeople.

As for the purchasing process, the bigger the purchase and the bigger the importance of these purchases are to consumers, the more important personal sales will be. Sales management activities suffer from short-term vision, as they tend to concentrate on immediate aspects and ignore strategic planning. This happens because it is an area directly connected to the company's survival and its results easily verified and put under pressure by shareholders. It is fundamental for a company's performance to have a sales management strategy derived from the organization's competitive strategy, assuming that sales are crucial in the whole process (Olson *et al.*, 2001; Ingram *et al.*, 2002).

The sales force is responsible for the implementation of the business strategy developed by the corporation, and it communicates important components of the business strategy which become visible and also provides the administration with information about the strategy success (Fletcher *et al.*, 2004; Dewsnap and Jobber, 2004). A gap between corporate strategy and sales strategy is serious, since at the time a sale is made, everything that was built in terms of production and market efforts can be lost (Rogers, 1993; Olson *et al.*, 2001), and it is even more important when analyzing the fundamental role of creating relationships with more profitable consumers (East *et al.*, 2004).

There is a relation between the strategies adopted at a corporate level and the sales force action. For example, Porter's generic strategies (1997) have different implications for the sales force (Table 9.1).

A more recent view, which in a certain way questions this traditional sequence, is stated by Ingram *et al.* (2002). The traditional view is that the corporate strategy defines the business strategy which, in turn, defines the marketing strategy such as segmentation,

Table 9.1 Porter's strategies and implications for the sales force

	Strategy	Sales force implications
Cost	• gains with scale; • cost reduction; • overhead control; • generally high market share.	• service large customers; • minimize expenses; • sales based on price.
Differentiation	• creation of something perceived as unique; • brand loyalty; • less sensitivity to price.	• sale of benefits; • generate orders; • service and response; • prospecting is meaningful; • high-quality salespeople.
Niche	• service to a select target market; • policies are developed for the niche in mind; • share may be low, but is dominant in the segment.	• expert in operations and opportunities associated with a target market; • considerable time allocation for the target market.

Source: Castro and Neves (2005)

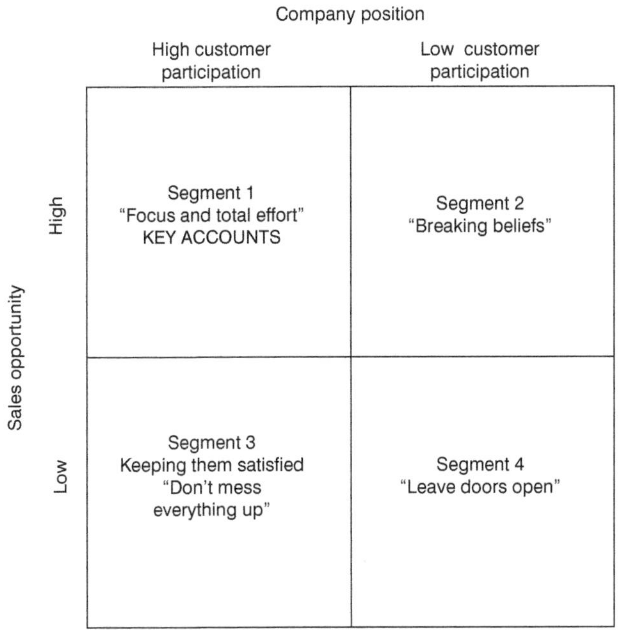

Company position

	High customer participation	Low customer participation

Figure 9.1 Establishing segments and operational focus
Source: Castro and Neves (2005)

choosing of the target market, definition of the marketing mix, the communications plan and the role of sales within the communications efforts. This is a vision that perhaps ignores the growing importance that sales has been gaining. With the growing importance of creating a relationship with customers, the customer relationship marketing (CRM) programs are getting more attention; Ingram *et al.* (2002) suggest that in the relationship with customers, sales should assume a more extensive and strategic role.

Sales strategy translates marketing strategy to an individual level. When marketing selects target markets, the sales force should know how to work within these segments, prospecting for and qualifying consumers and defining how the interaction with customers should be at a sales process level. Figure 9.1 suggests strategies for how this can be done in relation to the customer, separating out each salesperson's portfolio in terms of customer size and interaction with the customer.

Thinking about the level of relationship that a sales process should seek, the interaction can go from a transactional orientation at one extreme to the partnership orientation at the other; these are two distinct procedures with different types of sales and resource approach (Futrell, 2010; Weitz *et al.*, 2004; Ingram *et al.*, 2002).

A market entry model which considers the integration of communication and distribution tools, consumer behavior and market segmentation, following the same reasoning of the increase of the importance of sales in the strategic context, is presented by Zoltners *et al.* (2001), integrating different aspects, shown in Figure 9.2.

This model initially determines market segmentation. Next, market analysis is performed, as well as definition of sales channels, and a decision taken about direct and indirect sales for each of the target segments. In order to define the sales and communication channels

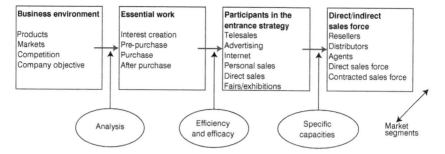

Figure 9.2 Market entry model
Source: Zoltners *et al.* (2001)

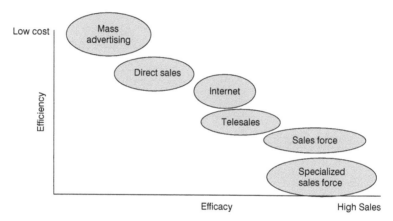

Figure 9.3 Efficiency and efficacy of alternative communication methods
Source: Zoltners *et al.* (2001)

used, consideration should be given to efficiency (cost of exposing to the target customer) and efficacy (sales made through exposition). This analysis should be made considering the specific market, product and external environment characteristics. Figure 9.3 shows some tools and their respective efficiency and efficacy.

This model is different from most models in planning, since it brings decisions about sales together with communications and distribution channels. It clearly studies consumers and defines ways of serving them, or the type of salesperson that will service the segment and discusses integration issues regarding these channels.

Organization of Sales Efforts

To organize the sales force means establishing criteria for the salesperson's operation and performance. The topics explored within the organization and their meanings are presented in Table 9.2.

The sales organization should allow for the division and specialization of the work, leading to more efficiency, stability and continuity in sales work. Note the negative correlation between specialization of the sales efforts and the need for coordination. The more specialized a team becomes the more need for integration and coordination so that

Table 9.2 Main decisions and descriptions in sales organization

Organization decisions	Decision description
1. Determination of sales targets	Establish sales objectives for the sales team.
2. Analysis of representative versus hired salesperson	The company should decide if the sales function will be an internal function (vertically integrated) or an external one (contractual relation) composed of sales agents or representatives.
3. Specialization or structuring of the sales force	This means specializing the function in five possible variables: (1) territories – where a certain area is divided into sales territories; (2) products – sales force works separately with one product line; (3) customers – teams specialized in different customers; (4) sales activity – each group specializes in one of the sales tasks, for example, market prospecting or customer visits; and (5) hybrid – the most common of this hybrid structure is the combination of geographical form with some other variable.
4. Definition of the number of salespeople	This is to determine the intensity with which the sales force will be used in conjunction with other marketing variables for the sought sales volume to be met.
5. Definition and alignment of the sales territory	The company operational territories are established: separate operation areas for salespeople and sales managers. These territories should be periodically evaluated and if necessary redefined.
6. Establish hierarchical levels and range of managerial control in sales	This is related to the vertical and horizontal range of the sales organizational structure: the number of hierarchical levels and the number of people within each level.
7. Set the role of the territorial sales manager	Define the necessary activities with respect to the territorial management.

Source: Castro and Neves (2005)

gains in efficiency are not lost with the increase of the coordination cost; for example, when making a team more specialized.

Determination of Sales Targets

The objective of establishing targets is in the first place to establish work incentives and direction for the sales force.

Targets need to be high enough to represent a true challenge, but low enough to be truly reachable. It is important also that the target be easy to understand, so that it is clear to salespeople what they should do and what the company wants from them. The targets must be complete, which means that they should have all the performance criteria that a company expects from a salesperson (Dalrymple and Cron, 1995). In order to establish targets, Churchill *et al.* (2000) set a three-step process: (1) determine the target type, (2) determine the relative importance of each type, and finally, (3) determine the level of each target type.

In a general way, sales volume goals direct salespeople excessively toward volume and generally they do not achieve them, or do not achieve them in the way they should. Administrative activities that could lead to future sales, including better ones, tend to be ignored. Activity goals have the potential of compensating an excessive orientation towards immediate results and do not establish a long-term vision for the salesperson.

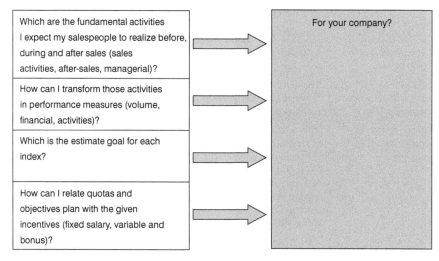

Figure 9.4 Stages in developing a target and incentive plan
Source: Castro and Neves (2005)

Financial targets generally give the team a direct idea about the profitability of the sales force activities.

After determining what will be part of the final target for the salesperson, it is necessary to define how important each of the variables are in calculating the final goal. According to Churchill *et al.* (2000) two forms are suggested, first through the calculation of a simple average of the percentages of each criteria, or even attributing weights to each of these variables. Finally, the calculation of the goal levels should be made in relation to the evaluation of historical data, the study of the potential of the territory (both mainly for the volume goals), based on the manager's experience (mainly activity goals) or the company profitability objectives (for financial goals).

Representative versus Employed Salesperson

Although both these different formats have been discussed, the theoretical discussion has focused on the decision between commercial representative and employed salesperson. Arguments in favor of the use of representatives and salespeople and contingency considerations are presented in Table 9.3.

Transaction cost economics (TCE) is used as a reference in the context of this decision, which, in a certain way, consolidates the arguments presented earlier and provides some guidance for managers about choosing between sales representatives or hired salespeople. The more specific the factors are in the relationship between the salesperson and the company (mainly the human factors, as highlighted by Anderson, 1985), the larger the uncertainty present in the relationship becomes, and TCE advocates that vertical integration (hiring of salespeople as employees) would be indicated instead of using commercial representatives.

Table 9.3 Arguments in favor of representatives, salespeople and contingency arguments

Arguments for the use of representatives	Arguments for the use of salespeople	Contingency arguments
• By combining different product lines from different manufacturers, the representative can generate synergies and make visits that a salesperson could not. • By using a representative, the manufacturer can obtain a trained sales force, already established local relationships without any fixed cost. • Costs of sales management are reduced. • It is not likely that they will be promoted or transferred; their jobs tend to stay in a certain territory. The stable presence allows continuity and an excellent knowledge about consumers. • They are entrepreneurs responsible for their business and income, therefore probably more motivated. • More flexibility is allowed, because it is easy to substitute a representative.	• They allow more control, which can be fundamental when the customer becomes loyal to the salesperson and not the company. • They are more willing to perform actions not related to sales. • They are more willing to sell products that are in the introduction phase of the life cycle or products whose life cycle is very long. • They commit more to the company because they probably want to progress within it. • They are easier to influence. • Salespeople are more loyal. • Salespeople have more knowledge of the products. • Exclusivity is possible.	Size: • If a company is small, it should use representatives because it can not pay the high fixed costs of a sales team. • If a company is average-sized it should use salespeople. • If the company keeps growing, reaching an extremely large size, because of bureaucracy and inertia, it will probably be better if it goes back to using representatives. • A company should use salespeople when average sales are large and less frequently purchased. • A company should use salespeople when the products are complex, less standardized or at the initial phase of the life cycle, requiring more sales effort.

Source: Castro and Neves (2005)

Specialization or Sales Force Structuring

Sales force structure is one of the most neglected parts of the sales force management, although frequently the impact of decisions about it is larger than decisions about the size of the sales force or the compensation plan. Table 9.4 summarizes factors which influence the choice of a certain structure.

In order to make this decision, the line of thought is to consider the increase of revenue arising from the team's higher specialization, and on the other hand, a high consequent cost. Figure 9.5 details where these costs and revenues can vary with this decision.

Defining the Number of Salespeople

The number of salespeople is an important issue in sales. It is about determining the intensity of the sales force that will be used in conjunction with other marketing variables to reach sales objectives. The following is a summary of some methods for reaching this decision (Zoltners *et al.*, 2001; Albers, 2000; Churchill *et al.*, 2000). Organizations should evaluate which is the most appropriate, taking into consideration the costs involved and the level of precision required in determining the ideal team size. These methods are:

Table 9.4 Considerations for sales structure organization

Structure by territory	Structure by product	Structure by customer	Structure by sales function
Appropriate for: • small companies; • simple product lines, which are not extensive or complex; • when divided by customer or product, but the total territory is extensive, use of the two variables is appropriate.	Appropriate for: • extensive or diverse product lines; • complex products; • different types of product produced by different factories; • products which are customized to meet the customers' specific needs; • when production and delivery time are key factors in competition; • new products when launched.	Appropriate for: • companies which work with different products for different customers; • very competitive environments with rapid changes; • companies entering a new market or one that has not been worked in; • where there are significant differences in sales approaches in use in different segments.	Appropriate for: • different types of sales activity requiring different abilities that are not easily combined from the salespeople

Source: Castro and Neves (2005)

Assuming this specialization, how much more will a salesperson sell making the same sales effort (number of visits and activities)? A) variation in the number of customers serviced by the team B) variation of the total revenue per customer Potential increase of sales with the same team separated by criteria (territory, product, clients): A x B	With the sales team divided by _____ (territories, products and clients), how much will the cost increase? C) increase in transportation costs D) increase in costs with technical support per product line E) increase in training and supervision costs per product line **Cost variation:** B + C + D + others

Figure 9.5 Decision model for sales specialization

• *Breakdown method:* the organization's objectives are divided by the sales potential of an average salesperson (productivity). In this way, salespeople should individually reach approximately their individual goal and consequently the organization reaches its goal, too.

• *Workload method:* after classifying customers into categories, the number of visits per category is estimated, and a total for the number of visits calculated; and from the number of visits a salesperson can make, the total number of salespeople to make all visits can be found.

• *Lodish model:* is similar to the workload model, although the elasticity of visits to sales are introduced to refine the calculation, estimating the number of visits necessary to maximize sales. This estimate is based on individual judgment using a mathematical optimization model.

• *Non-linear programming model:* maximizes profitability for differing sizes of the sales force, taking into consideration costs, visit elasticity and the profit generated.

• *Incremental method:* uses a principle that salespeople must be added if the marginal revenue generated is larger than the marginal cost, generating profits.

- *"Same level as last year" method:* this decision assumes last year's level should be maintained, giving the team stability.
- *Competition parity method:* matching the competition in terms of increase and decrease in the size of the sales force.
- *Available resources method:* the size of the team is determined by the resources the company has to invest in sales and the cost of an individual salesperson.
- *Expected profit method:* knowing the cost structure and margins sought, the cost of sales as a part of the margin is estimated in order to guarantee the expected profitability.

Discussed below are some considerations and methods to define and align territories, which is mainly undertaken after the decision about the number of salespeople is reached.

Definition and Alignment of the Territories

Generally, an appropriate definition of territories is sought in order to guarantee satisfaction of the sales force, good customer coverage, better service, better evaluation and control. Territory design has the objective of defining areas that have the same sales potential (which can be determined by demand forecast calculations) and the same workload. This ideal is hard or even impossible to reach, given that customers have different purchasing capacities (Zoltners and Lorimer, 2000).

The process of determining territories has the following steps (Chonko *et al.*, 1992; Churchill *et al.*, 2000; Heschel, 1977; Ingram and Laforge, 1992):

1   select a basic control unit: this will be the smallest possible unit for which sales potential and subsequently the amount of work can be calculated; it could be a neighborhood, city, region, state, country region, etc.;
2   estimate the market potential in each of these control units;
3   try to group smaller control units into sales territories with similar potentials;
4   analyze the workload in the territories formed;
5   make final adjustments (attempting to balance the workload with the potential sales, as well as considering natural conditions and the design practices);
6   allocate salespeople to the territories.

After determining the territories, it is important to generate data to add information about them. Two indexes can be developed, the market development index and the market penetration index. The first compares how is the company's geographical sales distribution with the industry geographical sales distribution, and the second compares the territories' potential sales with the sales made by the company in this territory. Table 9.5 illustrates this data.

Based on the hypothetical data in Table 9.5, area SP would be the territory where the company has made additional efforts (compared with the other areas) in its development; for example, area MG would be an area where the development is below average. Regarding the territory penetration index, it can be noticed that in SP the company has 50 percent whereas in RJ it is higher at 83 percent.

Establishing Hierarchical Levels and the Range of Sales Management Control

Generally three factors define the number of management levels and amount of control in the sales area. The amount of control should be smaller and the number of hierarchical

Table 9.5 Market development index and market penetration index

Sales area	Company revenue in the sales area (A)	Percentage of company sales in the area (Area/total)	Total sales potential in the sales area (of the market) (C)	Percentage of the area's potential in relation to the total market (D)	Market development index (B /D)	Market penetration index (A/C)
SP	10,000	20	20,000	15	1.33	50%
RJ	5,000	10	6,000	15	0.67	83%
MG	7,000	5	9,000	8	0.63	78%

levels larger when the sales process is complex, the impact of the profit resulting from each salesperson is high and the company's salespeople are professional and well-paid (Ingram and Laforge, 1992; Albers, 2000).

Regarding centralization, concentrating activities in the hands of the senior sales management, instead of delegating it to regional managers, favors coordination and integration of the sales force behavior; it helps in maintaining consistency between the sales plan and the marketing plan, in addition to, logically, decreasing the cost of activities such as hiring, selection or training. However, there will probably be difficulties in adapting to regional segments, to the different needs of customers and even to the different salespeople. Advances in communications technology tend to make these decentralization efforts more viable.

The Role of the Territorial Sales Manager

Generally acting as a bridge between the salesperson and the company, the sales manager has a fundamental role in the reaching of sales objectives, since salespeople generally work away from the daily routine of the company (Maxwell *et al.*, 2004). The sales manager's functions include: allocating sales force resources, final selection of the salespeople, training, defining salaries and bonuses, determining targets, evaluating and motivating sales staff, besides adapting the national sales program to the their territory.

In most cases, managers continue to use 15 percent of their time in sales, generally to large key account customers. There will always be a risk of managers concentrating on sales to the detriment of management activities (Ryans and Weinberg, 1981; Churchill *et al.*, 2000).

Human Resources in Sales

Human resources topics in sales are related to how to acquire, develop and keep talented salespeople motivated in the company. This involves recruitment and selection, training, motivation and compensation.

Recruitment and Selection of Salespeople

The main decisions and activities in recruitment and selection of salespeople are establishing policies of responsibility for it; in other words, who will participate in the process and who will have authority to make hiring decisions, analysis of work and determination of the selection criteria, job descriptions, description of the necessary qualifications, attracting internal and external candidates, and finally, the development and application of selection processes to evaluate the candidates using forms, interviews, formal tests and reference confirmation (Ingram and Laforge, 1992; Dalrymple and Cron, 1995; Chonko *et al.*, 1992).

It is essential to understand the main reasons causing salespeople to fail, in order not to ignore them during recruitment and selection. These characteristics are: poor ability to listen, poor capacity to plan and prioritize activities, wasting time, lack of effort, lack of ability in understanding customers' needs, lack of planning for sales presentations, inadequate knowledge about products and services, unreliability, unprofessional behavior and unreasonable expectations of customers (Ingram *et al.*, 2002; Futrell, 2010; Roman, 2004). Sale training, discussed in the following section, should be taken into consideration to try to minimize these factors.

Sales Training

Training is fundamental for the maintenance of the sales team. Sales training program objectives generally are: (1) to increase productivity by teaching skills, raising team morale (with training, salespeople become more aware of what is expected from them, bridging the gap between expectations and reality), (2) to lower staff turnover (by encouraging and motivating salespeople – especially younger ones – when difficulties appear) and (3) to improve time and territory management.

It is important to understand sales teams' needs regarding training. Understanding of these needs can be acquired by observing the team or even surveying customers about points for improvement. It is also important that training objectives be quantifiable, for example, attracting a certain number of new customers, or increasing sales of a product line to a certain level, so that analysis on returns on training can be made (Ingram and Laforge, 1992; Dalrymple and Cron, 1995; Chonko *et al.*, 1992).

Training programs generally deal with the following topics: knowledge of the company's offer, orientation on industry or market conditions, company internal policies, time and sales territory management, legal and ethical aspects of the sales process and activity, and the sales process itself (in other words, how to sell better) (Levy and Weitz, 2000; Churchill *et al.*, 2000; Kotler, 1997).

Motivation in Sales

Motivation in sales is defined as the amount of effort a salesperson is willing to invest in activities such as visiting customers, producing reports and post-sales activities. Individual motivation theory has various approaches, such as Maslow's hierarchy of needs, which states that physiological, safety, social, ego and self-realization needs are sought by people, although all of them are active all the time; Herzberg's motivation–hygiene theory, in which people seek to satisfy factors that are not covered in a satisfying way; and finally McGregor's X and Y theory, highlighting management styles in which X is controller and Y is motivator. According to this approach, the person's motivation is a consequence of the management style of senior management (Maximiano, 1997; Kotler, 1997).

Another theory that can be applied in sales is expectation theory, in which motivation occurs in a cycle. A person's capacity combined with their motivation defines their effort, which will determine a superior performance in certain aspects, resulting in reward and satisfaction, which in turn leads to greater motivation and so forth (Zoltners *et al.*, 2001).

Two points are fundamental for sales management using these concepts. The first is to identify what salespeople value in terms of rewards, and second is to relate these rewards with clear performance goals and the necessary or recommended activities to reach them (Zoltners *et al.*, 2001; Churchill *et al.*, 2000; Srivastava and Rangarajan, 2004).

Developing Reward and Incentive Plans

Many people have an intrinsic natural motivation to work, related to personal realization goals. In sales, due to the multiplicity of situations the salesperson faces and the function's instability, often extrinsic motivation must be provided as well. Monetary and non-monetary incentives represent ways of providing extrinsic motivation (Albers, 2000).

The rewards and benefits plan is one of the most important factors related to the salespeople's motivation. In order to develop a reward and incentive program it is first necessary to take into consideration the company's situation and its sales objectives and determine which aspects should be rewarded.

Sales force efforts should be directed so as to reach the company objectives as a whole. According to some studies, aspects that are rewarded should be easily understood, so a salesperson is clear about what in fact is related to good performance.

Regarding the latter issue, Table 9.6 lists the components of sales force evaluation and reward and a short description of each of the objectives.

Figure 9.6 summarizes the considerations about compensation in four stages to arrive at a salesperson's compensation, bearing in mind the proportion of commission to fixed salary, and highlighting the non-financial incentives as a component of the benefits package.

The first suggested stage is to calculate the total value of the compensation of a person in the sales function. For this it is necessary to consider the aspects highlighted in item 1. The second step is related with determining the fixed part of this total, taking into consideration the points listed in item 2. In summary, the more salespeople value safety, the more administrative tasks are part of their fundamental job, but the more the environment is uncertain and the more the company wants to control salespeople's activities, the more the fixed salary will be larger. The third stage is related to the need of providing additional incentives in terms of commissions to strengthen the salesperson's extrinsic motivation in the development of his activities. Finally the fourth stage is related with the selection of

Table 9.6 Components of a compensation plan and their respective objectives

Components	Objectives in the compensation plan
Sales contest	Stimulates additional effort for a short-term objective.
Incentive payment	Directs efforts to strategic objectives. Establishes additional rewards to the best salespeople. Encourages success in sales.
Commissions	Motivates a high level of sales efforts. Encourages success in sales.
Salary	Motivates efforts in activities not related to sales. May adjust differences between territories with different sales potentials. Rewards experience and competence.
Benefits	Satisfies the salesperson's need for safety. Prevents competitor hire offers.

Source: Castro and Neves (2005)

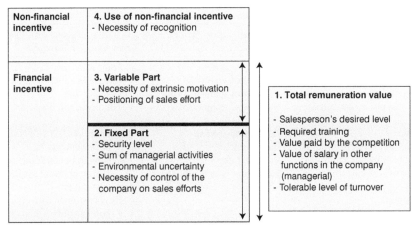

Figure 9.6 Structure for creating a compensation plan
Source: Castro and Neves (2005)

non-financial items, such as prizes, job promotion, and recognition when doing well in the function, that can be fundamental in the improvement of the salesperson's satisfaction in the company, and consequently, better motivation and results.

Evaluation and Control of Sales Results

It is a big challenge to evaluate the salespeoples' performance. How much of their results were influenced by their efforts? And how much by conditions beyond their control (which are uncontrollable variables for them)? This is the challenge sales executives have to face. In addition, although there is a belief that controlling salespeople can negatively impact on their sales performance, recent studies have shown positive aspects of following salespeople closely, leading to increased performance and also to increased satisfaction, commitment, and reduced expectation gaps and conflicts in the existing roles.

Sales analysis involves the collection, classification, comparison and study of company sales data. This can be done observing the evolution of data over time, or by cross referencing and comparing internal with external data sources (Zoltners *et al.*, 2001). Evaluation variables can be divided between input and output measures or even a combination of the two that are the sales indexes, as shown in Table 9.7.

Besides the measures presented earlier, subjective measures of salespeople's work can be developed with the objective of enriching their evaluation. Such criteria as the salesperson's knowledge about the company, its products and activities, territory management (visit planning, expense control, among others), company and consumer relations and personal characteristics can be used.

The sales audit is a broader form of evaluation and control. Using the same principles of evaluation and control, it encompasses the area's performance as a whole (Ingram and Laforge, 1992). Dubinsky and Hansen (1981) present an audit tool for sales management. Four elements of analysis are proposed in Table 9.8.

Table 9.7 Performance evaluation measures

Output evaluation factors (results)	Input evaluation factors (activities)	Measures commonly used to evaluate salespeople
Orders	*Visits*	*Sales expenses*
Number of orders	Number of visits	Expenses/value of sales
Average order	Number of planned visits	Cost per visit
Number of orders canceled	Number of unplanned visits	Total costs/number of visits
Customers	*Time management*	*Account and service*
Number of active customers	Days worked	*development*
Number of new customers	Visits per day	Customer penetration: active
Number of lost customers	Sales time versus non-sales	customers/total available
Number of prospective	time	customers
customers		New customer conversion:
	Expenses	number of new customers/
	Total.	number of total customers
	By type	Lost customers: customers that
	As a percentage of sales	did not buy/number of total
	As a percentage of the quota	customers
		Sales per customer index:
	Activities not related to sales	total sales/number of total
	Letters written to potential	customers
	customers	Average order value: value of
	Telephone calls made to	total tales/number of total
	customers	orders
	Number of formal proposals	Order cancellation: number of
	developed	canceled orders/number of
	Placing of sales displays	total orders
	Number of meetings with	
	distributors	*Visit activity and productivity*
	Amount of training developed	Visits per day: number of visits/
	for distributors or their	number of worked days
	employees	Visits per customer index:
	Number of customer service	number of visits/number of
	visits	customers
	Number of late payments	Planned visits: number of
	collected	planned visits/number of
		total visits
		Orders per visit index: number
		of orders/number of total
		visits

Source: Castro and Neves (2005)

Collective Actions in Sales Force Management

Just like distribution channels discussed earlier, sales management provides excellent opportunities for sharing activities with companies in the network. Customers, suppliers, competitors or companies offering complementary products can join sales forces or use sales strengths in other processes. Table 9.9 presents some suggestions in which these processes could happen to generate gains for the companies in the network.

In this way it is sought, with sales force planning, to manage the area with other marketing variables in a coordinated way, integrating communication, products and distribution and thinking on network actions. Next, the price variable will be examined in Chapter 10, using the same focus, which will practically finish the DDSP method proposed here.

Table 9.8 Sales audit model

Sales organization development	Sales management environment	Sales planning system	Sales management functions
Sales manager development Administrative development	Extra-organizational factors: • economic and demographic • political and legal • technological • competitive • market • consumers Intra-organizational factors: • company organization • integration of the sales department with marketing and other areas	Objectives. Sales management program Program implementation	Sales force organization Recruiting and selection Sales training Compensation and expenses Supervision, morale and motivation Sales forecasting Budgeting Quotas Territories and routing Sales analysis Cost and profitability analysis

Source: Castro and Neves (2005)

Activities for Developing the Sales Force Plan

In this chapter of the DDSP, we should make the following analyses:

* think strategically about the sales force using the cost, differentiation and niche views, as in Table 9.1;
* determine the main functions of salespeople in the company and whether they should coexist with other forms of access to the customers as in Figures 9.2 and 9.3.
* answer the questions in Figure 9.4, thinking about the key activities of salespeople, their objectives and their compensation;
* if the company considers the alternative of using commercial representatives, use Table 9.3 to orient the decision;
* to decide if the company should specialize the sales team in different ways, use Figure 9.5, estimating revenue and costs;
* estimate the number of salespeople, taking into consideration the most appropriate method for your business;
* create sales territories following the orientation in the section on definition of sales territories;
* invite specialized companies and look at all equipment, software and information technolgy available for sales force information management and control;
* if the company already has defined territories, create development and territory penetration indexes to evaluate their degree of utilization;
* use the considerations on sales recruitment, selection, training and motivation to rearrange the personal policies of this area;
* rethink the compensation plan using the outline of Figure 9.6;
* select from Table 9.7 complementary measures of control of the sales efforts;
* use Table 9.9 to think about possible collective actions with complementary companies, competitors, among others, that present synergies with the company's business.

Table 9.9 Opportunities for sales force collective actions in the network

Actions	Description	Ideas (actions) for your company
Companies with complementary offers sharing sales teams	Salespeople from different companies complement their product portfolio with products from the other company. Thus, the offer can be seen in a more complete form, adding convenience to consumers' purchasing process. However it is crucial to manage commissions in a careful way, distributing fairly the results between the two companies involved.	
Competing companies share commercial representatives in markets that are still unexplored	In international markets that are unexplored, two competing companies can decide to jointly contract international representatives for certain product lines to increase chances of success abroad and to dilute risk.	
Non-competing companies (with the same target market) sharing training	Training about customer characteristics (knowledge about customers' specific needs) can have costs divided by two or more companies, as well as motivation training, prizes and so forth. This could also be a way of increasing the trading of information among salespeople from different companies, possibly opening sales opportunities for salespeople for all companies involved.	
Non-competing companies share databases for visits	Companies can share sales and potential sales databases about their market, within legal and ethical limits, to increase knowledge of territories.	
Service companies (such as banks, insurance companies or logistics) and manufacturers share information and form a true business network	Several service companies also have access to customers and can also share their knowledge about customers. The collective action also goes in the direction of increasing the partnership between these facilitators, strengthening ties and forming a true network, as proposed in this book.	
Non-competing companies trade information regarding market potential	The study of potential markets in certain regions can be conducted jointly to make several sales organization decisions easier, such as the determination of the number of salespeople, alignment of territories and determination of targets.	
Non-competing companies form a package offer for a salesperson, making them truly into a business consultant	Companies can form true business consultancies with a complete offer by jointly training their salespeople and creating partnerships in the sales force with complementary products and services which will in fact represent the whole network which is supporting the sales team.	

Questions

1 What is the relation among business strategy, marketing strategy and the sales force management?
2 How does a company define its segments and operation focus in order to separate each salesperson's portfolio?
3 What are the main decisions in the sales organization?
4 What should be considered for a company to decide between representative or hired salesperson?
5 How does a company define the number of salespeople to be used for its operation?
6 What variables should be considered in drawing up the reward and incentive plans for its salesperson?
7 Is it possible for a company to have its salesperson activities measured? How could this be done?
8 Which partnerships with other companies can be used in the sales force decisions?
9 What are the most up-to-date technologies available for sales force information and activity management and control?

10   Price Decisions

After the analysis of the importance of sales force management in the organization and effort needed to obtain the required results from sales in the marketing strategy, understanding the price variable is crucial in the marketing mix. In this chapter, we will show how strategic management of an effective price can be achieved and its relationship with other variables in the marketing mix in the DDSP. In summary, the following analysis should be conducted at this stage:

- define company objectives in relation to price;
- analyze domestic and international demand;
- analyze and control production costs;
- analyze costs, prices and offers of competitors;
- choose a method to be used in price setting and in decisions about types of prices and which variations (regional, circumstantial, etc.) will be used;
- think about how the company should react to competition price changes.

Although other variables of the marketing mix have become important in the last few decades, price still remains as one of the fundamental elements affecting market share and profitability in companies. Lovelock (1996) comments that price is the only element of the marketing mix that produces revenue. The other variables, despite being essential for the company's success, in effect produce expenditure. Price is also one of the most flexible elements, for it can be altered quickly, unlike other components, such as changing a product or a commitment in the distribution channel. The flexibility competitors have in setting prices is one of the largest problems companies face.

Any exchange involves price, although it may not always be monetary. Price can be defined as a relationship that indicates the amount necessary to acquire a given quantity of goods or service (Lambin, 2000), and is simply the quantity in money and/or other items with the necessary usefulness to acquire a product (Etzel *et al.*, 2001). Or according to Czinkota (2010), price is the unit of value delivered by a party in exchange for something received from another party.

Price decisions are important, for they affect the sales volume of a company and how much revenue it receives. Some factors that have importance for price decisions in the marketing environment are taken into consideration by Lambin (2000), such as: price directly influences demand, directly determines the activity's profitability and influences the perception of the product, contributing to the brand positioning. Even with such importance, many companies do not handle price setting well. According to Kotler (1997) the most

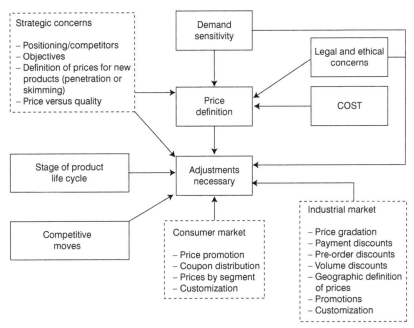

Figure 10.1 Factors which determine and influence price definitions
Source: Czinkota (2010: 443)

common errors are: prices overly oriented to costs, prices that are not revised frequently enough to capture market changes, and price setting that does not depend on the rest of the marketing mix and that doesn't vary according to different product items, market segments and purchase occasions.

The pricing decisions taken by a company should be well integrated with other marketing decisions, because that price should allow a company to generate enough returns to invest in communication strategies, product development and distribution channel strategies.

According to the contingency approach for pricing, Ingenbleek *et al.* (2004) state that a product's relative advantage alone will not lead to elevated margins. The company will reach elevated margins only when it uses appropriate pricing practices.

Lambin (2000) considers that the choice of a price strategy must have two types of coherence: internal coherence, which requires that the price set takes account of cost conditions and company profitability, and external coherence, which requires a compatible sensitivity to buyers with the price and with prices of the competition. Figure 10.1 presents the main variables involved in the price definition: strategic considerations, demand sensitivity, costs, and legal and ethical issues, followed by factors that influence the need to adjust prices.

This chapter of the DDSP will show how to set prices in a six-stage process. Once the price is established, the next step will be to develop appropriate price strategies and initiatives for price changes by competitors. Finally, we will see how the network approach can help the company to better price its products and services.

Price Setting

One of the most difficult decisions for companies is the pricing of its offers, including both products and services. An appropriate, sustainable and creative pricing strategy is based on

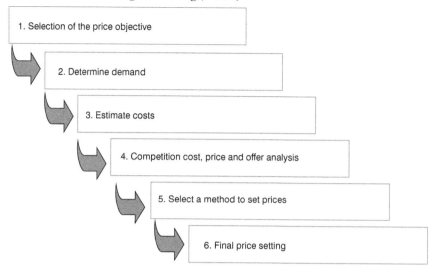

Figure 10.2 The price-setting process
Source: based on Kotler (1997) and Etzel *et al.* (2001)

the equilibrium of financial returns desired by companies and well-being of consumers in the tough competitive global arena.

Therefore, the price-setting objectives must be adjusted to the company's marketing objectives. A company should decide where to position its product in the market in terms of quality and price, possibly finding in the same market several price levels.

By establishing a price policy, the company should think about six steps: (1) select the price-setting objective, (2) determine demand, (3) estimate costs, (4) competition cost, price and offer analysis, (5) select a method to set prices, and (6) final price setting. Figure 10.2 illustrates the six steps of the price-setting process. Each one of these steps will be described in the following sections.

Selection of the Price Objective

The decision of where a company wishes to position its offer should be the first the company takes. For the clearer the marketing plan objectives are, the easier it will be to set prices. The price objectives must be decided before the price itself is set, although, as logical as it seems, few companies establish a price objective.

In general, there are five objectives in determining price (Kotler, 1997; Etzel *et al.*, 2001; Lambin, 2000; Czinkota, 2010): (1) *survival*, a short-term objective mainly practiced when there is surplus production, intense competition or a change in consumers' needs; (2) *profit maximization*, when the demand and costs are estimated for alternative prices, a level that maximizes profit is chosen, and a specific level of profit is established as objective; (3) *revenue maximization*, estimating only the demand and establishing the price that maximizes revenue or market share; (4) *maximization of sales growth* or maintenance and/or increase of market share, which due to the learning curve, can lead to smaller unit production costs; and (5) *maximization of market utilization*, used when there is a higher price; given the comparative benefits in relation to substitutes available, then the company reduces the price to conquer the segment immediately below, in other words, seeking price stability and alignment in relation to competitors. Which of your objectives is aligned with each of the company's products?

Determine Demand

Setting a price that only takes account of production cost is not sufficient. It is important that the organization identifies the level of demand over time. The estimation of demand in some cases is intuitively obvious, and in others the patterns only are revealed when studied and mapped correctly. Each price used by the company will result in a different level of demand, and consequently, cause different impacts in marketing objectives of a certain company. This relationship is shown by the demand curve using factors that affect the price sensitivity. Nagle and Holden (1994) indicate nine situations where the consumer's sensitivity to the company's prices can be reduced and a company can use these factors to create advantages to reduce these sensitivities.

The factors mentioned in Table 10.1 are valuable, because they can serve as guides. The issue of "how to reduce the consumer's price sensitivity" can have, in network actions, interesting paths to go down.

Table 10.1 Price sensitivity factors

Factors that reduce price sensitivity	How can your company use this factor?	Ideas for your company
1. The product is exclusive: unique value.	How to create unique value for the customer?	
2. Buyers have less knowledge of the existence of substitutes.	How to make substitute product comparison difficult?	
3. Buyers cannot compare the substitute's quality.	How to create a unique and superior category?	
4. The price is small in relation to total income.	How to make the company's product part of a larger expense in which the consumer does not directly evaluate its cost?	
5. The product's final benefit is large.	How to increase the customer's perception that the benefit created by the product is of great value?	
6. The product's cost is shared with a third party.	How to involve different partners in the sales negotiation?	
7. The product is used in conjunction with previously bought assets.	To which product already bought by the customer can we associate ours?	
8. The product presents more quality, prestige or exclusivity: price–quality.	How to create a unique value?	
9. Buyers cannot stock the product.	How to avoid having our customers stocking our product and therefore having more power to negotiate future purchases?	

Source: based on Nagle and Holden (1994)

Table 10.2 Impact of demand elasticity

Factors	How can your company use this factor?
Substitutes or competitors	How can we position our product or service as being unique and not comparable?
Larger price perception	How can customers be prevented from easily perceiving price increases (legally)?
Change in purchasing habits	How to establish purchasing habits in customers so they will not simply change supplier?
Justification in price increase	Which communications actions are fundamental to justify price increases?

Many companies seek to measure their demand curve using different methods, such as statistical analysis of price data and quantity sold, the systematic variation of prices in a store and variation analysis and research with buyers to discover how much of a given product they would buy at different price levels.

Finally to estimate demand, companies can study the level of demand elasticity, allowing a better understanding of the relation between prices and sales. Demand is less elastic the smaller the variation in demand for given variation in price. Kotler (1997) comments that the demand will be less elastic under the following conditions:

1   there are few or no substitutes, or no competitors;
2   buyers do not notice the higher price;
3   buyers are slow in changing purchasing habits and seeking lower prices;
4   buyers consider price increases justifiable because of the increase in quality, inflation, or other factors.

Using these factors Table 10.2 can be developed to help a company monitor its demand and establish control over it.

Measuring and Estimating Costs

According to McCarthy and Perreault (1997) there are basically three types of costs: (1) fixed costs, whose amount does not depend on volume, and within a certain period of activity these costs do not vary with production quantity; and (2) variable costs, which are those whose amount varies directly with production volume in proportion to the activity's volume within a certain production range. The sum of the fixed and variable costs result in the (3) total cost, which divided by the number of units produced, gives the unit or average cost.

Companies should be careful when using cost information in price policies. Ingenbleek *et al.* (2004) state that this type of information does not demonstrate the true value that consumers attribute to the product.

Costs generally vary with different levels of production. For good results in price setting, a company should know how its costs vary according with production levels (Kotler, 1997). Costs will be reduced with increases in the quantity produced because of dilution of fixed costs. But after a certain point the factory becomes inefficient, machines breaking more frequently and lack of physical space. Thus, there is for any given resource, an ideal production level.

The behavior of costs as a function of accumulated production is a result of the experience or learning curve. This occurs when a company reduces total average cost as a function of the learning gained with the increases in production and acquired experience: the company learns how to make products better; workers learn to reduce costs; the flow of raw materials and purchases are improved, among other factors (Henderson, 1984; Kotler, 1997). This strategy can be used when a company bases its price relying on the experience/learning curve and expands production. However, this is a risky strategy, because competitors can develop technology with lower costs and overtake the company.

Companies tend to adapt their offers and conditions to different buyers, resulting in different costs and profits for each segment of the market. To estimate the profitability of each transaction with a customer, the company should use cost accounting based on activities – activity-based costs (ABC) – which identifies the costs linked to meet each entity, through the decomposition of fixed and variable costs.

Setting of target costs consists of reducing costs by the concentrated efforts of designers, engineers and buyers in the company. The characteristics of a new product, such as the price for which it can be sold, are established through market research. After determining the desired profit margin, the team examines the cost components (design, engineering, production, sales, etc.), separates them into smaller units and considers ways to reduce them. The objective is to make cost projections which are adjusted to the target cost, and so with the target price, the target profit can be reached.

A cost type structure is presented by Lambin (2000) based on internal costs, without reference to market data. The author mentions three costs: minimum cost, which corresponds to the direct cost, only allowing the recovery of the product's replacement value, therefore, the margin is zero; technical cost, which corresponds to the activity level in which the company covers the direct and fixed costs, and allows the company not only to recover the product's value, but also to cover structural charges; and target cost or sufficient price, which includes besides the minimum and technical cost, a profit. All these methods ignore the demand sensitivity, in other words, market conditions; therefore, the desired margin will only be realized if the stipulated level of sales is met.

Analysis of the Competition's Cost, Price and Offer

The company needs to compare its costs with the competition's costs in order to know at which level it is operating, and whether the company has a cost advantage or disadvantage, (see the section on strategy at the start of Chapter 5). It is also necessary to know the price and quality of the competitor's offer. This will be a reference point for the price. The pricing strategy is strongly influenced by what competition is being faced, by the number of companies that operate in the same segment and by their products' perceived value, which results from the product differentiation aimed at reaching a competitive advantage. These dimensions are considered in Table 10.3 with two levels of intensity of competition relating to the perceived value of the product, thus defining four distinct situations for price decisions given the type of competition.

Selecting a Method to Set the Price

Given the consumer demand, the cost function, and the competing prices, a company will be prepared to select a method for price setting that includes one or more of these three factors. Generally, companies select a method to set prices taking into account the considerations

Table 10.3 Price decisions as a function of competition

Product perceived value	Intensity of the competition	
	Low	High
Higher	Monopoly or differentiated oligopoly	Monopolistic competition
Lower	Undifferentiated oligopoly	Pure or perfect competition

Source: based on Grant (2002), Lambin (2000), Porter (1992), Besanko *et al.* (2000)

presented in Table 10.3. Kotler (1997) defines at least six methods to set prices. These methods and their characteristics are presented in Table 10.4.

Final Price Selection

A company should consider additional factors in order to conduct the process of setting the final price for its products. These additional factors, according to Kotler (1997), are:

- *Psychological price*: the association of high price with quality leads the company to place its product with a price among the most expensive of the segment.
- *Influence from the other elements of the marketing mix*: the company should take into consideration brand and advertising quality in relation to the competition. There is a positive relationship between high price and advertising budget. Consumers generally are willing to pay more for known rather than unknown products. From this we see the importance of the demand driven strategic planning.
- *Company pricing policy*: the price should be consistent with company pricing policies, with the purpose of ensuring that the sales force works with prices that are attractive for customers, and profitable for the company.
- *Impact of prices on other members of the channel*: the company should take into consideration the reaction of the other interested parties in the chain, such as distributors and dealers.

After setting the price it is important that the company develop an appropriate pricing review structure to meet situations such as those discussed in the next section.

Strategies for Price Adjustment

In recent years, many companies, influenced by environmental variations, by market saturation with low growth rates, by global competition and by consumer movements, are using different forms of price adjustment. These companies develop price adjustment strategies that mainly reflect variations in demand and costs. Jain (2000) considers that a price adjustment strategy should be applied for products or quantities depending on the consumers' group or market segment. There are several strategies for price adjustment, such as geographical pricing, discounted pricing, promotional pricing, discriminatory pricing and product mix pricing, which are presented in Table 10.5.

Note that an appropriate marketing information system contributes, as well as looking at different factors, in carrying out of pricing adjustments.

Table 10.4 Methods for setting prices

Method	Concepts, characteristics and limitations	Advantages and disadvantages for your company's situation
Markup	• A method that simply adds the standard margin to the product's cost to create the sales price. • It is popular because: salespeople are more sure of costs rather than demand; the calculation is simple when costs change; when all companies use this method, prices tend to be similar. • Prices are higher on seasonal items (to cover the risk of getting stuck with stock), specialty items, slow turnover items with high stock and movement costs, items with inelastic demand, and prices are also high for products with hidden costs or that are highly variable.	
Target return price	• Companies set the price that ensures their target rate for the return on investment (ROI), the manufacturer will achieve the intended ROI if the estimates of costs and sales are precise. • The point of equilibrium calculation is important to know what will happen if the sales forecast is not fulfilled. • Ignores price elasticity and competing prices.	
Perceived value price	• The buyer's perceptions, not costs, are key factors to set prices. • The key to use the perceived value is to determine correctly, through market research, the market perception in relation to the offer's value. • Product positioning is fundamental. • Measure the perceived value of each of the product's benefits (pricing through the value components): durability, reliability, superior service, part warranties, among others. • It must be shown to the consumer why the product is more expensive, in other words, the value that the offer in fact represents.	
Value price	• Setting a low price in relation to the high quality of the product compared with the competitor. • It is not the simple price reduction, but an attempt to reduce costs without losing quality.	
Competitor follower price	• The company bases its price as a function of the prices charged by the competitors, paying little attention to costs or demand.	
Bidding price	• The setting of the price is strongly oriented to the competition. • The higher the price, the lower the chances of the company winning the bid. It is possible to calculate expected profits of alternative combinations of price and price winning probability.	

Source: developed from Kotler (1997) and Lambin (2000)

Table 10.5 Price adjustment strategies

Strategies	Considerations	Is this pricing strategy applicable to your company? If so, note necessary adjustments in the established policies
Geographical pricing	Considers transportation costs to the consumer, which grow in importance when the freight is a large component of the total variable cost. There are two geographical strategies: • By production point, when the product is picked up at the factory. • Flat delivery price, in which the quoted price is the same for all buyers regardless of their location.	
Discounts and concessions	Discounts for payments in cash, discounts for quantity, functional discounts (offered to the members of the distribution channel), seasonal discounts and concessions.	
Promotional pricing	Bait pricing, occasion pricing, discount coupons, low-interest finance, longer term payments, warranty and service contracts, psychological discount (use of an artificial high price which is reduced drastically).	
Discrimination pricing	Pricing by consumer segment, pricing by product version, image pricing, location pricing, period pricing. Segmentation must be possible, impossible to resell, must be legalized and attuned to the institutional environment.	
Product mix pricing	The product is part of a mix and the company seeks a price that maximizes this mix in the following ways: • Product line pricing: each successive version of the product has extra characteristics, allowing higher prices. • Subproduct pricing: sale of subproducts allows reduction of the price of the main product. • Package pricing: gathering of several products that are sold more cheaply than if sold separately.	

Source: developed from Kotler (1997) and Etzel *et al.* (2001)

Initiatives and Responses to Price Changes

Given the interdependence there is between competitors, generally there is a price in the market that serves as a reference point for these companies. This price set limits on company decisions when reducing, maintaining or raising their prices. There are several initiatives and answers which companies can develop given a change in prices (Lambin, 2000; Kotler, 1997; Jain, 2000):

• *Price maintenance*: a price maintenance strategy is appropriate in circumstances in which the price change is desirable, but the magnitude of this change is undetermined; if reactions of consumers and competitors to the price change are not possible to estimate, price maintenance is maybe the most appropriate measure. Many times the price change will cause a negative impact in the image of the product.

- *Price reduction initiatives*: some situations lead companies to reduce their prices, mainly when there is idle capacity in the production line or in conditions in which there is a decline in market share or even as a strategy to dominate the market through lower costs. Lambin (2000) considers two favorable situations for reducing prices: when the competitors have higher costs and cannot reduce them; or when the small companies are more apt to lower prices than large competitors, (because it represents a smaller loss, making large competitors prefer to keep prices stable, by increasing activity in a different market than that of the small companies). Jain (2000) adds one more situation in which price reduction may be a response the consumer needs, and this happens when the price reduction is a prerequisite for market growth.
- *Price increase*: this can considerably increase the company's profits, although the company should make sure that competitors will follow, otherwise it will lose market share; this is a typical case where there may be illegal collective action. Another important factor in increasing prices is excess demand, when a company cannot meet all orders. Kotler (1997) considers some methods of increasing prices, such as: (1) adopting a delivery date price, where the price is not set until the offer is delivered; (2) imposing price adjustment contract conditions; (3) breaking down products and services; and (4) reducing discounts offered to customers.

Jain (2000) adds other reasons for increasing prices, such as: (1) price adjustments in economies with high inflation to avoid losing margins; (2) when there is a monopoly of a certain brand in a certain segment or the brand has a competitive advantage and in a unique position in relation to the competition; (3) when the company is the price leader and the competitors are price followers; and (4) when the price increase will have repercussions in a positive perception on the consumer's behalf.

There are ways of avoiding increasing prices in view of the risks of lower demand or increase in costs, such as: reducing the product's size; substitute raw materials or cheaper packages; remove product and/or service characteristics; reduce the number of brands and creating new brands that are less costly. These need to be communicated well to consumers to avoid problems.

When there is a price change, customers, competitors, as well as partners in the distribution channel, such as distributors or even facilitator agents, may react. The company as a whole needs to be ready to respond.

Finally we need to discuss how the network approach can help the company to better price its products.

Network and Collective Actions Perspective for Prices

In order to suggest pricing actions based on this book's proposed network approach, four key issues linked to the variables of influence in price setting will be commented on. Table 10.6 shows these suggested actions, describing them and giving examples when possible.

The price variable in the marketing mix was seen through the topics above, such as the steps for setting prices, followed by price adjustment strategies that can be used by companies, and finally, actions in response to price changes from competitors. The next step to develop the DDSP will be the development of the budget, thinking about pricing practices, as well as the consolidation of the other variables of the marketing mix, such as product, communications, distribution channels and sales force.

Table 10.6 Motives for using the network and collective action perspective for pricing

Actions	Description and examples	Ideas for the company
To increase the value perceived by the customers	*Offer a package of products and services* A package of products and services has more value as it makes the purchasing process easier for the consumer, bringing more convenience. It also transmits more trust, for the package can be constructed especially for their needs. The example of bundling in the agricultural inputs area (products and services package offer) uses this strategy.	
To reduce the price sensitivity in segments served	*Offer a package of products and services* Following from earlier points, there is a significant chance that the customer's price sensitivity is reduced, allowing the company to charge more for the package, in comparison with separate products. *Joint loyalty programs* As strategies for joint discounts and network benefits, companies can share discounts (through loyalty cards, for example) where the benefit of using the network overcomes the competitor's offer. Airline companies have used this concept through associations with telephone companies, credit card companies, internet providers, newspapers, among several others. *Difficulty in comparing substitutes* The network offer makes the comparison with other offers harder, for networks are harder to compare than isolated products.	
To reduce costs	*Joint actions in reduction of marketing expenses* Promotional joint actions, in sales management, market research and so forth, have a great potential of saving expenses. *Outsourcing processes and activities* Process outsourcing or the use of private brands, for the company that produces as well as for companies that "order the production," has a good potential to reduce costs either because they optimize the production or because they focus on their core competencies. These processes demand, and benefit, from the network coordination. *Joint purchasing offices* Companies that buy jointly increase their bargain power with suppliers, besides benefiting from a common purchasing structure, they obtain scale advantages.	
To compare competition costs and prices	*Getting market information from other networks through members that cooperate with market information* The companies from the network can use one another to get privileged cost structure and price information from competing companies. Actions with non-exclusive distribution channels can facilitate obtaining information, as well as with non-exclusive suppliers. Legal and ethical limits should be scrupulously observed in such cases.	

Box 10.1 The Creative Pricing Strategy Method (CPS Method)

In this book a framework method is introduced that has three major phases in this creative pricing strategy (CPS) process. The first phase is the understanding of the initial value of the product or service to the consumer. The second is about increasing this value, and finally, the third is the strategic pricing movements.

a) Understanding the Initial Value to the Consumer

Before any pricing decision is taken, a company must analyze the external environment of economic income and demand conditions (1).

Next, a company should look at the target consumers to understand their behavior, their perception of a reasonable price (using surveys, experts, "food labs") and do initial pricing experiments through different marketing channels. Analysis of total consumer costs when buying the product (money, time spent, knowledge acquisition, training costs, and psychological costs) that may be working as "buying barriers" is needed. All the consumer's risks in buying the company's product or service should be taken into account (2).

The third analysis in this first phase of CPS process is related to competitors, competing products/solutions and their prices, and how the consumer values and compares competing product attributes (3). To finish this first phase, a company should establish objectives and understand its cost structure for different sales levels.

The analysis of consumer, competitors and economic environment will facilitate a company understanding the value of its product or service in consumers' initial perceptions. After this first phase – understanding – of the CPS framework, comes the second, where a company can try to change the initial view the consumer has of its products or services.

b) Increasing the Value Strategies

The idea is to search and create a unique value position. This can be reached by reducing the importance of substitutes for the product and the possibility of comparisons, deflecting consumers away from competitors (4).

Another opportunity is to compare the price of the product as a ratio of consumers' incomes or total expenditure they make in one category (5). Also, a company can use "lock-in" strategies, using the product as a complement to other items previously acquired by consumers (6).

It is important to try to communicate the importance of attributes the product and service has and the danger of having problems when these attributes, for instance, quality and safety, are ignored by competitors (7). A company may also think of the possibility of offering a "problem-solution driven" package of products and services to win consumers, this is sometimes called "bundling" (8).

The list of possibilities that mitigate consumer's buying risks of the product that was developed in Phase 1 is also an idea (9). Some markets offer the possibility of skimming price strategies for new solutions (using image, status, and exclusivity), capturing value from innovative consumers, early adopters and status-oriented market segments (10).

continued...

Box 10.1 *continued*

A final point in this second phase of CPS is to show economic benefits to consumers (like lower production costs to farms, in the case of farm suppliers' companies) in buying the solution from the company with simple messages and credible commitments (11).

The points raised in the second phase of the CPS framework are related to increasing value strategies.

c) Strategic Pricing movements

In this phase, a company should be monitoring and predicting the competition's pricing movements (12), establishing discount policies and promotions, analyzing seasonality and other factors (13), having an integrated product line approach with interacting pricing (14), thinking about the pricing adaptations needed when the market faces any macro environmental (economic) changes (15) and finally, using web-based strategies, solutions and experiences in pricing (16).

I have used this framework with companies, turning each of these 16 points into questions and answering them with executives and management of the companies. These questions are relevant for existing products and services, for new products, and even to help to suggest consumer research and other information seeking activity.

Activities to Develop a Pricing Strategy

- Use the section on pricing objectives to think about which is the central objective for pricing in the company;
- study demand and use Tables 10.1 and 10.2 to develop ideas of how to reduce the target consumer's price sensitivity;
- find the break-even point with price simulations in order to work out the price bases and realistic costs;
- use Table 10.4 to decide which is the best pricing method to use, after reflection and completion of this table;
- use Table 10.5 to discuss occasional price adjustment strategies for the company;
- use Table 10.6 to think of possible collective actions in the pricing area.

Questions

1   How can you describe the relation between pricing decisions and the other decisions in DDSP?
2   What factors, which determine and influence price definitions, can you describe for a company to use in its pricing decisions?
3   What are the steps for price setting that can be used by companies?
4   How can a company be competitive with its products pricing? Describe some price adjustment strategies.
5   For how long should a company keep its products prices?
6   What are the methods a company could use to establish its price?
7   What is the importance of measuring the price elasticity?
8   Which kind of collective actions can be made in price decisions?

11 Budget and Investment Analysis

Given the pressure to maximize contributions to business performance and company value, an appropriate budget in the DDSP has never been as relevant as it is in the current business environment. The decision about quantity and the allocation of resources in the budget context of the DDSP continues to be a fundamental and complex challenge for executives (Fuchs and Reinecke, 2004). Thus, performance measurment systems are formalized systems of routines, procedures and control, which supply information to maintain or modify the company's activities in order to reach the desired objectives (Sajtos and Berács, 2004).

According to Westwood (1995) the budget is a plan which emerges from what the company expects to sell in a certain period and the resources it needs to invest to obtain these results. Gitman (1997) considers the budget as a process that consists of evaluating and selecting long-term investments that are coherent with the company objectives of maximizing the owner's wealth. Welsch (1983) considers it in broad terms, as a systematic and formal approach of executing the planning, coordination and control of management responsibilities. The budget specifically involves the preparation and use of: (1) long-term objectives; (2) a general long-term results plan; (3) a detailed short-term results plan, according to different relevant levels of responsibility; and (4) a system of periodic performance reports for the various levels of responsibility.

Tung (1994) defines budget as the presentation of anticipated results of a plan, project or strategy established for a certain period. In order to have an appropriate understanding of the concept of budget, it is necessary to recognize that it is close to a systems concept which integrates all functional and operational aspects of a company. It is necessary to recognize that it is not about separate techniques that can be conceptualized and used independently from the management process as a whole. On the contrary, the general concept of a budget involves the integration of several marketing strategy approaches, such as: sales forecasting, communications budget, implementation feasibility studies for new channels, launching new products or the extending product lines, production planning and control; in summary, all the aspects considered in the DDSP.

For the DDSP's completion it is necessary to consider aspects of budget development and investment analysis so the results of the proposed objectives seen in Chapter 4 can be reached.

Welsch (1983) and Tung (1994) highlight the main advantages of establishing a budget as being the most rational use of company and third-party resources, to establish objectives and realistic standards, develop a sales plan, determine the responsibilities of each function within the company in a clear and controllable way, coordinate and integrate company sectors in the light of the strategic objectives, and strengthen management by perfecting systems for data recording, analysis and reporting, which are indispensable elements in making decisions.

The main limitations that need to be considered are the fact that budgets are based on estimates, not always constantly adapted to existing circumstances, and finally the difficulty in executing a budgetary plan once it has been developed.

Budget Characteristics

A budget has the purpose of creating a basis for forecasting and controlling future economic and financial events. Starting from this assumption, the budget has the following characteristics (Tung, 1994):

- it includes all company activities;
- it establishes the relationship between revenue, costs and expenses in a detailed way;
- it prioritizes activities that contribute to the objectives set in the company strategy.
- it compares results achieved and aims at achieving future company results.

In this way, the budget does not limit itself to making estimates and comparing future and previous results; it analyzes future possibilities of operation and establishes marketing objectives which are part of the plan the company is striving to acheive. This group of management decisions represents the company's plan as a whole; in other words, each decision reflects the plan for a certain moment in time, and the sum of the decisions represents the totality of the company's plan. Welsch (1983) considers two dimensions of the management budget process: the time dimension and the structural dimension.

Present decisions will only affect the future, and never the past. As all management decisions are oriented to the future, the time dimension of the global budget becomes a basic requisite for the budgetary process. The effective application of the budget requires the establishment of well-defined time dimensions for main and secondary decisions from executives.

Budget structural dimensions: in order to increase managerial and operational efficiency, companies should structure themselves in business units. The managers of business units have specific responsibility for activities relating to their area of operation in the company. Tung (1994) states that an organizational structure is the minimum necessary condition for the implementation of a budget. It is through these areas of responsibility for the business units that plans are executed, objectives are reached and control is exercised. This reference system with its objectives and plans for the various centers of responsibility, together make up the company's objectives and plans as a whole.

The organizational structure should not be considered as an end in itself, but as a management tool to reach the company's objectives. Thus, in well-managed companies, project plans are structured according to authority and responsibility levels and according to the product lines or services.

Budget Structuring and Implementation

In order to structure and implement the DDSP budget, the executives responsible should follow the same sequence as for financial planning. The budget is a plan that emerges as a consequence of what the company expects to sell in a certain period, and of resources it needs to invest to obtain these results (Westwood, 1995).

These resources are directed to the product, communications, distribution channels and sales force variables of the marketing mix. It is important to begin with the determination of the sales objectives, which are based on the general objectives established by the senior management in Chapter 4 of the DDSP.

As a consequence, global results plans are developed according to the following general standard:

- business units prepare changes in the resource requirements and submit them to senior management, which reviews and approves or rejects the requests;
- senior management establishes the general objectives and identifies assumptions;
- business units define objectives and strategies;
- units prepare the company and develop forecasts;
- senior management approves or alters objectives and strategy;
- units make changes in the resource requirements and submit them to senior management, which reviews and approves or rejects the requests.

A broad budgetary program involves much more than a periodic budget; it includes the application of several management concepts through technical approaches and successive stages. It implies applying global planning and control concepts to all of the company's operation phases and a systems approach. Budget structuring and implementation consists of five distinct stages, although they are interrelated, according to Gitman (1997): generation of proposals; evaluation and analysis; decision making; implementation; and follow-up. Each step of the process is important; however the evaluation, analysis and the decision making processes require more time and effort. Table 11.1 describes each of these stages.

Table 11.1 Stages of the DDSP budget process

Stages	Description
Generation of proposals (consolidated in Chapter 12 of the DDSP)	Made by people from all levels of the company Possibility of prizes for the best projects as an incentive Can go from a lower level to a higher level in the organization's hierarchy
Evaluation and analysis	Are made considering the global company's objectives and plans Verification of the economic feasibility, estimating costs and benefits Introduction of budgetary techniques to verify the budget's merit Incorporate aspects of risk to the economic analysis
Decision making	Definition of the level of management according to the magnitude of the expenditure and importance of the expense
Implementation	Depending on the importance of the expenditure, when it is small the implementation becomes a matter of routine. When it is large, it demands greater control to assure that what is proposed and approved is bought at the budgeted costs
Follow-up	Comparison of the true results with the estimated values; actions must be taken when the true results differ from what was projected

Source: developed from Gitman (1997)

The planning process should be revised and evaluated for each of the stages described in Table 11.1 with the intention of updating each element based on the management's judgment and true company performance since the beginning of the plan period. Some of these components will remain unaltered, while others should be modified. One should have in mind that the preparation of the planning proposals, the evaluation and analysis of project plans and the evaluation and analyses require annual adjustment.

Figure 11.1 is an example of a spreadsheet to develop a marketing budget. Note this is only a suggestion, because budgets are a tool that many companies use and each has its own specific form. All models contribute; the important thing is to plan and make a budget.

Investment Analysis of the Major Projects of the DDSP

Here we will only summarize project/investment indexes that should appear in the DDSP. It is not our intention to describe them explicitly, as there is a vast literature on the subject.

The main objective in developing a budget analysis is to estimate how much value will be created or not by the objectives set in the DDSP for the company; and consequently ascertain if the project is economically viable. To create value, according to Gitman (1997), means making assets have more value than the capital invested in the project. There are several techniques for analyzing a project based on cash flow throughout the period of the project, and according to determination of the variables described earlier. The most commonly used techniques are considered below, according to Gitman (1997) and Ross *et al.* (1995):

- *Payback period* refers to the time required for the capital invested in a project to be returned, starting from when cash inflows begin. It is generally expressed as a number of years. The wide use of this technique, mainly by small companies, is because it is simple to calculate and has intuitive appeal. Ross *et al.* (1995) identify at least three problems in using the payback period: (1) it does not take account of the distribution of cashflows within the recovery period; (2) it ignores all cashflows after the moment the investment is returned; and (3) a company needs a well-defined period to analyse return on investment.
- *Net present value (NPV)* is a technique that discounts company cashflows at a specified rate, frequently called opportunity cost or cost of capital, referring to the minimum return that needs to be obtained from a project, so that the company's market value is unaltered. The net present value is the subtraction of the initial project investment from the present value of cash inflows, discounting the opportunity cost rates used in the project itself. Both the cash inflows and outflows are translated into current monetary values. The NPV gives information about when the project is adding value to the owner. The following rationale is adopted when making decisions about projects: if the NPV is greater than zero, this means the company will obtain a larger return than its cost of capital, therefore the project is acceptable; in cases where the NPV is lower than zero, the project is not acceptable, as the return is smaller than the cost of capital used by the company in the project.
- *The internal rate of return (IRR)* is defined as the discount rate that equals the present value of cash inflows to the project's initial investment. In other words, the discount rate that makes the NPV of an investment opportunity equal to zero is always expressed in percentage terms. It is the most widely used technique in project decision making processes. Figures 11.2 and 11.3 demonstrate the calculations and formulas of the NPV and IRR.

	Jan	Feb	Mar	Apr	May	Jun	Jul	Aug	Sep	Oct	Nov	Dec	Q1	Q2	Q3	Q4	Q1	Q2	Q3	Q4
Current sales average	1000	1000	1000	1000	1000	1000	1000	1000	1000	1000	1000	1000	3000	3000	3000	3000	3000	3000	3000	3000
Sales forecast																				
Product A1	100	110	120	130	130	130	130	160	160	160	160	180	540	540	580	580	600	600	630	630
Product A2	100	110	130	150	200	200	200	230	230	230	230	240	720	720	760	760	770	770	800	800
....	550	560	600	620	680	680	680	790	790	790	790	820	2460	2460	2500	2500	2550	2550	2600	2600
Product C3	250	280	300	310	360	360	360	400	400	400	400	410	1230	1230	1350	1350	1360	1360	1400	1400
New product 1	0	0	0	90	130	130	130	220	220	220	220	250	750	750	810	810	820	820	870	870
Forecast total	1000	1060	1150	1300	1500	1500	1500	1800	1800	1800	1800	1900	5700	5700	6000	6000	6100	6100	6300	6300
Sales increase	0	60	150	300	500	500	500	800	800	800	800	900	2700	2700	3000	3000	3100	3100	3300	3300
Profit increase (12% of sales)	0	7.2	18	36	60	60	60	96	96	96	96	108	324	324	360	360	372	372	396	396
Marketing plan budget																				
Product plan																				
Packaging changes	5	3	3				3	3	2	5	10	2			25	7	7		5	5
....	15	15	10	20	10	10							5	4						
Product development and launch				1	2	2	1									10	5			
Product plan total	20	18	13	21	12	12	4	3	2	5	10	2	5	4	25	17	12	0	5	5
Communications plan																				
Advertising	2	2	3	5	5	5	7	2	2	2	5	6	14	14	10	10	15	15	20	15
....	2	3	3	4	4	5	5	4	4	4	4	4	10	10	12	5	5	10	10	15
Sales promotion	2	2	10	10	10	10	5	5	2	2	1	1	3	3	6	6	10	10	8	8
Communications plan total	6	7	16	19	19	20	17	11	8	8	10	11	27	27	28	21	30	35	38	38
Distribution plan																				
Distributor structuring	6	7	10	10	25	25	10	10	3	3	3	3	6			10	6	6		
....		2			2			4			4		10			10			10	
Distributor returns plan (1% revenue)	10	10.6	12	13	15	15	15	18	18	18	18	19	57	57	60	60	61	61	63	63
Distribution plan total	16	19.6	21.5	23	42	40	25	32	21	21	25	22	73	57	60	80	67	67	73	63
Sales force plan																				
Sales commission (2% revenue)	20	21.2	23	26	30	30	30	36	36	36	36	38	114	114	120	120	122	122	126	126
Training	10			15				15				20				35			30	
Sales force plan total	30	21.2	23	41	30	30	30	51	36	36	36	58	114	114	120	155	122	122	156	126
Total marketing budget	72	66	74	104	103	102	76	97	67	70	81	93	219	202	233	273	231	224	272	232

Figure 11.1 Example budget sheet

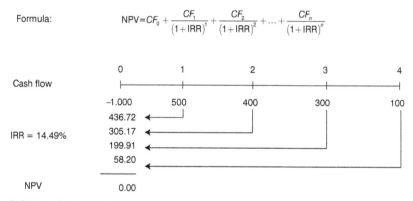

Formula:

$$NPV = CF_0 + \frac{CF_1}{(1+i)^1} + \frac{CF_2}{(1+i)^2} + \ldots + \frac{CF_n}{(1+i)^n}$$

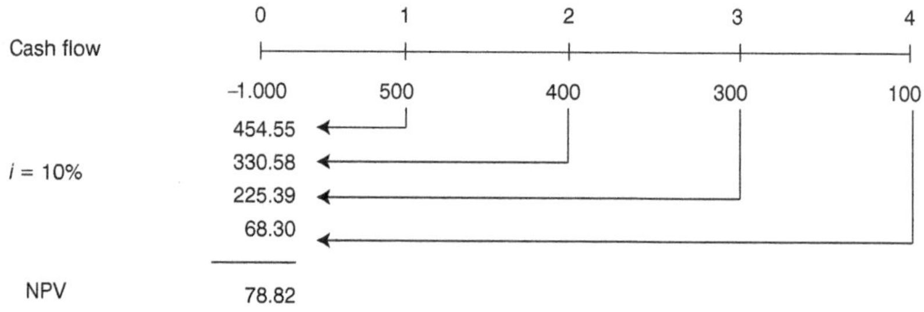

Definition: is the present value of future cash flows, discounted at a determined interest rate, less the present value of the investment cost

Figure 11.2 Formula and example NPV calculation
Source: adapted from Gitman (1997)

Formula:

$$NPV = CF_0 + \frac{CF_1}{(1+IRR)^1} + \frac{CF_2}{(1+IRR)^2} + \ldots + \frac{CF_n}{(1+IRR)^n}$$

Definition: it is the rate that makes the NPV nule; IRR represents the closest to NPV, not being the NPV itself.

Figure 11.3 Formula and example IRR calculation
Source: adapted from Gitman (1997)

Decision making with the IRR has the following rationale. When the IRR is higher than the cost of capital, then value is added, therefore the project is acceptable; in the case where the IRR is lower than the cost of capital, the project is not acceptable. Net present value and internal rate of return, generally, classify projects in different ways, because of the different cash inflow reinvestment assumptions they will generate. From the theoretical point of view, it is hard to determine which method is best to evaluate capital investments.

Gitman (1997) considers two factors in judging the NPV as the best investment analysis technique: (1) NPV considers that all cash inflows generated by the investment be reinvested at the company's cost of capital, while IRR presumes this reinvestment at a higher rate, given by the IRR itself, since the cost of capital tends to be a reasonable estimate of the rate at which the company could apply its inflows in the market; (2) certain mathematical

Table 11.2 Criteria for investment decisions

Criteria	Accept	Reject
Payback	if less than the maximum expected period	if greater than the maximum expected period
Net present value (NPV)	if greater than zero	if less than zero
Internal rate of return (IRR)	if greater than the discount rate	if less than the discount rate

Source: adapted from Gitman (1997)

properties could make unconventional cash flow projects present more than one IRR, a problem that does not happen when the NPV technique is used. Table 11.2 summarizes the main investment decisions.

Ross *et al.* (1995) mention three key attributes for the use of the NPV: it uses cashflows; it uses all the cashflows of the plan; and it discounts the corresponding cashflows. Other techniques ignore the value of resources during time when they process the cashflow.

Activities in Making the Budget

• To finish the marketing plan budget, the team should gather all budgets made for product and service plans (Chapter 6), communications (Chapter 7), distribution channels (Chapter 8) and sales force (Chapter 9), according to the spreadsheet in Table 11.1;
• from this information, the IRR, NPV and payback for the plan period can be calculated, using the formulas in Figures 11.2 and 11.3, in order to decide then about investments and possible adjustments, according to the decision diagram in Table 11.2;
• the budget can also be made for specific projects, as we will see next in the final chapter.

Questions

1 Considering the current situation of the companies, why is it relevant to have an appropriate budget in the DDSP?
2 What does it mean to have an appropriate budget in the DDSP? What variables should be considered?
3 What are the stages involved in the marketing budget process?
4 How does a company analyze its marketing investments?
5 Through the marketing investments analysis, when should a company accept the marketing investment proposed in the DDSP?

12   DDSP Management and Control

Every plan needs to become a reality. It is common to see cases where well-prepared and dense plans are not implemented for several reasons. This last stage of the DDSP tries to prevent the company from not applying the plan. Planning is of fundamental importance, so, however, is execution. We begin with the pitfalls identified by the planning literature, and afterwards, we show how the planning and marketing strategic management process can be implemented.

McDonald (2002) raises a series of pitfalls that are present in the planning process. They are organized in topics below. In the proposal made in the DDSP these have tried to be avoided.

- giving more emphasis to the analysis than the actual planning, leading managers to worry more about techniques and tools than being creative with objectives, positioning and strategy;
- information instead of decisions, where there is a great demand for information, but little emphasis on decision making;
- simplicity, the annual plan should be a gradual development of activities that have been performed by the company, rather than raising fundamental issues about ability, objectives or markets;
- vested interests, resulting in the emphasis of the maintenance of the status quo and in defending revenues and power within the organization, to the detriment of the interests of the company;
- conservative organizations, which refuse to accept plans that substitute well-accepted and well-known past proposals, giving rise to difficulty in breaking bad management habits;
- resistance to change by members of the management team;
- little control over the plan, whether it is lack of commitment or capacity;
- inadequate allocation of resources for the plan;
- focus on the planning process itself instead of planning and implementation; in other words, little capacity to execute what has been planned;
- reduced interest in the plan, resulting from past lack of credibility or the fact that the planning process has become just a meaningless and tiresome annual ritual which consumes time, or from previous negative experiences of the process;
- confusion between marketing tactics and marketing strategy, and the emphasis on easier and more predictable short-term points and performance to the detriment of more complex and uncertain ones in the long term; this is one of the points this book's model tries to emphasize, making marketing decisions more strategic;
- the separation of the marketing function and daily operations, as a result of the plan being developed without market contact;

- confusion between marketing as a function and marketing as a broader business concept; the implications being that marketing is viewed as synonymous with sales, or advertising, or customer service, instead of directing the organization's philosophy towards the markets where it operates;
- organizational barriers that result in the structuring of company activities in relation to functional activities instead of focusing on consumers;
- lack of knowledge and ability;
- failure in prioritizing objectives and their impact on the organization, their urgency and implications on resources;
- hostile corporate culture that views marketing, and consequently marketing planning, as less important than other parts of the company.

Gilligan and Wilson (2003) state that in order for the planning process to be efficient, it is not enough just to impose a planning structure on team members. On the contrary, it is first necessary to show that planning is a living and significant process, and second, that the plan is designed to be a working document; in other words, it is created to be used daily to guide and inform decision making.

When recognizing this, we recognize the fact that the format of planning needs to be standardized, so managers throughout the business are familiar with the process and structure, and there is a built-in flexibility so that when the external environment changes, the plan can be altered to meet these changes. The plan should also be based on strategic thinking and oriented to opportunities instead of being simply a reiteration of what has already happened. Finally, the priorities and strategies should not be hidden in the details of the plan, but immediately apparent.

Gilligan and Wilson state that it is possible to identify characteristics of companies in which the managers did not lose the meaning of strategic planning, for, in these companies there is a clear sense of purpose and direction, the strategies are clearly articulated, and there is a continuous investment in people, products, processes and markets. Efforts and resources are clearly focused on important elements which give or contribute to the competitive advantage, there is a long-term commitment, and the management team is determined to overcome obstacles, emphasizing implementation. Furthermore, managers are interested in creating their own future, instead of letting it be created by others. Gilligan and Wilson (2003) suggest six dangerous situations that can make the implementation ineffective:

- separation between planning and market management activities; products and day-to-day brands are an incentive for putting away the plan;
- having an excessive optimism that leads to the development of plans that are almost totally separated from reality;
- finding out too late about points associated with the plan's implementation, resulting in the inability to continue without new resources, capacities, systems or people;
- denying the existence of possible implementation problems (this is mainly manifested by managers through the thought "if we say it's going to be this way, then this is the way it's going to be"); with a lack of commitment, even the most logical plans will not be fully implemented;
- how the plan was to be implemented was a late addition rather something that was fully part of the planning process from the beginning;
- any barriers or possible implementation problems identified, but not analyzed in detail, and managers who either react beyond what is necessary or inappropriately.

Table 12.1   Important aspects for the effective implementation of the strategic marketing plan and the planning process as a whole

Component	Specific Tasks
Build an organization that is capable of executing the strategy	Create an organizational structure of support for the strategy. Develop abilities and distinct competencies on which strategy is based. Select people for key positions.
Establish a budgetary support strategy	See that each organizational unit has a budget to conduct its part of the strategic plan. Make sure that resources are being used efficiently.
Construct internal management support systems	Establish and manage policies and procedures which facilitate the strategy. Develop management and operational systems to provide critical capacities to the organization's strategy.
Distribute prizes and incentives that are strongly connected to the objectives and strategy	Motivate organizational units and individuals to carry out the strategy. Designate prizes and incentives that lead to the employee's desired performance. Promote orientation to results.
Mold corporate culture to adjust to the strategy	Establish shared values. Define ethical standards. Create a work environment that supports the strategy.
Exercise strategic leadership	Lead the process of creating values, modeling culture and motivating the creation of of the strategy. Keep the organization innovative, responsive and alert to market opportunities. Lead strategy policies, creating consensus. Reinforce ethical and behavioral standards. Initiate corrective actions to improve the strategy's execution.

Source: Thompson and Strickland (1990)

The authors state that in order to try to overcome these problems, the plan should be turned upside down. Begin with what executives consider the most critical points. Work with these points towards the beginning, creating a strategic plan, create executive committees for the plan, demand explicit strategies with implementation costs and research for each key item, and finally, reject any strategic plan which does not show how the plan benefits from the commitment of the people who run the business, or which ignore the importance of the consistency between what should be done and what the company is trying to do. Table 12.1 summarizes important aspects for an effective implementation of a plan.

In summary, for an effective implementation of the plan it is "important that the plan is important." This statement may seem simple, but it is the essence of appropriate management. When the plan is required only to satisfy headquarters or senior management, the planning philosophy and strategic marketing management are typically not given importance. Depending on the organization, there may be a period in the year where the process gets more intense, however it should be permanent.

A lot of organizations use the end of the year to intensify discussions about strategy and to start January with an updated document, a guide of actions for the current year and strategic direction for the next five years. This document is revised each month or every other month, by the strategy committee, and the revision should include those who have day-to-day involvment in the execution of the plan.

Transformation of the Plan into Project Management

The plan must be capable of adjusting itself to people's agendas, so that it is not forgotten. The more the agendas converge to the plan, the more likely the plan is to be kept alive in the marketing and strategy teams. The plan must evolve for the implementation of project management.

For example, the person responsible for implementation of the communications plan should be concerned with building a project structure. A project is a group of coordinated activities, with established objectives and deadlines, and a finite duration. A project involves several functional areas and levels of management and it goes beyond the routine of the company. Figure 12.1 shows a project schematically.

A strategy committee can be established to implement the plan. The committee must be defined by its members; it is a small group of decision makers, where projects can be evaluated and adjusted in monthly meetings within the routine management of the company. The clear objective of the strategy committee is to conduct the implementation of the actions in the plan. The fact that there is a meeting where people "should" present development of the plan's implementation helps actions determined by the plan "to be on the agenda" of the people involved. Another thing that can be done in the strategic marketing meetings of this committee is to have businesses and professionals from outside the organization attending (i.e., consultants, marketing academics and researchers, guests from non-competing industries) to form what can be called a "strategic marketing committee."

Not all projects can be implemented in the first year or the first cycle of the plan implementation, therefore it is instructive to carry out a prioritization exercise, in conjunction with managers, to decide what is more urgent and relevant, by assigning scores from 0 to 10. The multiplication of these two criteria (urgency and relevance) gives scores for projects, so that in the initial period those which are the most important (relevance) and urgent (cannot be postponed to later) are done first.

In fact, there is a difference between the determination of a strategic action in a company and its implementation. For this, project management is fundamental. Each group of planning activities is transformed into projects to be implemented.

Other essential topics that should be in a project are listed in Table 12.3.

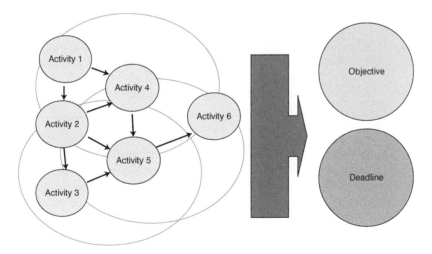

Figure 12.1 Scheme for structuring a project
Source: Pensa

Table 12.2 Project priority tool

Project/actions	Urgency (need for rapid implementation)	Relevance (impact on company results)	A × B
Project B	10	10	100 points
Project C	7	9	63 points
Project F	8	6	48 points

Table 12.3 Fundamental topics in project management

Detailed description of the plan developed in the concept phase	
Coordinator and team	Definition of a coordinator for the project. Appoint a team or someone committed to getting the project going.
Objectives	The project must have clear objectives. In the same way the objectives of the strategic plan were made, the project (operational) objectives must be defined.
Scope	Define the outline (project boundaries). List the actions that are part of the project. Make clear what is not a part of the project (in cases where boundaries are not very clear).
Results	The results expected from the actions to be developed must be clear and well defined; it is the expectation at the end of the project.
Expected schedule	Make a time matrix scheduling the project's activities. Define activities in an analytical structure which successively decomposes the project's final result into stages and sub-stages, until a level is reached where activities are sufficiently small for deadline estimates to be defined.
Points of control (indicators)	Indicate the important points for the committee to follow up on the project. For example, the end of an economic analysis, a technical essay, the opinion of a specialist, etc. Indicators: point out items that will evaluate the efficacy of the project's result. For example: • Cost: reduce ABCD's production cost by x% • Margin: increase EFGH's product line margin by y% • Quality: reduce the contamination index to z% • Image: change to w% the positive image evaluation index of products, according to perception research
Budget/ resource balance	A large percentage of all projects will involve expenses in order to implement defined actions. Therefore, the budget of what will be spent should be discussed by the committee and the expenses approved.
Contingency plan	Actions to be taken can be highlighted where there are unexpected or undesirable events.

Source: based on Pensa Projects and contributions from Roberto Waack

In this way, each project should move towards implementation in an ordered sequence of actions. Making a project happen demands a coordinator with leadership and purpose, who is responsible for the whole team's activities and who represents them on the managing committee, thus promoting the integrated participation of all members of the committe. He should be capable of awakening the team's interest, as well as recognizing interference and difficulties during the process.

There will be connections between several projects within a strategic marketing plan, since everything is interrelated and some activities can even be sequential. A relationship matrix between the projects can show these interrelations, as in Table 12.4.

Table 12.4 Interrelationships between the projects

Projects	1	2	3	4	5	6	7	8	9	10
1	O	X					X			
2	X	O			X		X	X	X	
3		X	O			X	X		X	X
4		X		O	X	X	X		X	
5	X	X		X	O		X	X	X	
6	X		X			O	X		X	X
7	X	X	X	X	X	X	O	X	X	X
8	X	X			X		X	O		
9		X		X	X	X	X		O	
10		X	X			X	X		X	O

Table 12.5 Project management control tool

Project actions	Responsible person	Deadline

Management meetings between the coordinator with his team should be opportunities for internal delegation and discussion of obstacles and proposals of solutions. It is important that each meeting be accompanied by management spreadsheets, as in Table 12.5, where the people involved record actions to be taken over a certain time period. This is also a management tool for the coordinator to control what should be done and what was in fact done in the evolution of the project that is being coordinated.

The team, in turn, should actively participate in technical and interdisciplinary contributions, by representing their area of expertise and by being committed to the results.

At the end of the first implementation cycle of the DDSP, which can coincide with the first year of the project implementation, the company can evaluate the achievements and results and make necessary corrections. The objective as a whole is to make the company more market oriented and to reach the objectives established by the strategies.

DDSP Control: A Marketing Dashboard Perspective

All marketing programs need to be measured and controlled in order to better contribute to marketing planning. This process considers brand, customer and cash flow perspectives, as shown in the previous chapter. However, in order to control the set of activities involved in the marketing planning, these perspectives must be integrated.

A dashboard represents the possibility for integrating the different perspectives for the DDSP control, composed by a set of indicators that allow managers to control their plan. When this concept is applied to the marketing field, it means that the demand driven strategic plan (Lapointe, 2005):

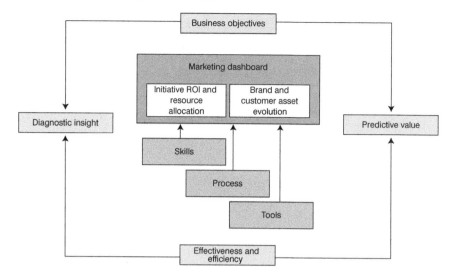

Figure 12.2 The marketing dashboard
Source: Lapointe (2005: 27)

- aligns marketing objectives to company objectives and corporate strategy;
- creates organizational alignment, clarifying the relationships between marketing and the other functional areas;
- provides better resource allocation and it creates a learning organization;
- shows transparency in marketing goals and strategies, helping the other departments to create synergies with the marketing area.

Figure 12.2 shows the marketing dashboard and its constituent parts. Dashboards are the key in looking at the results from the DDSP plan. Moreover, with an increasing availability of data, they can be set up in a more consistent way. That is, today more than ever before, organizations must perform this kind of analysis in order to provide managers with structured and consistent information, helping them to make decisions in their DDSP.

The DDSP Tools

To finish this chapter, Table 12.6 is presented which summarizes important tools for the companies to develop its DDSP, based on tools and methods as shown in the book. By means of this tool the development of the DDSP can be controlled.

Questions

1   Why is the DDSP management and control process relevant for business strategy? Why is a dashboard perspective important in this sense?
2   What are the common business challenges before, during and after the execution of the DDSP activities?
3   How can a company make the DDSP management and control?
4   What are some of the fundamental topics in project management?
5   What do you think are marketing/strategy trends for 2030?

Table 12.6 Summary of the tools and methods to be used for the company during the DDSP

Figure/ table	Title	Was the tool used for the company
Chapter 2: Analyzing the company's environment and market (external analysis)		
Figure 2.1	Company network and main variables	
Table 2.2	Market evolution	
Table 2.3	Market evolution by region	
Table 2.4	Drivers of change and actions that must be implemented	
Figure 2.2	Consolidation of the project and actions based on the STEP analysis	
Figure 2.3	Determinants of the competition's intensity – the five forces model	
Table 2.7	Analyzing the purchase decision process of your customers/ consumers	
Table 2.8	Matrix of collective actions between the members of a network	
Chapter 3: Analyzing the company and the competition		
Table 3.1	Evaluation of the company's customer orientation	
Table 3.3	Description of the company's main competitors	
Table 3.4	Internal analysis versus competition	
Figure 3.3	Components of the created value	
Table 3.5	Comparison and weighting of the critical success factors	
Figure 3.6	Consolidation of the project and actions based on the competition analysis	
Chapter 4: Establishing company objectives		
Table 4.2	Worksheet showing the main DDSP objectives of a company	
Table 4.3	Worksheet showing geographical distribution of sales objectives	
Table 4.4	Worksheet showing main product line sales objectives	
Table 4.5	Worksheet showing major growth rate objectives by target segment	
Chapter 5: Strategies to reach the objectives		
Figure 5.1	Generic business strategies	
Table 5.2	Matrix of strategic alternatives	
Figure 5.2	Segmentation matrix	
Table 5.4	Differentiation options for companies	
Table 5.6	Main growth opportunities	
Figure 5.3	Growth strategies (product/market expansion grid)	
Figure 5.4	BCG Growth–Share Matrix	
Figure 5.5	GE/McKinsey Market Attractiveness Matrix	
Table 5.9	Actions to create and maintain a competitive advantage	
Chapter 6: Product. service, brand, and packaging decisions		
Figure 6.1	Product line analysis	
Figure 6.2	Product comparison: volume vs margin vs revenue	
Figure 6.3	Product life cycle and marketing strategies	
Table 6.1	New product launch evaluation matrix	
Table 6.2	Main brand decisions	
Table 6.3	Package amplitude and decisions (ideas) for the company	
Table 6.4	Opportunities for the use of collective actions in products, services, brands and packages	

Figure/ table	*Title*	*Was the tool used for the company*
Chapter 7: Communications decisions		
Table 7.1	Definition of the target market and communications actions	
Table 7.2	Establishing communication objectives	
Table 7.4	Main communications tools	
Table 7.6	Communications budget creation methods	
Table 7.7	Example communications budget and schedule	
Table 7.8	Collective actions opportunities	
Table 7.9	Definition of the target public and communication actions	
Chapter 8: Distribution channel decisions		
Table 8.1	Distribution channels flow	
Table 8.3	Criteria for the selection of channel members	
Table 8.4	Advantages and disadvantages of coordination via the market	
Table 8.5	Advantages and risks in strategic alliances (joint ventures)	
Table 8.6	Advantages and risks in franchises	
Table 8.7	Factors to consider and risks in the vertical integration	
Table 8.8	Distribution channel network approach	
Chapter 9: Sales force decisions		
Table 9.1	Porter's strategies and implications for the sales force	
Figure 9.1	Establishing segments and operational focus	
Table 9.2	Main decisions and descriptions in sales organization	
Figure 9.4	Stages in developing a quota and incentive plan	
Table 9.3	Arguments in favor of representatives, salespeople and contingency arguments	
Figure 9.5	Decision model for sales specialization	
Table 9.5	Market development index and market penetration index	
Table 9.6	Components of a compensation plan and their respective objectives	
Table 9.7	Performance evaluation measures	
Table 9.9	Opportunities for sales force collective actions in the network	
Chapter 10: Price decisions		
Table 10.1	Price sensitivity factors	
Table 10.2	Impact of demand elasticity	
Table 10.4	Methods for setting prices	
Table 10.5	Price adjustment strategies	
Table 10.6	Motives for using the network and collective action perspective for pricing	
Chapter 11: Budget and investment analysis		
Figure 11.1	Example budget sheet	
Table 11.2	Criteria for investment decisions	
Chapter 12: DDSP management and control		
Table 12.2	Project priority tool	
Table 12.3	Fundamental topics in project management	
Table 12.4	Interrelationships between the projects	
Table 12.5	Project management control tool	

Planning Strategies for 2013–2022

In this section, the object is to outline 10 important topics for the next 10 years, ranging from strategic planning processes, to overall positioning strategies of companies, consumers and governments.

1   *Empowerment:* In the next 10 years, companies, networks and productive chains will be more valued by consumers. How to build sustainable incentives for associations and cooperatives will be a central task for governments.

2   *Economic integration:* A more integrated economy gives importance to developing countries' supply chains, as sources/alternatives for supplying consumers in the developed world. This integration also brings prominence to the marketing channels in developing countries through which products made in the developed world could be sold to the emerging consumers.

3   *Income distribution:* There is a huge internal market growing in several parts of the world, and these emerging consumers should be studied more by companies for their positioning. The impact of these new consumers on the planet's capacity to produce (from grains to proteins) is a major issue.

4   *Climate and environmental protection:* This topic will be even more important in the next 10 years, since climate change is a reality. The following are essential: attention to low carbon networks (carbon footprint and carbon management), network adaptation to climate change, renewable energy networks, environmental certification, resource usage efficiency, network reversal (material reuse and recycling) and network integration to optimize use of byproducts.

5   *Technology:* As the driver of cost reduction, consumers will not only value network transparency, information exchange and technology systems but also consumer "hi-tech" networks. Companies and their networks should really be driven by consumers and communicate with consumers on an individual basis.

6   *Industry mergers:* The next 10 years will be especially marked by industry mergers; this has happened in mobile phones which now are cameras, computers, watches, voice recorders, radios and other equipment. The world will see the growth of nutra-ceutical networks (food and pharmaceutical), nutri-cosmetics networks (food and cosmetics), nutri-touristic networks (food and tourism business), nutri-car networks (food and biofuels).

7   *Risk management:* An integrated network of risk management and mitigation will be of fundamental importance in this connected world. Several risks are present in a global perspective, such as financial crisis, diseases, sustainability, security and others.

8   *Communications:* Communications will experience crucial changes, with new media network communication, and proactive network communication with stakeholders. Communicating with high-tech consumers will be a challenge for companies.

9   *Era of simplicity:* Simplicity will be valued, in terms of the company network management, market segmentation, new product launches, brand management, services, costumer focus, sales management and others. Simplicity is the watch-word for the next 10 years.

10 *Network value engineering:* The next 10 years will an era of integrated company networks, which include the promotion of permanent supply chain redesign, the value capture of marketing channels, closeness to customers, contract evaluation and reliable relationship building.

Final comments

We have now reached the end of this book. I hope you have enjoyed it and that it will be useful for you and your organization. If so, my dream (which has lasted almost ten years) of seeing my blackboards from classes transformed into a published book has come true.

Thank you for your attention throughout these chapters, which have a mix of theory and practice. I wish you success in your professional career.

Marcos Fava Neves
Ribeirão Preto, Brazil
10 May 2012

References and Further Reading

Aaker, D. A. (1991) *Managing brand equity: capitalizing on the value of a brand name.* New York: Free Press.

Aaker, D. A. (1996) *Building strong brands.* New York: Free Press.

Abell, D. F. (1980) *Defining the business: the starting point of strategic planning.* Upper Saddle River, NJ: Prentice Hall.

Achrol, R. S. and Stern, L. W. (1988) Environmental determinants of decision making: uncertainty in marketing channels. *Journal of Marketing Research,* 25: 36–50.

Ailawad, K. L., Borin, N. and Farris, P. W. (1995) Market power and performance: a cross-industry analysis of manufacturers and retailers. *Journal of Retailing,* 71(3): 211–248.

Albers, S. (2000) Sales-force management. In Blois, K. (ed.) *The Oxford textbook of marketing.* Oxford: Oxford University Press.

Alderson, W. and Halbert, M. (1971) *Homens, motivos e mercados.* São Paulo: Atlas.

AMA – American Marketing Association (n.d.) Marketing definitions. Available online at http://www.marketingpower.com.

Amato Neto, J. (2000) *Redes de cooperação produtiva e clusters regionais.* São Paulo: Atlas.

Ambrósio, V. and Siqueira, R. (2002) *Plano de marketing: passo a passo serviços.* Rio de Janeiro: Reichmann & Affonso.

Anderson, E. and Coughlan, A. T. (1987) International market entry and expansion via independent or integrated channels of distribution. *Journal of Marketing,* 51: 71–82.

Anderson, E. and Weitz, B. A. (1986) Make-or-buy decisions: vertical integration and marketing productivity. *Sloan Management Review,* Spiring: 3–19.

Andreasen, A. R. and Kotler, P. (1996) *Strategic marketing for nonprofit organizations.* 5th edn. Upper Saddle River, NJ: Prentice Hall.

Andrews, K. J., Bower, C. R., Christensen, R., Hamermesh, R. G. and Porter, M. E. (1986) *Business policy: text and cases.* 6th edn. Homewood, IL: Richard D. Irwin.

Andrews, K. R. (1987) *The concept of corporate strategy.* 3rd edn. Homewood, IL: Richard D. Irwin.

Ansoff, H. I. (1965) *Corporate strategy: an analytic approach to business police for growth and expansion.* New York: McGraw-Hill.

Ansoff, H. I., Declerck, R. P. and Hayes, R. L. (1976) *From strategic planning to strategic management.* London: Wiley.

Axelsson, B. and Easton G. (eds) (1992) *Industrial networks: a new view of reality.* London: Routledge.

Azevedo, P. F. (1996) *Integração vertical e barganha.* Doctoral thesis, Depto. de Economia, FEA/USP, São Paulo.

Bain, J. (1968) *Industrial organization.* 2nd edn. New York: John Wiley.

Ballou, R. H. (2001) *Gerenciamento da cadeia de suprimentos.* Porto Alegre: Bookman.

Bateman, Thomas S. and Snell, Scott A. (1998) *Administração: construindo vantagem competitiva.* São Paulo: Atlas.

Belch, G.E. and Belch, M.A. (2008) *Propaganda e promoção.* 7th edn. São Paulo: McGraw-Hill.

Berman, B. (1996) *Marketing channels*. New York: John Wiley.

Besanko, D., Dranove, D. and Shanley, M. (2000) *Economics of strategy*. 2nd edn. New York: John Wiley.

Biong, H., Wathne, K. and Parvatiyar, A. (1997) Why do some companies not want to engage in partnering relationships?. In Gemünden, H. G., Ritter, T. and Walter, A. (eds) *Relationships and networks in international markets*. Oxford: Pergamon.

Bonoma, T. and Shapiro, B. P. (1983) *Segmenting the industrial marketing*. Lexington, KY: Lexington Books.

Boonee, L. E. and Kurtz, D. L. (1998) *Marketing contemporâneo*. Rio de Janeiro: LTC.

Borghini, S., Azoulay, A., Sherry, J. F. and Kozinets, R. V. (2004) Making it mine: consumers' attachments to their favorite brands. In *Proceedings of the 33rd European Marketing Academy Conference (EMAC)*, 18-21 May, Murcia.

Bower, J. L. (1986) *Managing the resource allocation process*. Cambridge, MA: Harvard Business School Press.

Boyle, B., Dwyer, F. R., Robicheaux, R. A. and Simpson, J.T. (1992) Influence strategies in marketing channels: measures and use in different relationship structures. *Journal of Marketing Research*, 24: 462–473.

Brandt, C., Mortanges, C. P., Bluemelhuber, C., van Riel, A. C. R. (2010) Associative networks: a new approach to market segmentation. *International Journal of Market Research*, 53(2): 187–207.

Bridgewater, S. and Egan, C. (2002) *International marketing relationships*. London: Palgrave.

Bucklin, L. P. and Sengupta, S. (1993) Organizing successful co-marketing alliances. *Journal of Marketing*, 57(2): 32–46.

Campomar, M. C. (1982a) Contribuições ao estudo de planejamento e confecção de planos em marketing: uma aplicação em concessionárias de automóveis. Livre-docência thesis, FEA/USP, São Paulo.

Campomar, M. C. (1982b) Pesquisa de marketing: um auxílio à decisão. *Briefing*, 43(April): 20–22.

Campomar, M. C. (1984) O sistema de marketing. *Marketing*, 18(131) 43–45.

Castro, L. T. and Neves, M. F. (2005) *Administração de vendas: Planejamento, estratégia e gestão*. São Paulo: Atlas.

Chandler, A. D. (1966) *Strategy and structure*. New York: Doubleday.

Chonko, L. B., Enis, B. M. and Tanner, J. F. (1992) *Managing salespeople*. Boston, MA: Allyn and Bacon.

Churchill, A. G., Ford, N. M., Walker, O. C., Johnston, M. W. and Tanner, J. F. (2000) *Sales force management*. 6th edn. Boston, MA: McGraw-Hill.

Coase, R. H. (1991) The nature of the firm. In Williamson, Oliver E. and Winter, Sidney (eds) *The nature of the firm: origins, evolution, development*. New York: Oxford University Press.

Cobra, M. (1992) *Administração de marketing*. 2nd edn. São Paulo: Atlas.

Coelho, F., Easingwood, C. and Coelho, A. (2003) Exploratory evidence of channel performance in single vs multiple channel strategies. *International Journal of Retailing and Distribution Management*, 31(11): 561–574.

Collis, D. J. and Montgomery, C. A. (1995) Competing on resources: strategy in the 1990s. *Harvard Business Review*. July–August: 118–128.

Consoli, M. A. (2005) Proposta de um sistema de análise de captura de valor nos canais de distribuição com base nos fluxos de marketing. Master's thesis, Faculdade de Economia, Administração e Contabilidade, Universidade de São Paulo, São Paulo.

Cooper, J. and Lane, P. (1997) *Practical marketing planning*. London: Macmillan Press.

Corstjens, M., Umblijs, A. and Wang, C. (2011) The power of inertia: conservatism in marketing resource allocation. *Journal of Advertising Research*, 51(2): 356–372.

Coughlan, A., Anderson, E., Stern, L. W. and El-Ansary, A. (2002) *Canais de marketing e distribuição*. 6th edn. Porto Alegre: Bookman.

Czinkota, M. (2001) *Marketing: as melhores práticas*. Porto Alegre: Bookman.

Czinkota, M. (2010) *International Marketing*. 9th edn. New York: Cengage Learning.

Dalrymple, D. J. and Cron, W. L. (1995) *Sales management: concepts and cases*. 5th edn. New York: John Wiley.

David, F. R. (2001) *Strategic management: concept and cases*. 8th edn. Upper Saddle River, NJ: Prentice Hall.

Day, G. S. (1994) The capabilities of market-driven organizations. *Journal of Marketing*, 58(3): 37–52.

Dewsnap, B. and Jobber, D. (2004) The antecedents of sales-marketing collaboration: an empirical investigation. In *Proceedings of the 33rd European Marketing Academy Conference (EMAC)*, 18–21 May, Murcia.

Dowell, G. (2006) Product line strategies of new entrants in an established industry: evidence from the U.S. bicycle industry. *Strategic Management Journal*, 27: 959–979.

Doyle, P. (2000) *Value-based marketing: marketing strategies for corporate growth and shareholder value*. Chichester: John Wiley.

Dubinsky, A. J. and Hansen, R. W. (1981) The sales force management audit. *California Management Review*, 24(2): 86–95.

Easingwood, C. and Coelho F. (2003) Single versus multiple channel strategies: typologies and drivers. *The Service Industries Journal*, 23(2): 31–46.

East, R., Wright, M. and Riley, D. (2004) Are long-term customers more valuable? In *Proceedings of the 33rd European Marketing Academy Conference (EMAC)*, 18–21 May, Murcia.

Engel, James F. (1995) *Consumer Behavior*. 8th ed. Forth Worth: Dryden.

Etzel, M. J., Walker, B. J. and Stanton, W. J. (2001) *Marketing*. São Paulo: Makron Books.

Farina, M. M. Q., Azevedo F. and Saes, S. M. (1997) *Competitividade: mercado, estado e organizações*. São Paulo: Singular.

Fill, C. (199) *Marketing communications: contexts, strategies and applications*. 2nd edn. Edinburgh: Prentice Hall.

Fletcher, K., Wright, G. and Donaldson, B. (2004) The relationship of strategic and organizational factors to sales force automation sophistication: an empirical study of the UK financial services industry. In *Proceedings of the 33rd European Marketing Academy Conference (EMAC)*, 18–21 May, Murcia.

Ford, D. (1998) Two decades of interaction, relationships and networks. In Naudé, P. and Turnbull, P. W. (eds) *Network dynamics in international marketing*. Oxford: Pergamon.

Friedman, L. G. and Furey, T. R. (2000) *The channel advantage*. Oxford: Butterworth Heinemann.

Fuchs, D. and Reinecke, S. (2004) Marketing budgeting sophistication, stakeholders' satisfaction with marketing budgeting, marketing performance. In *Proceedings of the 33rd European Marketing Academy Conference (EMAC)*, 18–21 May, Murcia.

Fuller, C. B. (1983) The implications of the 'learning curve' for firm strategy and public policy. *Applied Economics*, 15(4): 541–552.

Futrell, Charles M. (2010) *Fundamentals of selling*, 12th ed. Homewood, IL: Irwin McGraw-Hill.

Gadde, L. E. and Hakansson, H. (2001) *Supply network strategies*. New York: John Wiley.

Galbraith, J. R. and Kazanjian, R. K. (1987) *Strategy implementation: structure, systems and process*. San Francisco, CA: West Publishing Company.

Garvin, D. A. (1987) Competing on the eight dimensions of quality. *Harvard Business Review*, 65(Nov./Dec.): 92–100.

Gattorna, J. L. and Walters, D. W. (1996) *Managing the supply chain*. New York: Macmillan.

Gemünden, H. G., Ritter, T. and Walter, A. (eds) (1997) *Relationships and networks in international markets*. Oxford: Pergamon.

Gilligan, C. and Wilson, R. M. S. (2003) *Strategic marketing planning*. Oxford: Butterworth-Heinemann.

Gitman, L. J. (1997) *Princípios da administração financeira*. 7th edn. São Paulo: Harbra.

Gonzalis, A. V. (1998) Marcas próprias – o que está se passando com os produtos. *Super Hiper*, XX(March): 64–66.

Gonzalez, S. and Trespalacios, J. A. (2004) Relationalism and dependence in industrial marketing channels: worldwide marketing? In *Proceedings of the 33rd European Marketing Academy Conference (EMAC)*, 18–21 May, Murcia.

Granovetter, M. (1985) Economic action and social structure: the problem of embeddedness. *American Journal of Sociology*, 91(Nov.): 481–501.

Grant, R. M. (1991) The resource-based theory of competitive advantage: implications for strategy formulation. *California Management Review*, 33(March): 114–135.

Grant, R. M. (2002) *Contemporary strategy analysis: concepts, techniques and applications*. 4th edn. Oxford: Blackwell Business.

Grönroos, C. (2004) The relationship marketing process: communication, interaction, dialogue, value. *Journal of Business & Industrial Marketing*, 19(2): 99–113.

Guissoni, L. A. and Neves, M. F. (2011) *Comunicação integrada de marketing baseada em valor*. São Paulo: Atlas.

Guissoni, L. A., Neves, M. F. and Bonizio, R. C. (2010) Proposta de avaliação dos resultados do programa de comunicações de marketing sob a perspectiva da criação de valor para as organizações. *Revista Brasileira de Marketing – ReMark*, 9(2): 137–165.

Gulati, R. (1998) Alliances and networks. *Strategic Management Journal*, 19: 293–317.

Gulati, R., Nohria, N.. and Zaheer, Z. (2000) Strategic networks. *Strategic Management Journal*, 21(3): 203–215.

Hair, J. F., Anderson, R. E., Tatham, R. L. and Black, W. C. (1995) *Multivariate data analysis with readings*. 4th edn. Englewood Cliffs, NJ: Prentice Hall.

Hakansson, H. and Snehota, I. (1993) The burden of relationships: who is next? In Naudé, P. and Turnbull, P. W. (eds) *Network dynamics in international marketing*. London: Pergamon.

Hamermesh, R. G. (1986a) *Making strategy work: how senior managers produce results*. New York: John Wiley.

Hamermesh, R. G. (1986b) Making planning strategic. *Harvard Business Review*, 64(4): 115–120.

Hamermesh, R. G. (1996) *Fad-free management*. Santa Monica, CA: Knowledge Exchange.

Hammer, M. (1990) Reengineering work: don't automate, obliterate. *Harvard Business Review*, 68(4): 104–112.

Harrigan, K. R. (1980) *Strategies for declining businesses*. Lexington, KY: Lexington Books.

Harrigan, K. R. (1983) A framework for looking at vertical integration. *Journal of Business Strategy*, 3: 30–37.

Hart, O. (1995) *Firms, contracts, and financial structure*. New York: Oxford University Press.

Hax, A. C. and Majluf, N. S. (1991) *The strategy concept and process: a pragmatic approach*. Upper Saddle River, NJ: Prentice Hall.

Hayek, F. (1945) The use of knowledge in society. *American Economic Review*, 35(Sept.): 519–530.

Heide, J. B. (1994) Interorganizational governance in marketing channels. *Journal of Marketing*, 58(Jan.): 71–85.

Heide, J. B. and John, G. (1990) Alliances in industrial purchasing: the determinants of joint action in buyer–supplier relationships. *Journal of Marketing Research*, 27: 24–36.

Hendersen, B. D. (1984) *The logic of business strategy*. Cambridge, MA: Ballinger.

Hendersen, B. D. (1989) The origin of strategy. *Harvard Business Review*, 67(6): 139–143.

Heschel, M. S. (1977) Effective sales territory development. *Journal of Marketing*, 41(2): 39–43.

Heydebreck, P. and Maier, J. C. (1997) Need bundles of innovation-oriented services and resources. In Gemünden, H. G., Ritter, T. and Walter, A. (eds) *Relationships and networks in international markets*. Oxford: Pergamon.

Hofer, C. W. and Schendel, D. (1977) *Strategy formulation: analytical concepts*. St. Paul, MN: West Publishing.

Hofstede, G. J. (2004) Globalization, culture and netchains. In Bremmers, H. J., Omta, S. W. F., Trienekens, J. H. and Wubben, E. F. M. (eds) *Dynamics in chain and networks*. Wageningen: Wageningen Academic Publishers.

Hooley, G. J., Beracs, J., Cadogan, J. W. *et al.* (2004a) Marketing assets, capabilities and competitive positioning. In *Proceedings of the 33rd European Marketing Academy Conference (EMAC)*, 18–21 May, Murcia.

Hooley, G. J., Saunders, J. A. and Piercy, N. F. (2004b) *Marketing strategy and competitive positioning.* 3rd edn. Harlow: Pearson Education.

Hunt, S. D. and Deroizer, C. (2004) The normative imperatives of business and marketing strategy: grounding strategy in resource-advantage theory. *Journal of Business & Industrial Marketing,* 19(1): 5–22.

Hunt, S. D. and Nevin, J. R. (1974) Power in a channel of distribution: sources and consequences. *Journal of Marketing Research,* 11: 186–193.

Iacobucci, D. (ed.) (2001) *Os desafios do marketing.* São Paulo: Futura.

Ingenbleek, P., Frambach, T. R. and Verhallen, T. M. (2004) Increasing profit margins of innovations: an empirical analysis of firm' pricing practices. In *Proceedings of the 33rd European Marketing Academy Conference (EMAC),* 18-21 May, Murcia.

Ingram, T. N. and Laforge, R.W. (1992) *Sales management: analysis and decision making.* 2nd edn. Orlando, TX: HBJ.

Ingram, T. N., Laforge, R. W. and Leigh, T. W. (2002) Selling in the new millennium: a joint agenda. *Industrial Marketing Management,* 31: 559–567.

Jackson, D. M. and D'Amico, M. F. (1989) Products and markets served by distributors and agents. *Industrial Marketing Management,* 18: 27–33.

Jain, S. C. (2000) *Marketing planning and strategy.* 6th edn. Cincinnati, OH: Thomson Learning.

John, G. (1984) An empirical investigation of some antecedents of opportunism in a marketing channel. *Journal of Marketing Research,* 21: 278–289.

Johnson, G. and Scholes, H. K. (2008) *Exploring corporate strategy.* 7th edn. Hemel Hempstead: Prentice Hall.

Juttner, U., Christopher, M. and Baker, S. (2007) Demand chain management: integrating marketing and supply chain management. *Industrial Marketing Management,* 36: 377–392.

Kaplan, R. S. and Norton, D. P. (1997) *A estratégia em ação.* Rio de Janeiro: Campus.

Kaplan, R. S. and Norton, D. P. (2004) Measuring the strategic readiness of intangible assets. *Harvard Business Review,* 82(2): 52–63.

Keller, K. L. (1993) Conceptualizing, measuring, and managing customer-based brand equity. *Journal of Marketing,* 57: 1–22.

Kelley, W. T. (1970) The sales promotion program. In Buell, U. P. and Heyel, C. (eds) *Handbook of modern marketing.* New York: McGraw-Hill.

Klein, B. (1995) The economics of franchise contracts. *Journal of Corporate Finance,* 2: 9–37.

Konus, U., Verhoef, P. C. and Neslin, S. A. (2008) Multichannel shopper segments and their covariates. *Journal of Retailing,* 84(4): 398–413.

Kotler, P. (1997) *Marketing management: analysis, planning, implementation and control.* 9th edn. São Paulo: Atlas.

Kotler, P. and Levy, S. J. (1969) Broadening the concept of marketing. *Journal of Marketing,* 33: 10–15.

Kotler, P. and Levy, S. J. (2000) *Administração de marketing: análise, planejamento, implementação e controle.* São Paulo: Prentice Hall.

Kotler, P., Kartajaya, H. and Setiawan, I. (2010) *Marketing 3.0: from products to customers to the human spirit.* Hoboken, NJ: John Wiley and Sons.

Lambin, J. J. (2000) *Marketing estratégico.* 4th edn. Lisbon: McGraw-Hill.

Lapointe, P. (2005) *Marketing by the dashboard light.* New York: Marketing NPV/Association of National Advertisers.

Lapointe, P. (2011) The rock in the pond: how online buzz and offline WOM can make a strong message even more powerful. *Journal of Advertising Research,* 51(3): 456–457.

Las Casas, A. L. (1999) *Plano de marketing para micro e pequena empresa.* São Paulo: Atlas.

Lassar, W. M. and Kerr, J. L. (1996) Strategy and control in supplier-distributor relationships: an agency perspective. *Strategic Management Journal,* 17: 613–632.

Lazzarini, S. G., Chaddad, F. R. and Cook, M. (2001) Integrating supply and network analysis: the study of netchains. *Journal on Chain and Network Science,* 1(1): 7–22.

Levy, M. and Weitz, B. A. (2000) *Administração de varejo.* São Paulo: Atlas.

Lovelock, C. H. (1996) *Services marketing.* 3rd edn. Upper Saddle River, NJ: Prentice Hall.

Lusch, R. F. (1976) Sources of power: their impact on intrachannel conflict. *Journal of Marketing Research*, 13: 382–390.

Lusch, R. F. and Brown, J. R. (1996) Interdependency, contracting and relational behaviour in marketing channels. *Journal of Marketing*, 60: 19–38.

Lynch, R. P. (1993) *Business alliance guide.* New York: John Wiley.

Machado Filho, C. A. P., Spers, E. E., Chaddad, F. R. and Neves, M. F. (1996) *Agribusiness europeu.* São Paulo: Pioneira.

MacNeil, I. R. (1974) The many futures of contracts. *Southern California Law Review*, 47: 691–816.

Mahoney, J. and Pandian, J. R. (1992) The resource based view within the conversation of strategic management. *Strategic Management Journal*, 13: 363–380.

Malhotra, N. (2001) *Pesquisa de marketing: uma orientação aplicada.* São Paulo: Bookman.

Martinelli, D. P. (2002) *Negociação empresarial: em busca de uma visão sistêmica na negociação.* Barueri: Manole.

Mattsson, L. (1997) Relationship marketing in a network perspective. In Gemünden, H. G., Ritter, T. and Walter, A. (eds) *Relationships and networks in international markets.* Oxford: Pergamon.

Maximiano, A. C. A. (1997) *Teoria geral da administração: da escola científica à competitividade em economia globalizada.* São Paulo: Atlas.

Maxwell, S., Reed, G., Saker, J. and Story, V. (2004) The playfulness of sales managers: its effects on sales reps' organizational commitment and job satisfaction. In *Proceedings of the 33rd European Marketing Academy Conference (EMAC)*, 18–21 May, Murcia.

Mazzon, J. A. (1978) Formulação de um modelo de avaliação e comparação de modelos em marketing. Master's thesis, FEA/USP, São Paulo.

McCarthy, E. J. (1982) *Marketing.* Rio de Janeiro: Campus.

McCarthy, E. J. and Perreault, W. D. (1997) *Marketing essencial: uma abordagem gerencial e global.* São Paulo.

McDonald, M. (2002) *Marketing plans: how to prepare them, how to use them.* 5th edn. Oxford: Butterworth-Heinemann.

Mestriner, F. (2001) *Design de embalagem: curso básico.* São Paulo: Makron Books.

Michels, R. (1962) *Political parties.* Glencoe, IL: Free Press.

Mintzberg, H. (1973) *The nature of managerial work.* New York: Harper & Row.

Mintzberg, H. (1987) Crafting strategy. *Harvard Business Review*, 65(Jul/Aug): 66–75.

Mintzberg, H. (1993) *Structure in fives: designing effective organizations.* Englewood Cliffs, NJ: Prentice Hall.

Mintzberg, H. (1994a) The fall and rise of strategic planning. *Harvard Business Review*, 71(1): 107–114.

Mintzberg, H. (1994b) *The rise and fall of strategic planning.* Englewood Cliffs, NJ: Prentice Hall.

Mintzberg, H. and Quinn, J. B. (1996) *The strategy process: concepts, contexts and cases.* 3rd edn. Upper Saddle River, NJ: Prentice Hall.

Moore, J. L. (1992) *Writers on strategy and strategic management.* London: Penguin Books.

Morgan, R. E. and Ambler, T. (2001) Strategic orientation and export development: a resource-based perspective. *Proceedings of the 30th European Marketing Academy (EMAC) Conference*, Bergen, 8–11 May.

Morgan, R. M. and Hunt, S. D. (1994) The commitment–trust theory of relationship marketing. *Journal of Marketing*, 58(July): 20–38.

Nagle, T. T. and Holden, R. K. (1994) *The strategic and tactics of pricing.* 2nd edn. Upper Saddle River, NJ: Prentice Hall.

Naudé, P. and Turnbull, P. W. (1998) *Network dynamics in international marketing.* London: Pergamon.

Neves, M. F. (1999) Um modelo para planejamento de canais de distribuição no setor de alimentos. Doctoral thesis, Faculdade de Economia, Administração e Contabilidade, Universidade de São Paulo.

Neves, M. F. (2003) Marketing and network contracts (agreements). *Journal of Chain and Network Science*, 3(1) 7–19.

Neves, M. F. and Castro, L. T. (2003) *Marketing e estratégia em agronegócios e alimentos*. São Paulo: Atlas.

Neves, M. F., Zuurbier, P. and Campomar, M. C. A. (2001) A model for the distribution channels planning process. *Journal of Business and Industrial Marketing*, 16(7): 518–539.

Noonan, C. (1999) *Export marketing: the Chartered Institute of Marketing*. Oxford: Butterworth Heinemann.

North, D. C. (1990) *Institutions, institutional change and economic performance*. Cambridge: Cambridge University Press.

Oksanen, E. (2000) Organizational roles of sales people in the network marketing context. *Proceedings of the 16th Industrial Marketing and Purchasing Group Conference*, September, Bath.

Oksanen, E. (2001) Search of networking sales people. *Proceedings of the 30th European Marketing Academy (EMAC) Conference*, Bergen, 8–11 May.

de Oliveira, D. P. R. (2002) *Planejamento estratégico: conceitos, metodologia e práticas*. 17th edn. São Paulo: Atlas.

Olson, M. (1999) *A lógica da ação coletiva: os benefícios públicos e uma teoria dos grupos sociais*. Fabio Fernandez (trans). São Paulo: Edusp.

Olson, M., Cravens D. W. and Slater, S. F. (2001) Competitiveness and sales management: a marriage of strategies. *Business Horizons*, March/April: 25–30.

Omta, O., Trienekens, J. and Beers, G. (2001) Chain and network science: a research framework. *Journal on Chain and Network Science*, 1(1): 1–6.

Ozsomer, A. (2004) Capabilities for managing economic crisis: the role of market orientation and organizational learning. In *Proceedings of the 33rd European Marketing Academy Conference (EMAC)*, 18–21 May, Murcia.

Palmer, A. (2000) *Principles of marketing*. Oxford: Oxford University Press.

Pancrazio, P. D. S. (2000) *Promoção de vendas: o gatilho do marketing*. São Paulo: Futura.

Parasuraman, A., Zeithaml, V. A. and Berry, L. L. (1985) A conceptual model of service quality and its implications for future research. *Journal of Marketing*, 49: 41–50.

Parente, J. (2000) *Varejo no Brasil: gestão e estratégia*. São Paulo: Atlas.

Pearce, J. A. (1988) *Strategic management: strategy formulation and implementation*. 3rd edn. Homewood, IL: Richard D. Irwin.

Pearce, J. A. (1996) *An industry approach to cases in strategic management*. 2nd edn. Homewood, IL: Richard D. Irwin.

Pearce, J. A. (2003) *Strategic management: strategy formulation, implementation and control*. 8th edn. Chicago, IL: Richard D. Irwin.

Pearce, J. A. and Robinson, R. B. (2003) *Formulation, implementation and control of competitive strategy*. 8th edn. Chicago, IL: Richard D. Irwin.

Peattie, K. and Peattie, S. (1994) Sales promotion: a missed opportunity for services marketers? *International Journal of Service Industry Management*, 6(1): 22–39.

Pelton, L. E., Strutton, D. and Lumpkin, J. R. (1997) *Marketing channels: a relationship management approach*. London: Times Mirror Books.

Planet Retail (2010) *Power shift in FMCG: how retailers are in control and what suppliers can do about it*. London: Planet Retail Limited.

Porter, M. E. (1974) Consumer behavior, retailer power and performance in consumer goods industries. *Review of Economics and Statistics*, 56(November): 419–436.

Porter, M. E. (1992) *Vantagem competitiva: criando e sustentando um desempenho superior*. Rio de Janeiro: Campus.

Porter, M. E. (1997) *Estratégia competitiva: técnicas para análise de indústrias e da concorrência*. 7th edn. Rio de Janeiro: Campus.

Prahalad, C. K. and Hamel, G. (1990) The core competences of the corporation. *Harvard Business Review*, 68(May/June): 79–91.

Qu, R. and Ennew, C. (2004) Does business environment matter to the development of a market orientation? In *Proceedings of the 33rd European Marketing Academy Conference (EMAC)*, 18–21 May, Murcia.

Quinn, J. B. (1980) *Strategies for change: logical incrementalism*. Homewood, IL: Richard D. Irwin.

Rangan, V. K., Corey, R. and Cespedes, F. (1993) Transaction cost theory: inferences from clinical field research on downstream vertical integration. *Organization Science*, 4(3): 454–475.

Ries, A. and Trout, J. (1981) *Positioning: the battle for your mind*. New York: Warner Books.

Rindfleisch, A. and Heide, J. B. (1997) Transaction cost analysis: past, present and future applications. *Journal of Marketing*, 61(Oct.): 30–54.

Rogers, L. (1993) *Administração de vendas e marketing*. São Paulo: Makron Books.

Roman, S. (2004) Personal antecedents of adaptive selling and adaptive selling influence on performance: an alternative perspective. In *Proceedings of the 33rd European Marketing Academy Conference (EMAC)*, 18–21 May, Murcia.

Rosenbloon, B. (1999) *Marketing channels*. 6th edn. New York: Dryden Press.

Ross, David R. (1986) Learning to dominate. *The Journal of Industrial Economics*, 34(4): 337–353.

Ross, S. A., Westerfield, R. W. and Jaffe, J. F. (1995) *Administração financeira*. São Paulo: Atlas.

Rubin, Edward (1995) The non-judicial life of contract: beyond the shadow of the law. *North-Western University Law Review*, 90(Fall): 107–131.

Rubio, A. G. and Redondo, Y. P. (2001) The impact of launch strategies on new product success. *Proceedings of the 30th European Marketing Academy (EMAC) Conference*, Bergen, 8–11 May.

Rumelt, R. P. (1986) *Strategy, structure and economic performance*. Cambridge, MA: Harvard Business School Press.

Runkel, K. E. and Brymer, C. (1997) *The nature of the brands, in brand valuation*. London: Premier Books.

Rust, R. T. and Oliver, R. W. (1994) The death of advertising. *Journal of Advertising*, 23(4): 71–78.

Ryans, A. B. and Weinberg, C. B. (1981) Sales force management: integrating research advances. *California Management Review*, 24(1): 75–89.

Saes, M. S. M. (2000) Organizações e instituições. In Zylbersztajn, D. and Neves, M. F. (eds). *Economia e gestão dos negócios agroalimentares*. São Paulo: Pioneira.

Sajtos, L. and Berács, J. (2004) Developing a multidimensional marketing performance measurement. In *Proceedings of the 33rd European Marketing Academy Conference (EMAC)*, 18–21 May, Murcia.

Salter, M. S. and Weinhold, W. A. (1979) *Diversification through acquisition: strategies for creating economic value*. New York: The Free Press.

Scare, R. F., Afonso, R. A., Campos, E. M. and Takahashi, S. (2005) Planning and management of projects portfolio. V PENSA Conference, 27–29 July, FEARP USP, Ribeirão Preto.

Schultz, D. E. and Barnes, B. E. (2001) *Campanhas estratégicas de comunicação de marca*. Rio de Janeiro: Qualitmark.

Semenik, R. J. and Bamossy, G. J. (1995) *Princípios de marketing: uma perspectiva global*. São Paulo: Makron Books.

Simon, H. (1947) *Administrative behavior*. New York: Macmillan.

Sinha, P. and Zoltners, A. A. Sales-force decision models: insights from 25 years of implementation. *Interfaces*, 31(3): 8–44.

Specht, G. and Willrodt, K. (2004) Brand management and competence-based view. In *Proceedings of the 33rd European Marketing Academy Conference (EMAC)*, 18–21 May, Murcia.

Spers, E. E. (1991) Organizations and markets. *Journal of Economic Perspectives*, 5(Spring): 25–44.

Spers, E. E. (2003) Mecanismos da regulação da qualidade e segurança em alimentos. Doctoral thesis, FEA/USP, São Paulo.

Srinivasan, S., Dekimpe, M. G., Hanssens, D. M. and Pauwels, K. (2001) Do promotions increase profitability and for whom? *Proceedings of the 30th European Marketing Academy (EMAC) Conference*, Bergen, 8–11 May.

Srivastava, R. and Rangarajan, D. (2004) Salesperson job perception and the feedback-satisfaction relationship. In *Proceedings of the 33rd European Marketing Academy Conference (EMAC)*, 18–21 May, Murcia.

Stalk, G., Evans, P. and Shulman, L. (1992) Competing capabilities: the new rules of corporate strategy. *Harvard Business Review*, 70(Mar./Apr.): 57–69.

Stern, L., El-Ansary, A. I. and Coughlan, A. (1996) *Marketing channels*. 5th edn. New York: Prentice Hall.

Sternquist, B. (1998) *International retailing*. New York: Fairchild Publications.

Swaminathan, V. and Moorman, C. (2009) Marketing alliances, firm networks, and firm value creation. *Journal of Marketing*, 73: 52–69.

Thompson, A. A. and Strickland, A. J. (1990) *Strategic management: concepts and cases*. Homewood, IL: Richard D. Irwin.

Toledo, G. L. (1973) Segmentação de mercado e estratégia de marketing. Doctoral thesis. Faculdade de Economia, Administração e Contabilidade, Universidade de São Paulo, São Paulo.

Toledo, G. L. (1978) *Marketing bancário: análise, planejamento e processo decisório*. São Paulo: Atlas.

Toledo, G. L., Neves, M. F. and Machado Filho, C. A. P. (1997) Marketing estratégico e varejo: o caso europeu. *Revista de Administração*, 32: 47–57.

Trainor, K. J., Rapp, A., Beitelspacher, L. S. and Schillewaert, N. (2011) Integrating information technology and marketing: an examination of the drivers and outcomes of e-marketing capability. *Industrial Marketing Management*, 40: 162–174.

Tung, Nguyen H. (1994) *Orçamento empresarial e custo padrão*. 4th edn. São Paulo: Universidade Empresa.

Urdan, A. T. (1993) Qualidade de serviço: um modelo integrativo. Doctoral thesis, Faculdade de Economia, Administração e Contabilidade, Universidade de São Paulo, São Paulo.

Walters, G. C. (1974) *Marketing channels*. New York: Ronald Press.

Webb, K. L. (2002) Managing channels of distribution in the age of electronic commerce. *Industrial Marketing Management*, 31(2): 95.

Webster, F. E. (1992) The changing role of marketing in the corporation. *Journal of Marketing*, 56: 1–17.

Webster, F. E. (1998) The rediscovery of the marketing concept. *Business Horizons*, May/June: 29–39.

Weitz, B. A., Castleberry, S. B. and Tanner, J. F. (2004) *Selling: building partnerships*. New York: McGraw-Hill.

Welsch, G. A. (1983) *Orçamento empresarial*. 4th edn. São Paulo: Atlas.

Welsch, G. A., Hilton, R. W. and Gordon, P. N. (1997) *Budgeting profit planning control*. 5th edn. São Paulo: Prentice Hall.

Wernerfelt, B. A. (1984) Resource view of the firm. *Strategic Management Journal*, 5(2) Apr–Jun: 171–180.

Westwood, J. (1995) *Plano de marketing*. São Paulo: Makron Books.

Wiertz, C., Ruyter, K., Keen, C. and Streukens, S. (2004) Cooperating for service excellence in multichannel service systems: an empirical assessment. *Journal of Business Research*, 57(4): 424.

Wilkinson, I. (2001) A history of network and channels thinking in marketing in the 20th century. *Australasian Journal of Marketing*, 9(2): 23–53.

Williamson, O. E. (1975) *Markets and hierarchies: analysis and antitrust implications*. New York: Free Press.

Wilson, E. J. and Vlosky, R. P. (1997) Partnering relationship activities: building theory from case study research. *Journal of Business Research*, 39: 59–70.

Wilson, H., Street, R. and Bruce, L. (2008) *The multichannel challenge: integrating customer experiences for profit*. Oxford: Butterworth- Heinemann.

Wright, P., Kroll, M. K. and Parnell, J. (2000) *Administração estratégica: conceitos*. São Paulo: Atlas.

Zoltners, A. A. and Lorimer, S. E. (2000) Sales territory alignment: an overlooked productivity tool. *Journal of Personal Selling & Sales Management*, 20(3): 139–150.

Zoltners, A. A., Sinha, P. and Zoltners, G. A. (2001) *The complete guide to accelerating sales force performance*. New York: Amacom.

Zylbersztajn, D. (1995) Estruturas de governança e coordenação do agribusiness: uma aplicação da nova economia das instituições. Livre-docência thesis, Faculdade de Economia, Administração e Contabilidade, Universidade de São Paulo, São Paulo.

Zylbersztajn, D. and Farina, E. M. M. Q. (1999) Strictly coordinated food systems: exploring the limits of the Coasian firm. *International Food and Agribusiness Management Review*, 2(2): 249–265.

About the Author

Born in 1968, Marcos Fava Neves is Professor of Planning and Strategy at the School of Business (FEARP) at the University of São Paulo, Brazil and an international expert on global agribusiness issues. He was Head of the Business Department of FEARP/USP in 2000–2002 and 2010–2012.

He graduated as an agronomic engineer from ESALQ/USP in 1991, as Master of Science in 1995 and received his PhD in management (with a focus on "Demand Driven Planning and Management") from the FEA/USP School of Economics and Business in 1999. He completed postgraduate studies on European agribusiness and marketing in France (1995) and on marketing channels and networks in the Netherlands (1998/1999). He also lived in the USA in 1977 and 1978, where he had his first job as a paperboy.

He specializes in strategic planning processes for companies and food production chains and is a board member of PENSA and other public and private organizations in Brazil. In 2004, he created the Markestrat Think Tank Group, doing international projects, studies and research in strategic planning and management for more than 40 organizations. Since then he has supervised more than 20 PhD theses and MSc dissertations. In 2008 he became CEO of Brazil's second largest biofuel holding company, a position occupied until 2009.

Following the boom of agribusiness in Brazil and the emerging position of Brazil in world food business, he has given more than 400 presentations in Brazil and 150 in 15 other countries.

His writing is strongly focused on supplying methods for business, publishing 70 articles in international journals and proceedings and has been author and editor of 30 books by 10 different publishers in Brazil, Uruguay, Argentina, South Africa, Netherlands, China, United Kingdom and the USA. He is a regular contributor for *China Daily* and *Folha de São Paulo* in Brazil and, in 2009 and 2010, wrote two case studies for Harvard Business School.

He lives in Ribeirão Preto, São Paulo State, Brazil, and is married with three daughters.

Index

T - #0109 - 230425 - C0 - 246/174/10 - PB - 9780415626392 - Gloss Lamination